NORTHERN PASSAGE

ETHNOGRAPHY AND APPRENTICESHIP AMONG THE SUBARCTIC DENE

ROBERT JARVENPA

State University of New York, Albany

WAVELAND

PRESS, INC.

Long Grove, Illinois

For information about this book, contact:
Waveland Press, Inc.
4180 IL Route 83, Suite 101
Long Grove, IL 60047-9580
(847) 634-0081
info@waveland.com
www.waveland.com

For Hetty Jo

Contents

Acknowledgements

This book is a result of the kindness, wisdom and patient guidance of the Han people of Dawson City, Yukon Territory and Eagle, Alaska and of the Chipewyan people of Patuanak, Dipper Lake, Primeau Lake, Knee Lake and Cree Lake, Saskatchewan. To my friends and mentors in those communities I owe an immense debt. Thank you for showing an apprentice the way. *Maci^{n}cho* and *Marci cho*.

Certain individuals and families deserve recognition for their special assistance. I am grateful to Charlie Isaac, Slim Marcelin, Mary Marcelin, Joe Henry, Annie Henry, Harry David, Bessie David, Willie Juneby, Adeline Juneby, Isaac Juneby, Sarah Malcolm, Joe Joseph, Richard Martin, Dick North, Mary McLeod, Albert Bernard, Marius Paul, George Paul, Catherine Paul, Gordon Tcho, Abraham Tcho, Frank Rat, Sarazine Rat, Rene Janvier, Joe Black, George Black, Cecile Black, Etienne Black, Rose Black, Isaac Black, Albert Black, Mary Black, Peter Cunningham, Linda Cunningham, Frank McIntyre, Beatrice McIntyre, J. B. McIntyre, Cecile McIntyre, Noel McIntyre, Celina McIntyre, Rene McIntyre, Moise McIntyre, Pierre Lariviere, John Lariviere, Christine Lariviere, J. B. Sandypoint, Gabriel Djonaire, Mary Djonaire, Mathias Maurice, Norbert George, Clara George, Amable George, Eugene George, Christine George, Paul LaPointe, Patti LaPointe, Jonas Aubichon, Joe Roy, Peterson Maurice, Andrea Maurice, Daniel Wolverine, Phillip Wolverine, Ovide Wolverine, Albert Wolverine, Louis Wolverine, Michael Wolverine, Louis Wolverine Jr., Martin Wolverine, Albertine Wolverine, Gilbert Wolverine, Gregoire Campbell, Rose Campbell, J. B. Campbell, Pat Campbell, Marayzine Campbell, Frank Mispounas, Victor Mispounas, Rodrick Apesis, Cyrill Gunn, Harry Gunn, Christine Gunn, Harry Gunn Jr., Marie Gunn, Joe Gunn, Maurice Gran, Ethel Gran, Lawrence John, Dean Steuck, Louison Rose Black, Angele Solomon, J.B. Gar, and Clementine Gar.

A portion of the author's royalities from the sale of this book will be donated to education programs of the English River First Nation (formerly the English River Band), Trondek Hwech'in (formerly the Dawson Band), and the Eagle Village Council.

Field research was supported by grants from the National Museums of Canada (now the Canadian Museum of Civilization), and the National Institute of General Medical Sciences administered through the Department of Anthropology at the University of Minnesota.

My professors at the University of Minnesota and other institutions provided me with rich intellectual nourishment and the tools to embark on my first fieldwork. I am deeply grateful to the late Robert F. Spencer, Pertti Pelto, Catharine McClellan, the late Elden Johnson, Eugene Ogan, the late Roy Rappaport, Robert Kiste, and Yi-Fu Tuan. A stimulating interchange with colleagues in subarctic and arctic research over the years has enhanced my scholarship, broadened my perspective and, in many ways, prepared me for writing *Northern Passage*. I am especially grateful to Hetty Jo Brumbach for a long period of insightful and productive collaboration in the North, a research partnership which continues, and for her critical reading of this manuscript. Joel Savishinsky also has my sincere thanks for providing a thoughtful assessment of the manuscript. In addition, I am very grateful to Karla Poewe for writing an exceptionally well-crafted study guide. Her insightful, thought-provoking guide enhances the reading of this book. I also wish to thank Charles Bishop, Annette McFadyen Clark, Julie Cruikshank, June Helm, Robert Janes, Shepard Krech III, Jukka Pennanen, Arthur Ray, Henry S. Sharp, David M. Smith, the late James G. E. Smith, William Schneider, and James VanStone. Students and colleagues at SUNY-Albany have kindly supported my efforts from start to finish. Finally, I am forever indebted to my grandparents for setting my sights northward, and to my parents for encouraging my scholarly pursuits.

The germ of an idea for *Northern Passage* emerged many years ago after I read Cornelius Osgood's *Winter*, a riveting retrospective account of his early field experiences published in 1953, long before reflexive, experimental and literary approaches became fashionable in cultural anthropology. I owe a special debt to George Gmelch and Sharon Gmelch for their friendship and intellectual support, and for directing me to Waveland Press. I am deeply grateful to Tom Curtin at Waveland for his cogent advice, skillful editing, and encouragement to complete the project. Jeni Ogilvie at Waveland deserves special thanks for her fine handling of the copy editing and production process. Any shortcomings in this book are my responsibility alone.

Prologue

The days were growing long again in northern Canada. Even in late May pockets of snow survived in the forest's dark recesses, but the swollen Ithingo River was finally free of ice. My two Chipewyan Indian companions, Norbert Ptarmigan and Gregoire Stonypoint, scanned the shore for a good camping spot. I had been traveling and living with them for months now in the bush as they hunted for food and furs for their families. With five fat beaver in the bottom of their wooden skiff, the men were elated as they put ashore. Their good mood buoyed my own spirits. I was beginning to feel more like an accepted friend and less like an interloper in Chipewyan country.

Norbert and Gregoire quickly butchered their day's catch and built a fire. As the twilight lingered, we enjoyed a leisurely meal. It wasn't an ordinary meal, even by bush standards. Since the men were hungry after several days of hard travel, they celebrated with a banquet of boiled beaver that had been lightly smoked over an aspen wood fire. Chunks of rich fat meat and the internal organs lay simmering in a large kettle along with a bit of lard and flour to thicken the broth. Norbert fished out the head and began to eat. Gregoire attacked a hindquarter, and I started on the other one. As was customary, the tail had been roasted and eaten first. Seeing the pleasure on the mens' faces as they savored this meal was oddly spellbinding. We ate until the kettle was half empty.

"*Dastloze* [little beard], come here, I want to show you something!" Norbert addressed me by my Chipewyan name. It was a clever reference to my beard and stature. It had become the Chipewyans' way of distinguishing me from one of the few other white men in the community, a taller man with a beard who became known as *Dastlocok* or "big beard." For better or worse, I would always be Dastloze here. Norbert had a wry sense of humor, and I thought he had some joke prepared for me. But his expression was serious as he handed me one of the bones from the beaver we had just eaten. It was a femur, an extraordinarily thick stubby

1

thigh bone. "Go ahead, try to break it. You ate the beaver, so now you must try to break the bone with your hands."

As instructed, I wrapped my hands in cloth for a better grip. I exerted all the force I could muster, but this was like trying to break a steel bolt. My best effort failed. I passed the bone to Gregoire. His face mirrored the strain as he attacked the femur with his powerful hands, but it still remained intact.

Norbert then studied the bone for a few seconds, gripped it tightly and began twisting. There was an audible snap. Norbert humbly displayed the broken femur. What was his secret? Had we weakened the bone for him? At the time, it all seemed like delightful after-dinner amusement. Later I learned that this was only one of the Chipewyans' many delicate gestures of respect for a slain or sacrificed animal. The ritual atones for the taking of the beaver's life, and it also insures its future reproduction. Later that evening the men noted that the femur breaking had an added benefit. It was a form of hunting magic that would provide Norbert with success in pursuing other beavers. And much later, back in the village, I would discover that such acts insured Norbert's reputation as a powerful man in the community.

The bone business was both momentous and inexplicable. Some hidden door to other people's knowledge had been opened, if just a crack. Norbert, Gregoire and I spent the rest of the evening in relaxed conversation around the fire, smoking, drinking mugs of hot tea and listening to sounds on the river.

"Dastloze," Gregoire asked, "do you know that we call this river 'Ithingo' after one of our old relatives? Ethengoo Campbell lived around here years ago. *Ethengoo*, that means 'caribou tooth' in Chip, and that's what our relatives called him. And now that's what we call this river."

Listening to an account of Ethengoo Campbell's life, and his connection to Gregoire and Norbert's ancestors, a feeling of sublime contentment spread over me. I felt privileged to hear my companions' stories, share their food and fellowship, and witness the ritual rebirth of the beaver. Silently I wondered. Had I come to the North for this very experience?

This book is meant to be a "journey" in two ways. On the one hand, it is about becoming a cultural anthropologist. Like a child being socialized to adulthood, the anthropologist is metaphorically an infant who must learn a strange society's rules or an alien culture's logic anew. Viewed from the perspective of many years, this private journey has a life crisis quality as the anthropologist passes through cycles of doubt, revelation and reflection. This book focuses upon my earliest experiences as a neophyte confronting the complexities and ambiguities of fieldwork among subarctic native people, first as a graduate student apprentice and, shortly thereafter, as a lone researcher working on a dissertation. Responding to the recent interest in reflexive and critical writing, part of my goal is to help demystify the research process. What is it like living among and learning about the lifeways of other people for the first time? Confusion, humiliation and fear, as well as joy, discovery, and enlightenment are constant companions in the humbling quest called "ethnographic fieldwork." More than 25 years after the fact, certain private experiences and emotions from my first fieldwork remain vividly etched in my memory. This burden of memory, a perpetual replay of sights, sounds, moods, and intense feelings, takes on a life of its own in the consciousness of the anthropologist and structures one's understanding of other people's cultures.

On the other hand, this book is an account of actual events and people's lives in a subarctic North that few outsiders see. The emphasis is upon situations that I found uniquely revealing, heroic, perplexing, disturbing or dramatic, not only for storytelling appeal but also for illustrating fundamental truths about life as lived in the subarctic. In a sense, these are "behind-the scenes" accounts, the other reality beyond the formal prose of anthropological monographs and journal articles. While the names of most individuals have been fictionalized, and some dialogue reconstructed or modified, I have attempted to faithfully convey the circumstances and drama of people's everyday experiences.

The people and places in the vastness called the *subarctic* hold an allure and sense of mystery for me. It is a huge circumpolar belt, covered mostly by boreal forest and some tundra, that includes much of northern Canada, interior Alaska, much of Scandinavia, and large parts of Russia and Siberia. Covering one-ninth of the earth's land surface, it has less than one-thousandth of the world's population. Historically, the subarctic North was one of the last great regions to evade the imprint of Western culture and the capitalist world system. Lying beyond the limits of most agricultural production, Europeans have viewed the subarctic, especially in North America, as an extractive frontier from which to remove furs and mineral wealth, not as a place to settle. While this philosophy continues in the current era of oil and gas pipelines, hydroelectric dams and other "mega-projects," much of the subarctic still lies beyond the reach of roads, cities and industrial development.

Yet, for thousands of years indigenous peoples have made the subarctic North their home, adapting to its demanding conditions with nomadic hunting and fishing lifestyles and small flexible communities. Comparatively speaking, the culture and history of these native northerners are poorly known to outsiders. By contrast, an extensive literature exists regarding the Inuit or Eskimo in the adjacent high arctic as well as Native American groups of the Northwest Coast, the Plains, the Southwest and other regions.

The events in this book take place in the western subarctic of
North America, a vast region extending from Hudson Bay in central
Canada westward into interior Alaska. It is the homeland of the *Dene* or
northern Athapaskan-speaking Indians. According to some interpretations, the ancestors of Athapaskans ultimately may be traced back to
peoples who migrated from eastern Siberia into interior Alaska between
11,000 and 10,000 years ago during the terminal Pleistocene. Those
early migrants are often associated with archaeological residues of the
Paleo-Arctic microblade tradition (Clark 1991; Greenberg, Turner and
Zegura 1986; Turner 1988).

Yet, the diversification of the various Athapaskan languages and
speakers occurred much more recently. They probably diverged from a
common origin in the upper Yukon River area within the past 2,000
years and then spread into the farthest reaches of the western subarctic
(Fowler 1977; Krauss 1973, 1988). Nonetheless, contemporary languages of the Dene or northern Athapaskans form an open-ended
dialect complex. This flexibility in communication reflects a cultural
adaptation based upon mobility of small groups of people hunting and
fishing over large territories. The prevailing social organization of these
groups has been the *band*, that is, a nomadic community of closely
related kin which is relatively egalitarian, politically autonomous, and
marked by short-term, de facto leadership rather than formal, central-
ized authority. People like the *Han* and the *Chipewyan*, of central
concern in this book, are only two among 26 or so regional Athapaskan
groups known in recent historical times.

In commenting upon the environment of the Chipewyan Indians in
the late 1700s, the Hudson's Bay Company explorer Samuel Hearne
(1795:315, 327) noted:

> Those poor people live in such an inhospitable part of the globe,
> that for want of firing they are frequently obliged to eat their vict-
> uals quite raw . . . the land throughout that whole track of country
> is scarcely any thing but one solid mass of rocks and stones.

Few would dispute that the western subarctic is a demanding environment of fragile slow-growth boreal forest and tundra communities,
dramatic extremes in climate, and immense territory coupled with low
densities of both food resources and human populations. Expressions
like "simple," "harsh," "marginal," or "low-energy" are often used as a
shorthand to convey these realities.

Unfortunately, similar language sometimes has been used by
scholars in referring to the people themselves. Notions that northern
Athapaskan cultures are "meager," "marginal," or somehow "impov-
erished," held meaning for an earlier generation of anthropologists
comparing material culture and sociopolitical organization across the
continent (Koolage 1975; Kroeber 1939:222). Yet such abstract, distant

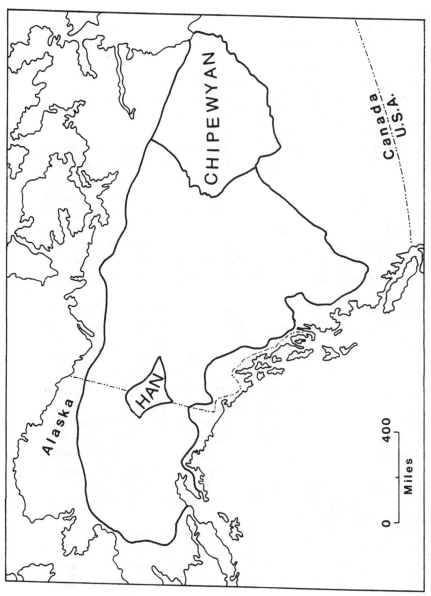

Distribution of the subarctic Dene or Athapaskan peoples of interior Alaska and northwestern Canada. Locations of the Han and Chipewyan are highlighted (base map adapted from Osgood, 1936, and VanStone, 1974).

characterizations add little to our comprehension of the complex lives and livelihoods of real people or their own understandings of environment and culture.

In discussing the landscape near his hunting area, one of my Chipewyan friends remarked:

> There's no more beautiful place in the world than going along *ethundeze* [deer river or caribou river] in the fall or spring time . . . when I get to my trapline I'll have lots of beaver and whitefish, and maybe moose and caribou to eat. Boy, my mouth is just going to be covered with fat!

Thus, some caution is needed in balancing external views from native interpretations of both the natural and social world. At the same time, a sense of historical context is essential. Environments, no less than the people adapting to them, are parts of resilient, dynamic systems. Athapaskan patterns of resource use, and the social arrangements facilitating those patterns, have shifted in complex and novel ways as the political economy of the northlands has changed during the past several centuries of relations with fur traders, missionaries, mineral prospectors, treaty agents, industrial developers, and government bureaucracies.

Anthropologists have attempted to classify and subdivide the northern Athapaskan peoples in different ways by emphasizing variable features of environment, economy and social life. Cornelius Osgood's (1936) pioneer studies and mapping of northern Athapaskan groups drew a distinction between "Pacific Drainage Culture" and "Arctic Drainage Culture." This called attention to the availability of migratory salmon species and their utilization by people in the far western watersheds, namely the Yukon River and its major tributaries. Among other things, salmon exploitation was thought to nourish relatively sedentary communities with *matrilineal* social structure (kinship groups such as lineages, sibs or clans, and moieties based on descent through the maternal line) and more elaborate aesthetic and ceremonial forms (such as funerary *potlatching*), features prominent in the west but lacking in the east.

However, other scholars have found the salmon hypothesis and associated Pacific/Arctic division inadequate (McClellan 1964:8–11; McKennan 1969:96–98). Pointedly addressing regional differences in ecology, Catharine McClellan (1970) developed a five-part classification which, among other things, assigns 13 groups along the interior mountain spine of northern British Columbia, the Yukon Territory and northeastern Alaska to a "Cordilleran" category. The Cordilleran's prominence in this scheme reflects McClellan's (1970:x) own view that the "Athapaskans can best be understood basically as a mountain people, who have in some places spilled off the great Cordillera."

In turn, James VanStone (1974) effectively utilized McClellan's framework to examine the cultural ecology of northern Athapaskan peoples. While he discovered considerable diversity in the interplay of subsistence practices, settlement systems and community organization, VanStone (1974:122–24) sees the hallmarks of northern Athapaskan adaptation at large as embedded in individualism, flexibility and accommodation. In particular, he suggests that *bilateral kinship* (tracing relationships through both father's and mother's families) may be more flexible and adaptive to the rigors of life in the subarctic than a matrilineal system because, as VanStone argues, "it makes available a greater number of relatives to help the individual when the need arises." Indeed, VanStone's view is reinforced by the findings of June Helm (1965, 1969a, 1969b). Her detailed studies of kinship and marriage among Athapaskans in the Mackenzie drainage demonstrate how bilateral kinship provides a highly flexible system of social ties for creating relationships and recruiting members into communities.

Yet other scholars have noted the importance of careful historical research to reveal the ways that interactions with Europeans have transformed livelihoods and socio-cultural patterns of northern Athapaskan peoples over the past two centuries or more (Hosley 1977; Krech 1984). Earlier notions of a universal "patrilocal band" model (Service 1962), for example, have long been dismissed as ethnographically and historically misinformed for the Athapaskans.

Early estimates placed the entire northern Athapaskan aboriginal population at about 34,000 scattered over a landscape of nearly 4 million square kilometers (Kroeber 1939:141–43; Mooney 1928). This yields a population density of less than one person per 100 square kilometers, possibly the lowest density for hunting, fishing or foraging people anywhere in the world. Allowing for future revision of these baseline figures, the densities clearly reflect the severity of the western subarctic environment. In the late nineteenth/early twentieth century, for example, the 150 or so *Kesyehot'ine* ("aspen house people"), a southern Chipewyan regional band, ranged over 49,700 square kilometers, a territory the size of West Virginia. That is roughly .30 persons per 100 km^2. Given the immense spaces and distances involved, one can appreciate why a premium on mobility weighs heavily in the social and cultural configuration of the northern Athapaskans.

Popular notions of a "spruce-goose-moose" habitat or a land of "feast and famine" convey some of the limitations of subarctic ecosystems. Compared with temperate and tropical environments, species diversity in the subarctic is low and food chains are simple in structure. Thus, while feeding habits of northern animals may be broad and flexible, boreal forest ecosystems are quite fragile since foodwebs composed of few species are easily upset or compromised by change (Pruitt

1978:48–52). Reproduction rates for many animal species are rather unstable, mortality frequently being very high, with considerable loss of life characteristic at the time of catastrophic weather, food shortage, and stressful migrations (Formazov 1970).

Dramatic population fluctuations are notable in the four-year cycles of lemmings and the well-known nine- to ten-year hare-lynx cycle. Some animals have developed special adaptations like the barren-ground caribou's long-distance seasonal migration across the forest-tundra ecotone (Kelsall 1968:106–42). Thus, the abundance of food animals can vary markedly by time and place, and their availability to Athapaskan hunters, fishers and trappers is necessarily enhanced by strategies of scheduling and mobility.

Some contemporary Athapaskan groups have retained a remarkable degree of geographical mobility despite political-economic changes ushered in by federal treaty provisions and despite a new era of settlement nucleation and service centralization emerging after World War II. The seasonal exchange of trapping camp for fishing camp, long-distance travel by water routes and forest trails, and the eating of freshly procured game are not simply mundane activities. Such movement and activity become an important means of relieving social sources of stress (Savishinsky 1994). They are also among the most highly valued cultural experiences.

For example, among the Chipewyan to be regarded as a "great walker" is a high compliment:

> Yah, that Antoine Whitefish was a great walker, you know. He could walk anywhere all day long, for many days and not get tired.

Such individuals not only walk tirelessly over great tracts of forest and barrenland but also have the knowledge to lead their families and companions out of difficulty.

In recent years, as settled life, wage labor and other market forces diminish annual nomadic cycles, the notion of a mobile "bush" lifestyle takes on added weight at a symbolic level as a primordial characteristic of Athapaskan culture and identity (Jarvenpa 1976:68, 1990:198). In this sense, remnants of seasonal bush living, and the geographical mobility they signify, continue to be a strongly conservative force in northern Athapaskan culture.

To the outsider, much of the subarctic landscape may appear "empty" or "unoccupied." This notion holds little meaning for Athapaskans who see virtually all their surroundings as active, alive or occupied in some fashion. Almost any space, whether within or beyond the confines of currently inhabited settlements or camps, may have functioned previously as a culturally meaningful landscape where events transpired and activities occurred.

A fine-grained understanding of the landscape is symbolically cod-
ified in language. Athapaskan place name terminologies recognize a
myriad of geographical features over extensive regions (Kari and Fall
1988; Osgood 1975). Many of these are trenchant descriptions of environmental features and processes. The Chipewyan expression *ts'ankwi
ttheba* ("old woman rapids") not only denotes a particularly turbulent
section of the Mudjatik River but also evokes the circumstances of a
tragic death at that location generations ago. In this way, conventional
language and discourse continually situate the topographical landscape
in terms of peoples' history and lore.

Robin Ridington (1988:107) perceptively notes that Athapaskans
and other northern forest people are "well aware that their means of
production are mental as well as material." Hence, knowledge, power
and individual competence and flexibility are essential to understanding how people use resources and adapt to environmental constraints
and opportunities. Some Beaver or *Dunneza* "hunt chiefs," for example,
visualize and coordinate an overall hunt strategy through *dreaming*,
even though ultimate success depends upon the individual's grasp of
animal behaviors and environmental processes (Ridington 1987).

Similarly, McClellan and Denniston (1981:377) comment on the
mental and ideological aspects of mobile hunting behavior among Cordilleran Athapaskans:

> The successful hunter had to know the landscape, the habits of his
> prey, and the probable course of the weather. Equally essential to
> his mind was the knowledge of how to behave in a personalized uni-
> verse in which many animal spirits were thought to be more pow-
> erful than humans.

Generalizing to all northern Athapaskans, we can argue that the moral
distance between humans and other organisms is negligible. A delicate
material-spiritual symbiosis between humans and food animals is a
fundamental means of interpreting causality. For example, there is a
tendency to interpret major historical changes in animal distribution or
abundance as withdrawals or withholdings due to flagrant "disrespect"
by hunters. One's ability to hunt, to cure illness, to engage in sorcery,
and to impact the behavior of other people is affected by the state of
one's "supernatural" knowledge and power, or what the Chipewyan
term *inkonze* (Sharp 1988; Smith 1973, 1982).

The foregoing comments have highlighted some key features of the
socionatural world and cultural orientation of the northern Athapaskans, at least in recent history. Specific variations on these themes,
including the often erosive changes of the modern era, appear in the rest
of the book. Also, this overture serves as background and context for
understanding the chapters that follow. The material is arranged in two
major parts, Klondike Novitiate and Trail of the Chipewyan, which

examine sequentially my earliest fieldwork experiences in the Yukon Territory and northern Saskatchewan respectively. I was a young anthropologist just learning my craft in the early 1970s. The North beckoned.

PART I

Klondike Novitiate

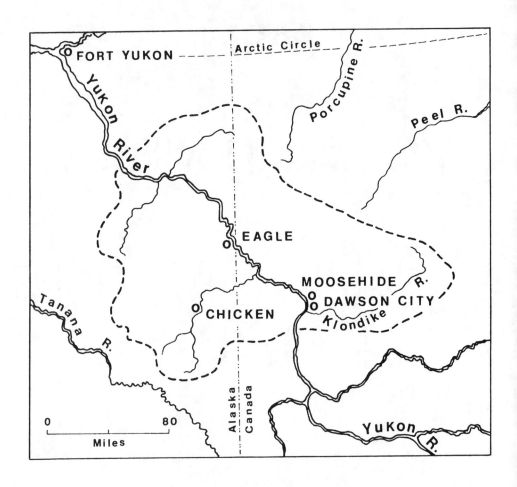

Han country in the upper Yukon River drainage (base map adapted from Osgood 1971).

Chapter One

Han Country

The visitor held a one-sided skin drum in her hands as she walked down the slope toward the lake. Clouds of white aromatic smoke billowed up from a settlement near the shore where an old woman was smoke-tanning a moosehide over a smudge fire. A pile of freshly caught whitefish glistened in the late afternoon sun. Kneeling before the bounty, another woman was cleaning the fish with quick knife strokes and hanging the thin-cut sections on a drying rack. At an adjacent fire an elderly man was bringing a kettle of tea to a boil. When the trio looked up, the visitor began chanting softly in accompaniment to a steady beat of the drum. With each step forward the drummer subtly increased her pace and volume until arriving at the camp, whereupon the old man leaped to his feet with startling agility. Taking the drum from the visitor, he reciprocated with his own energetic song. The women tittered at this turnabout, and then quickly averted their gaze and resumed their work.

The poignant greeting was unfolding in the small Tutchone Indian community at Burwash Landing on the shores of Kluane Lake in the Yukon Territory. The visiting drummer was not a Tutchone, however. Dr. Catharine McClellan, an anthropologist and an old friend of local families, was renewing cherished ties.

It was the summer of 1970. I could scarcely believe my luck in returning to enchanting Kluane Lake. The previous summer I had hitchhiked to Alaska from Minneapolis, passing by this very locale, an impulsive misadventure which whetted my appetite for the North. I was an anthropology graduate student at the University of Minnesota, and between summers I had attended the Universities of Michigan and Wisconsin, being fortunate at the latter place to have studied with Dr. McClellan. Having worked with native communities in the southern Yukon and adjacent Alaska for over twenty years, she had an immense knowledge of and fondness for the country and its people. And she was a leading authority on northern Athapaskan cultures. A fellow graduate student, Susanne Williams, and I were now serving as her research assistants. This would be our first prolonged exposure to the mysteries of *ethnographic fieldwork*, the art and science of understanding other societies by observing and participating at close range.

Indeed, a central element in the collective identity of sociocultural anthropologists, and a feature which often distinguishes them from other social scientists, is the method of obtaining information through *participant observation.* Since the time of Bronislaw Malinowski's (1922) pioneering fieldwork among the Trobriand Islanders of Melanesia, participant observation has come to mean, in its most basic sense, long-term immersion in communities or societies where the ethnographer both observes and participates in the day-to-day activities of the people being studied. As such, this style of field research has evolved into a rite of passage whereby novitiates earn their status as full-fledged anthropologists (Epstein 1967:vii).

While participant observation may be conducted in a variety of ways, the fieldworker often finds himself/herself cast in the role of an uneducated child. In reviewing his research among the Lugbara of Uganda, John Middleton (1970:230) once remarked:

> . . . an anthropologist learns the culture he is studying as does a child who is learning about his society, by acquiring kin and neighbors who become parts of a pattern of social relations of which he is at the center: another way of saying this would be that an anthropologist can only gain knowledge of the ways which people conceive their social experience (which is, after all, his main task) in one way, by being socialized as is a child.

A return to "childhood" in this sense can be simultaneously humbling and revealing for the researcher. Some fieldworkers may be unprepared for such an emotional step and consequent feelings of vulnerability. Yet, the payoffs in empathy for and understanding of other people's lives and cultural realities can be enormous. Perhaps it is the sense of awe and wonder with which young children regard their parents and elders, translated to the anthropologist's experience, which builds true empathy.

On a more pragmatic level, participant observation serves as a basic platform from which to mobilize an array of specific data-gathering procedures. In addition to keeping a body of general field notes on a myriad of daily activities and conversations unfolding around them, ethnographers may conduct both informal and structured interviews, collect statistical and census data, carry out psychological tests, compile geneaological data, construct maps of settlements and households, and photograph, film or tape-record rituals and ceremonies, among other things (Holy 1984:23; Pelto and Pelto 1978:69).

Witnessing Dr. McClellan's reunion with her friends was one of those seminal moments not easily forgotten. After all, cultural anthropologists could be rather circumspect and secretive about their fieldwork. Doctoral students often embarked on their first major research with little prior experience hoping to endure, if not survive, a year or more of solitary fieldwork as a rite of passage into the profession.

Graduate student folklore ran rampant with accounts, exaggerated or otherwise, of malaria-stricken neophytes abandoned by villagers in New Guinea, of unfortunate souls caught between leftist guerrillas and right-wing armies in Latin America, and of ill-prepared or insensitive researchers getting kicked off of Indian reservations. For such reasons, it was a privilege to watch an experienced mentor ply her trade. Hoping that the lesson would not go to waste, I hung on Dr. McClellan's every move and utterance.

With the greeting songs over, there ensued a long period of leisurely conversation and reminiscing uninterrupted by the women's deft fish handling. An elderly couple, Joe and Annie Jacob, and their friend Mary, were genuinely pleased to see "Kitty," as Dr. McClellan was affectionately called. Susanne and I, while kindly received, sat silently on the margins. There were lengthy pauses in conversation, in any case. If this was customary, I was very grateful since I felt far too reticent and awkward to initiate conversation here. What would one say? I knew perhaps three words of Tutchone, although most of the conversation was conducted in broken English.

For a man in his 80s, Joe appeared remarkably vigorous, although he was hard of hearing. He wore an old grey wool suit coat and trousers that contrasted with a new pair of Tangerine brand basketball shoes made in The People's Republic of China. As Dr. McClellan became absorbed in discussion with Mary, Joe slowly swiveled around on his wooden bench until he was directly facing me. He opened his mouth as if to speak, but then looked away lost in thought.

Minutes dragged by. Then, to my surprise, perhaps prompted by a sudden memory, Joe began talking. And talking. He carried on for a half hour nonstop in a free-form monologue. Possibly because of his deafness, he expected no exchange or interruption. He spoke matter of factly about two moose he had killed on the opposite shore of Kluane Lake the previous year, and of his esteemed father, Chief Jacob of the Aishihik area, who had witnessed some of the first incursions of whites in that part of the Yukon in the late 1800s. Given Joe's age, that was certainly possible, but the information still astounded me. I was listening to a man who was barely one generation removed from European contact.

Looking around, I hoped to catch Dr. McClellan's attention, but she had retired to the Jacob's cabin with Annie and Mary. No doubt, she had heard Joe's stories many times, but I was fearful that some new twist or pearl of wisdom was being lost, especially since Joe's English was larded with quaint idioms and Tutchone phrases.

But Joe was already winding down. His voice grew somber as he ended on an ominous note that would come back to haunt me in the months ahead: "Too much drinking, you know. Too many people die. Yah, too many young people die here in Burwash. My relatives dying from drinking. Too many young Indian people dying all over Yukon. Because of drinking. Then just oldtimers like me left here, but then pretty soon we die too. Then no more Indian people, eh?"

Burwash Landing was not our ultimate destination. The game plan was to deposit Susanne and me farther north in the heart of Han Indian country. We would be left there for several months to learn what we could about the Han. Dr. McClellan had commitments back in Wisconsin, and while she would be supervising our efforts from afar, we would be in the field on our own.

The enormity of the country we were facing had not really registered. Extending from the 60th latitude northward to the Beaufort Sea and Arctic Ocean, the Yukon Territory embraced more than 207,000 square miles of trackless boreal forest, windswept tundra, formidable mountain ranges, and rampaging rivers. Less than 20,000 people lived there; it would be like scattering 20,000 people over an area the size of France. One of North America's mightiest torrents, the Yukon River, originated in high mountain lakes along the territory's southern border and then raced 1,900 miles northwestward into Alaska and out to the Bering Sea. Now, in early June, with nearly 20 hours of sunlight and midday temperatures pushing into the 60s and 70s, the land was deceptively inviting. One could easily forget that midwinter here would bring 20 hours of daily darkness and the continent's coldest recorded temperatures, including a bone-chilling −81°F.

The forests and mountains were home to moose, caribou, grizzly and black bears, mountain goats and mountain sheep, as well as wolves, foxes, lynx, beaver and a variety of smaller mammals and birds. Most of this vast region was roadless. The few gravel tracks that existed were recently constructed spur roads off the Alaska Highway in the southwest corner of the territory. We hoped to follow some of them on a somewhat elliptical path northwestward into a sliver of Alaska, curving back eastward into the Yukon at our destination of Dawson City.

As a kind of warm-up exercise, we were spending a couple weeks on the road. We had rented a vehicle in Whitehorse, the territorial capital, and were now renewing ties with Dr. McClellan's old friends and contacts. Like young chicks imprinting on a mother hen, we followed our professor on a round of visits, internalizing her modus operandi. That image was reinforced by Dr. McClellan's commanding presence. Although fiftyish in age, and sporting a shock of silver-grey hair, she looked younger. Her athletic frame towered over students and Indians alike.

Dr. McClellan had an unflappably cheerful disposition which could be contagious and immediately put a roomful of people at ease. And over the years she had built up an impressive number of fictive kin relations. Referring to people as "auntie" or "my daughter," or whatever, was delightfully personable and seemed so anthropologically correct. Given my own reserved persona, I worried that I would never acquire the proper "bedside" or fieldside manner. Could I walk into a village beating a drum?

At a nearby craft shop Dr. McClellan found a beaded eagle pendant for Susanne. As the Eagle was an alternate identity for one of the Tutchone's major matrilineal kin groups, the Wolf moiety, it was decided that henceforth Susanne was to "be a Wolf." Perhaps that would serve as some sort of gambit or entree. It struck me that the Indians might take this as effrontery. But what did I know? At least the Jacobs at Burwash Landing approved.

We would be passing through dozens of communities, and many of the Pacific-drainage Athapaskan peoples in far western Canada and interior Alaska had a *moiety* system, or perhaps had one in recent history. It was quite literally a halving of society. People were born either Wolves or Ravens, for example, in accordance with their mother's affiliation and line of descent. Such duality set in motion a web of reciprocal acts and obligations. Wolves had to marry Ravens, and vice versa, following a preference for *exogamous* marriage, that is, finding a mate outside one's own descent group. A tripartite division may have prevailed among some Athapaskans, although the position and function of the "third" unit in such kinship systems has been obscured by recent demographic and social change.

In turn, moieties were composed of a number of smaller matrilineal descent groups, *sibs* or *clans* which also tended to be exogamous. Seven sibs comprise the Crow (*Naltsina*) moiety and 10 sibs make-up the Sea Gull (*Tc'ia*) moiety among the Upper Tanana, for example. People host their opposite moiety members at important community feasts and celebrations such as the *potlatch*, thereby reaffirming the dual structure of society. While Athapaskan potlatches have sometimes been interpreted primarily as funerary commemorations to honor the dead, they are rather complex social and ceremonial occasions functioning to redistribute wealth, enhance the prestige of aspiring leaders, and serve as an outlet for community identity and creativity, among other things (Guedon 1974:64–83, 204–34; VanStone 1974:54–57).

For the sake of symmetry, it was decided that I should take on the affiliation of the opposing moiety, Raven, colloquially known in these parts as "Crow." Adolescent instincts took over immediately.

"Wolves are much more powerful than Crows, you know," Susanne teased.

"Oh yeah, did you ever see a Wolf fly?" I parried.

"No, what I mean is we Wolves have more supernatural power, more medicine. More all around power."

"That's what a Wolf *would* think! We Ravens are tricksters from way back. We can outsmart the bejeezus out of a Wolf any day. You don't want to fool with a Raven or a Crow, man!"

Crow? Raven? How fitting! I laughed inwardly as dark feathered comrades fluttered through my mind. The previous summer I had encountered many of these vocal, intelligent creatures whenever I was stranded on the road. Then, shortly after visiting the Tutchone fishing village at Klukshu, I had an unsettling dream in which a group of ravens demanded, in plain English, that I give them the salmon I was about to eat. A year later, I still felt vaguely indebted to those birds, but at least now I was on their side! Should I say something about those peculiar dreams? I was tempted but held my tongue. It was too early in the game to reveal such weirdness. Dr. McClellan might be less than amused and send me packing.

As we traveled westward toward the Yukon-Alaska border we were entering a region that lay at the intersection of at least three major Athapaskan groups: Tutchone to the east, Upper Tanana or Nabesna to the west, and Han to the north. The intricacies of all this were driven home in one household in Beaver Creek where three women responded to Dr. McClellan's requests for native vocabulary.

"How do you say crow in your language?"

"Ts'an."

"Ts'an? Okay, how do you say tobacco?"

After some cursory comparisons of word lists it was evident that the woman of the house, Sadie George, spoke an Upper Tanana dialect. But her two neighbors, who had dropped by for a visit, spoke northern and southern variants of Tutchone. All of this seemed consistent with the women's varying family histories and identities and their farflung communities of origin. After all, Athapaskans were renowned as mobile hunters and great travelers. Perhaps it was not unusual to find native people of different backgrounds mixing in such remote locales.

I was reminded of the words of a Tutchone man we had met earlier near the Snag cut-off: "Yup, it's pretty complicated up here. You'll find a new language about every 80 miles along the Alaska Highway." Indeed, one wondered how the highway itself, nearly 30 years old, had disrupted native communities and moved people about.

Our musings on language seemed trivial compared to Sadie's problems, however. She appeared somewhat hungover and had a nasty cut and welt over one eye. She gingerly lowered the collar of her sweater to reveal a horrible inflammation. The right side of her neck looked like a bruised over-ripe eggplant. My immediate sense was that the poor woman had barely survived a strangling. Had her intoxication saved her? Perhaps she had passed out before some brute could finish a throttling. These thoughts embarrassed me. For all we knew, the woman had a rare skin ailment. At Sadie's suggestion, Dr. McClellan drove her to a woman who dispensed drugs in the white section of town. After Sadie received a penicillin shot and other medication, we parted company and resumed our journey.

Near the international border Dr. McClellan was hoping to contact an old acquaintance, an Upper Tanana man known, fittingly, as White River Johnny or Border Johnny. In fact, the man was a well-known mineral prospector in the White River country and adjacent districts. At his camp along the highway a lone tent was occupied by a few young Indian men on break between shifts. A couple dogs slinked about outside, but unfortunately Johnny was out working somewhere in the bush.

Pushing west into Alaska a cold drizzle enveloped us, eroding any desire to pitch our tents beside the road for the night. Instead, we moved on to Tetlin Junction and treated ourselves to a rented cabin and a warm meal at a local roadhouse. The latter was especially welcome as our normal diet leaned heavily toward pilot biscuits covered with jam, peanut butter, raisins or whatever was handy.

"Yech! I know you scavenger Crows will eat almost any filthy thing, living or dead, but what is that garbage you're eating now?" Susanne assumed a look of mock revulsion from across the table, as I brought the fork to my mouth. A couple at a neighboring table was giving us peculiar looks.

"You've never seen chicken-fried steak before? Hey, don't talk to me about filthy. It's you Wolves who gorge yourselves on gore and then throw it up later for the kiddies to eat." I affected a tone of utter disgust. The neighboring couple was searching for another table. Apparently, they knew nothing of Crows and Wolves. This rivalry-joking thing will wear thin in a hurry, I thought. It could be a long summer. If Dr. McClellan found the antics objectionable, however, she wasn't letting on.

My eyes throbbed painfully from the glare of fresh snow. An early June squall had caught us by surprise. As it subsided, shafts of sunlight penetrated the disintegrating cloud cover to illuminate white patches of tundra. It was a startling transition. The snow-free spruce forests of the Tanana valley had suddenly given way to mostly treeless alpine country.

We were in the vicinity of Mount Fairplay on the Taylor Highway. The latter was a 160-mile gravel road that spurred north off the Alaska Highway traversing a 5,000-foot range of mountains that separated the Tanana and Yukon drainages. Moving gradually northward the deep-cut tributary canyons of the Fortymile River came into view. These were the various "forks," including the West Fork and the Mosquito Fork and the Walker Fork of the

Fortymile, among others. Like dark fissures on a craggy weathered face, their forested recesses contrasted with barren plateaus and ridges above.

A roadside marker ("Caribou Harvest Tickets Required") was a reminder that one of the largest barrenground caribou populations in Alaska, the Fortymile herd, with about 40,000 animals, migrated southward through this region every fall, sometimes to wintering grounds in the adjacent Yukon Territory. I longed to witness the spectacle and wondered how I could lengthen my stay in the field to accomplish that.

Except for a couple gold mining settlements, now largely faded to obscurity, the upper Fortymile country was unpopulated. It was also a land of some mystery. There was uncertainty, at least among anthropologists, regarding its native people, or lack thereof.

"We're entering terra incognita," Dr. McClellan announced as she parked the car on a high windy ridge. "It's not clear what Indians occupied this area in recent history. McKennan says it was Nabesna or Upper Tanana people from the Tanacross area who came up here to do their winter hunting. But Osgood claims wintering Han Indians from the Yukon valley utilized the area as part of their hunting grounds. Who knows? There hasn't been a native presence in the vicinity for many years now. Well, maybe *you* two can shed some light on this." Dr. McClellan gave us a knowing glance.

Was this our first field assignment? Solving an ethnographic riddle might be exciting. Han or Nabesna? Nabesna or Han? Robert McKennan or Cornelius Osgood? The latter two were well known pioneering anthropologists among Alaskan Athapaskans, people like the Tanana, Chandalar Kutchin, Ingalik and Tanaina. I had avidly read their monographs but was unaware of this particular debate.

McKennan's (1959) research on the Upper Tanana was published. But Osgood's (1971) work on the Han, the very people we were hoping to study, was still unpublished at this point. Even so, the Han had been of secondary interest to him. Osgood's three weeks of fieldwork in Han country were back in 1932, and not many researchers had ventured this way since that time, which was precisely why *we* were here, or so it seemed.

"Han or Nabesna? Nabesna or Han?" I quietly chanted the query over and over. It sounded like an incantation.

"What did you say? Is that you Crow? What's the matter, you can't talk now? Your beak must be crammed with that foul food," Susanne jibed.

"No, no. Just working with some sacred knowledge here. Much too refined for a Wolf to comprehend. Dangerous too. If you heard it your ears would turn into lichens and your brain would rot."

"Sacred? Ha! Everything a Wolf does is sacred. Eating, sleeping, dreaming, all is sacred."

"Yeah, I'd say you're dreaming all right."

Han or Nabsena? Nabesna or Han? The question nagged as we descended deeper into the Fortymile valley. Why not both? Indeed, why not somebody else altogether? The boundaries on "tribal" distribution maps often had a chimerical quality. And what about those three women in Beaver Creek? Contemporary Athapaskans seemed to move around a lot, and their ancestors must have done so in the past when their livelihood was more firmly anchored to hunting, fishing and fur trading. Who was to say where "traditional" Nabesna country left off and Han country began? And at what point in history?

"Unless I'm dreaming this must be Chicken," Dr. McClellan announced.

Chicken? A forlorn collection of dusty buildings, mostly abandoned and in disrepair, hugged the bank of a small stream. Gold had been discovered in the vicinity of Chicken Creek in the mid-1880s, but in subsequent years the mining community had declined and now seemed in its death throes. A menacing-looking contraption the size of a small airplane hangar lay dormant on the edge of town. The gold dredger, a colossal earth-eating machine, had been out of commission for several years. It had left in its wake a valley full of dredging piles, great mounds of churned-up stream gravel that imparted an air of lunar bleakness.

No one seemed to be stirring in Chicken. But a couple miles out of town we encountered an elderly white woman walking slowly along the shoulder of the road. She was peering intently at the ground, but looked up as we approached: "Howdy! I'm just hunting rocks."

Hunting rocks. Was that a euphemism for prospecting? Maybe Chicken wasn't dead yet. The woman was Emily West, a veteran school teacher who had spent much of the past 40 years in the Yukon. Her husband, of part Eskimo ancestry, had died five years before, and they had adopted two girls of mixed Indian-white parentage. In an earlier era this somewhat unusual family life had stirred intolerant sentiments among at least some locals who referred to Mrs. West derisively as the "polka dot lady."

"Oh, I've seen a lot in my time here, that's for sure," Mrs. West reflected. She had a dauntless manner, penetrating eyes, a wiry physique, and she spoke in determined no-nonsense terms. "I have a lot of respect for the Indian culture. I've seen the people around here go through hard times. But things are changing. All the white man's vices have been thrust upon them: murder, rape, alcoholism. So many Indians are drunk. They were once a proud people, but no longer."

Joe Jacob's haunting speech surfaced in my mind: "Too much drinking. Too many people die."

"So you folks are anthropologists, eh? Do you know the archaeologist Ivar Skarland? And the paleontologist Otto Geist? Housed both of them when they were digging up here back in the 40s. You'd find this area interesting. You know, there was once an old caribou fence that stretched for 80 miles, all the way from O'Brien Creek to Ketchumstuck. That's how the Indians used to catch the animals during their migrations. If you walk back into these mountains you'll find pieces of that old fence still standing!" Mrs. West beamed with admiration.

The information was staggering. Many subarctic peoples had used "drift fences," rows of sticks or barriers of brush and branches, sometimes leading to circular enclosures from which entrapped caribou could be snared or speared or shot with arrows. But those were structures of modest size, maybe a few thousand yards or a few miles in length. But 80 miles?! That was gargantuan, a veritable Great Wall of caribou fences. I was sorely tempted to take to the bush and examine the evidence firsthand, but our tight schedule prevented such excursions. I penned a reminder in my notebook to check into it later.

The reference to "Ketchumstuck" did not escape us. It was an abandoned settlement off the road on the Mosquito Fork and part of McKennan and Osgood's disputed hunting hinterland. Mrs. West seemed to have some firsthand knowledge of the place: "Oh, Ketchumstuck was a thriving Indian community in the 1920s, no doubt about that. There could've been as many as 80 people there at that time. It's sad, but the place pretty much died away in the 30s. Wiped out by TB."

"Tell me, Mrs. West, do you recall what kind of Indians were living at Ketchumstuck?" Perhaps this was an inane-sounding question, but I could not resist a point blank query. After all, Dr. McClellan was expecting us to show some initiative. We'd be cast out on our own in a few days.

"What *kind* of Indians? Hmmm. Well, the Ketchumstuck people had lots of relatives in Eagle and Dawson City."

Aha! Eagle and Dawson City were certainly Han strongholds. Maybe Ketchumstuck was Han country after all. Score one for Osgood.

Chapter Two

Subarctic Skid Row

A week later it was time to sink or swim. A diesel-powered ferry churned through the powerful Yukon River heading for Dawson City on the far east bank. Much of the river's murky burden of silt came from glacier-fed tributaries to the south, like the White River. The massive volume of chilled water raced by at an alarming eight miles per hour. Falling overboard could mean instant hypothermia, not to mention a quick ride downriver toward Alaska.

Dr. McClellan's departure time was due, leaving Susanne and me to fend for ourselves. Dawson City was to be our field base for several months. It was an exhilarating moment, on the brink of a great unknown. Could we learn anything worthwhile? Were we up to the task at hand?

Privately, my emotions were mixed. On the one hand, it was a heady feeling to be embarking on my own research. I felt well prepared. Dr. McClellan had trained us in taking rigorously systematic field notes, a keystone to any quality ethnographic work. We had even become fairly practiced at writing the difficult Athapaskan vocabularies in proper phonetic notation, although I knew that linguistic transcription was not my forte.

On the other hand, I was ambivalent about the ostensible mission of our project, to investigate "traditional" Han society and culture. I had nothing against ethnohistorical work or "salvage ethnography" per se. It was a venerable mainstay of anthropology to reconstruct indigenous cultures as they were at a particular historical timeline, often at or just prior to first European contact. How the Han lived in the 1870s, for example. I had no quarrel with this. My discomfort stemmed from the simple realization that I was becoming more interested in the social realities of the present than in any conjectural past.

In a few brief weeks I had seen enough to make me wonder what impact roads and mines were having on lives and livelihoods. Were people still hunting and fishing for food? Why the omnipresent reference to drinking? How did Indians and whites interact? What were people's hopes and fears in the here and now? What did young Han see in their futures? Such thoughts preoccupied me.

And then there was that troubling statement in an unpublished draft written by Cornelius Osgood (1971:14) about his early Han research, also an exercise in cultural reconstruction: "It was not a country for quick intellectual rewards, for the wealth of the culture, like the gold in the creeks, was no longer readily available." If one could come to such dismal conclusions in 1932, pray tell, what could we hope to find 40 years later?

I kept these misgivings to myself. After a few days helping us get our bearings and introducing us to a few contacts Dr. McClellan was ready to leave. She offered a parting word of advice which gave me pause: "Don't drink with your informants."

At that moment, we were standing on Third Avenue across from the Westminster Hotel with its beer parlor and Cabaret cocktail lounge, popular watering holes for local Indians and whites alike. Surely Dr. McClellan had our welfare in mind, but was it realistic to avoid drinking in a place like Dawson City? With the gritty street life unfolding before us, I was filled with doubts. True, there were some rough and disheveled characters guzzling from open containers along the boardwalks and in the back alleys. One wouldn't expect them to sit politely for interviews over tea and biscuits. But good or bad, drinking seemed to be a passion that enveloped the community, drawing people of all ages, backgrounds and walks of life. If there was a social epicenter, it might well be in the Westminster. And if we couldn't approach people who drank, I wondered, who would be left?

After weeks on the road I was feeling restless and in need of diversion. While Susanne attended to other matters, I grabbed a packsack and bushwhacked up Midnight Dome, a small mountain east of town. Moving through thickets of scraggly spruce and poplar, I paused occasionally to collect botanical specimens. In a small clearing I was pleased to find a dense carpet of bearberry (*Arctostaphylos uva-ursi*). Many Native American peoples were known to use its dark shiny leaves for tea and as a substitute for, or a mixture with, tobacco. I filled a small pouch to smoke later in my own pipe. If nothing else, a collection of plants might inspire some local sage to talk about the flora or traditional medicines.

Barely 3,000 feet high, the mountain's crown protruded above the treeline and on this day was exposed to a refreshing breeze. Falling away to the west was a magnificent panorama of the Yukon River, slicing through its geologically youthful valley like a raw knife cut. Some 2,000 feet below, Dawson City looked like a toy town. Its rectangular grid pattern of streets covered what once had been a swampy patch of flood plain. But the town's tidiness was an illusion. Faintly visible were its scores of ramshackle and deteriorating buildings, stark remnants of the frenzied activity of the Klondike gold rush over 70 years before.

Joining the Yukon at the south edge of town was a swift-flowing tributary, the famed Klondike River. It drained a vast watershed of gold-bearing creeks that had fueled the world-renowned rush. Even from my distant vantage point, the Klondike had a ravaged desert-like appearance. Its valley bottom was denuded for miles eastward. The river channel itself was lost in a labyrinth of enormous gravel piles heaped up by mechanical dredgers in post-rush times.

The dramatic, if sometimes depressing, scenery stirred my thoughts. As far as one could gaze in any direction was solely the Han's domain in the mid-1800s. At that time they may have numbered 1,000 and were localized in several bands along the Yukon River, from the Klondike confluence in the southeast to the mouth of the Kandik River to the northwest in Alaskan territory.

Han were always river-oriented people. Indeed, the term Han means "river," and *Han Kutchin* "people of the river," in the language of the neighboring Peel River Kutchin Indians from whom the expression derives. Not surprisingly, Han society was heavily influenced by summer exploitation of fish, especially migratory king salmon and dog salmon which reached the upper Yukon waters between July and September. This permitted prolonged residence in riverine settlements with rather abbreviated dispersal of families into surrounding mountains and valleys for the hunting of moose and caribou in early fall and late winter.

Han man dip-netting salmon on the Yukon River near *Klat-ol-klin'*, or Johnny's Village, in 1883, a few miles upstream from present-day Eagle, Alaska (from Schwatka, 1892).

But what of Europeans? Until the early 1870s there were no permanent European outposts in Han territory. The region remained remote from the centers of Russian fur trade in western Alaska and from the expanding English, French and Canadian trades in central Canada. The Han would be among the very last of the northern Athapaskan peoples to deal directly with whites.

True, there were some stirrings of the fur trade on the periphery. The English-controlled Hudson's Bay Company had established its Fort Yukon post in 1847 to the northwest in Yukon Flats Kutchin country, and its Fort Selkirk post in 1848 to the south in Tutchone territory (Murray 1910). The former establishment served as a distant and irregular point of trade for some Han until its closure in 1869 after the United States had purchased Alaska from Russia. Then, in the mid-1870s to early 1880s rival firms established the first, albeit short-lived, trading posts within Han territory at Fort Reliance and Belle Isle (Mercier 1986:1–11). Ignoring the new international border, the Alaska Commercial Company sent traders, like Leroy "Jack" McQuesten (1952), into this region capitalizing on the vacuum left by the Hudson's Bay Company (Coates 1985:63–64). These developments brought the fur trade and a livelihood based upon commercial trapping more firmly into the annual economic cycle of the Han.

But the outside world's thirst for mineral wealth, rather than furs, ultimately would have a larger impact. White prospectors created ephemeral gold mining settlements up and down the Yukon squarely in the Han's homeland. Frequently, the refugees from worked-out claims in a dying settlement became the colonists of new camps. Arranged in a linear fashion along the Yukon River, places like Seventy Mile (or Nation), Sixty Mile, Forty Mile, Twelve Mile, Eagle City (or Eagle), Star City, and Circle City enjoyed brief booms in the last quarter of the nineteenth century. Among these, only Eagle would survive to the present day. While these placer mining settlements attracted few native residents, they reinforced the growing infrastructure of commercial trade in the region (McConnell 1891).

Yet places like Forty Mile were a mere prelude to the monster boom and the gaudy cosmopolitan mining camp culture emerging nearby. The discovery of rich placer deposits in the southern tributaries of the Klondike River in 1896 triggered an unparalleled stampede which peaked in 1898 and was essentially over by 1900.

The magnitude of the event was reflected in the size of Dawson City which became the commercial focus of the Klondike rush. Despite its isolated location, it was the largest population center west of Winnipeg and north of Seattle at the end of the nineteenth century. As many as 18,000 new arrivals crowded into the new town site by the summer of 1898. Perhaps another 5,000 miners inundated the Klondike valley

(Adeny 1900:386). While many of the ephemeral gold hunters were American men, prospectors and fortune seekers from all over the world made the often perilous journey to the Klondike.

Would-be miners scrambled northward via a variety of routes, including a punishing trek out of Edmonton and across northern Alberta and British Columbia, or up the Yukon River by steamboat during its short ice-free season. Perhaps the most popular entree to the Klondike was via Taiya Inlet at the northern end of the Lynn Canal on Alaska's southeast coast. During the winter of 1897–98 thousands passed through the coastal gateway towns of Skagway and Dyea and then lugged their supplies up the 3,550-foot Chilkoot Pass, the last half-mile of which had steps chiseled out of sheer ice. Those who survived the pass pushed on to Lake Lindemann and Lake Bennett where local timber could be used to construct boats. When the ice-choked waters finally broke free in the last days of May, 1898, a ragtag assortment of more than 7,000 hastily built craft began the 500-mile journey down the Yukon River toward Dawson City (Berton 1958).

For the Han Indians, the "Stampede of '98" could have been no less traumatic than an invasion force of Martians. For generations the Han had followed the quiet and timeless rhythms of the river and the salmon harvest. Then, in a mere lightning flash of time, their country was overrun by hordes of strangers who stripped down forests, overhunted game, staked claims and devoured the earth in a frantic quest for yellow metal.

An alien landscape emerged, replete with hotels, rooming houses, trading stores, liveries, restaurants, mortuaries, gambling houses, dance halls, saloons and brothels. To relieve the tedium of the goldfields the "sourdoughs," or experienced miners, came to town for their occasional "sprees." Maintaining order in this remote corner of Canada was the watchful eye of the North West Mounted Police (Morrison 1985; Stone 1979).

For a brief moment the world's attention was riveted on the Klondike. Privileged visitors and travelers were creating an imagery and mythology of the gold rush which would take on a life of its own. This was true whether one read the *Harper's Illustrated Weekly* reports of correspondents like Edwin Tappan Adeny (1900), the compelling prose of Jack London (1903), early travel guides and prospectors' manuals (Harris 1897), or the romanticized poetry of Robert Service (1907, 1909). After all, it was Service (1909:14) who gushed:

> Men of the High North, fierce mountains love you,
> Proud rivers leap when you ride on their breast.

The compelling image was that of the lone EuroAmerican or EuroCanadian enduring the isolation and privation of a "savage" frontier, privations sometimes ameliorated by the flamboyant, rollicking ambience of Dawson City.

Fearful of the corrupting vices of Dawson City, however, Anglican missionary William Bompas sought to segregate the Indians from the miners. Although no treaties were signed with the Canadian government, a small residential reserve called Moosehide was established three miles downstream from Dawson City. Those Han who had traditionally occupied the mouth of the Klondike River were removed to Moosehide (Coates 1988:239–40).

Then, in another lightning flash of time, the great spectacle was over. By 1911 Dawson City's population had declined to about 3,000, and it dropped further in ensuing years as gold production diminished (Dominion Bureau of Statistics 1957). In the meantime, the lives of native residents had been shattered. The environment of the Klondike River drainage had been degraded by deforestation and overhunting so that the traditional livelihood of the Han (especially the Klondike band) was curtailed without providing viable alternatives, save for occasional work as laborers and guides. They were further ravaged by introduced diseases such as influenza, measles and mumps.

At the same time, Indians from other Athapaskan groups in the vast interior of northwestern Canada had been attracted by the phenomenon of Dawson City (McClellan and Denniston 1981; Slobodin 1963). Minimally, these included Tutchone, Tagish, Hare, Upper Tanana, and especially Peel River Kutchin (or *Gwich'in*). In this sense, the native community was becoming more heterogeneous as the Euro-Canadian population rapidly declined in post-rush years. In addition, the completion of a road link southward to the Alaska Highway effectively ended steamboat freighting, which, with the removal of the territorial government from Dawson City to Whitehorse in 1953, contributed further to the former community's economic and demographic decline.

Apparently, a half-century of segregation was enough. In the late 1950s and through the 1960s most Moosehide families moved back to Dawson City to acquire government-sponsored houses and to be near other services and amenities. But now, in 1970, Dawson City had barely 700 residents during its summer employment peak. About 200 of those were of native ancestry, most of them having federal status as members of the Dawson Band (Yukon Indian Agency 1969). Small-scale miners were still working claims, but with gold selling for only $36 per ounce, the big dredging companies, like Yukon Consolidated Gold Corporation Limited, were no longer operating (Findlay 1969:91–92).

In view of the population's heavy dependence on federal financial assistance for roads, schools, hospitals and other basic services, some analysts regarded Dawson City as a "welfare community" (Lotz

1964:189). Relief and transfer payments were becoming an important form of support for many white and Indian residents alike. During the long harsh winters mineral exploration, mining and a fledgling tourist trade ebbed dramatically, producing a marked seasonal out-migration of workforce and population.

From the top of Midnight Dome one could barely see the Indian houses on the north end of town. They were modest pre-fab units in beige, mint green and other pastel shades. Set down in a row on Front Street near the ferry landing, they vaguely resembled a suburban tract. Ironically, the Indians were segregated once again, this time in a corner of Dawson City disparagingly called "Indian row" by some whites. Some things never changed.

"Hey mate! Want a ride back?"

The voice startled me out of my ruminations. I turned around to find a middle-aged man with thick red hair and khaki attire grinning at me.

"Just heading back into town. Thought you might like a ride. Rain's moving in, eh?"

In my blissful solitude I had forgotten about the five-mile road that snaked up the backside of the mountain. This chap had simply driven up for the view.

Dawson City and the upper Yukon River valley.

Ned Estcourt and his wife Betsy were from New Zealand, and they were driving a rented Ford from Whitehorse, a reminder that summer tourism was now the hoped for Mother Lode in Dawson City that gold had once been. I was grateful for the lift. It would spare me a drenching. Driving down the mountain we shared our first impressions of the Klondike.

"Say, do you mind if we make a quick stop here? Won't be long." Betsy was already out the door and pushing through a tangle of under-brush beside the road. Ned had parked in the unsettled outskirts just east of town, and he was quickly on Betsy's heels. Strange they should be stopping here to relieve themselves.

Stepping a few yards off the road, I peered into the bush. Familiar shapes loomed in the tall grass. Crosses. Row upon row of unadorned wooden grave markers. Splayed out at odd angles from frost, and with inscriptions largely faded away, the monuments were apparently part of a white cemetery now gone to seed. Was this where the Men of the High North ended up?

"Over here! C'mon take a look!" The Estcourts were beckoning from a dense clump of willows.

"My dear granddad lies here," Betsy whispered excitedly. She pointed to a fragile cross that was losing its battle with the elements. Ned furiously stamped down the weeds around the marker. A name was no longer visible, and I wondered how she could be certain of its rightful owner. Perhaps the date of death, January 3, 1899, was the tip-off.

"Yah, Granddad was quite a traveler. He was in Halifax when news broke about the gold discovery, and he came out here in the Stampede of 1898. Poor Granddad never got rich though."

The same could be said for about 29,000 other hapless prospectors, I thought. For all its acclaim, the Klondike yielded riches to very few individuals. Few of those who made wealth held on to it. And, as with Betsy's unfortunate grandfather, some never made it out alive.

"Indians? Hell, if you want to find out about the local Indians go to the bars. I'd hang out at the Westminster if I were you. 'Moccasin Square Garden' or the 'Snake Pit' is what we call it." The man squinted at me from beneath the brim of his greasy railroad cap, waiting for my reac-tion. While his demeanor was deadly serious, everything he said was laced with sarcasm.

"Are you sure about the bars?" I asked.

"Does a bear shit in the woods?" The man's incredulous stare made me feel like a moron. "Of course the bars. You've got to go where people are. Hey, it's fun to see the Indians at play in the Westminster. You can get knocked around some when they start dancing. Oh, you'll get information from them when they're reasonably sober, but when they're drunk . . ."

He didn't complete the sentence, leaving the dangers to one's imagination. I felt he was taunting me, testing my gullibility. Already I was beholden to this gruff enigmatic man. He was my landlord. And I had spent the better part of two days tracking him down to arrange for a water hookup. Fiftyish, of Swedish descent and born in Dawson City, Karl Swenson worked at the local power plant and collected garbage as a sideline. Entrepreneurial, he also rented out properties, including our ramshackle two-story wooden affair on Third Avenue. It had been a shoe repair shop during the gold rush but was now surrounded by long-abandoned buildings falling apart after years of neglect and exposure to the elements. Despite the bleak surroundings, it was a blessing to live in anything other than a tent. Since I had vague plans of moving on to Eagle, Alaska, the other Han stronghold, I would at least temporarily share the shoeshop field headquarters with Susanne.

"Don't worry about your water, we'll get it hooked up. Hey, jump in. I'm making a run." Karl pushed open the passenger door of his dump truck. Having no pressing plans, I climbed aboard. Seeing a community through its trash, so to speak, could be revealing. Perhaps I was a closet archaeologist.

"I'd never rent my place to Indians, you know. I've been burnt too many times," Karl observed as he wheeled his ancient truck down a dusty alley. "Sometimes you'll get these white guys who want to work out at the Clinton Creek mine looking for a place to stay here in Dawson. But I check 'em out. If I see a squaw in the car with kids, no way I'm renting. They'd have my placed messed up in no time."

"You say the Indians . . .?"

"Don't get me wrong," Karl cut me off. "Indians have their good points. You can bet that everything they have they share with each other. If somebody shoots a moose, all the relatives get some meat. No white man would do that."

Karl parked in back of St. Mary's Catholic church and yelled for "Father Bill" through an open back door. There was no reply, so we tossed several barrels of church rubbish into the truck. "Father Bill's been preaching in the Yukon for a long time," Karl noted, "but he's struggling for followers. This town's sewed up by the Anglicans. What's your church?"

"Well, I was raised a Methodist mostly." I neglected to mention that my family had been at various times Lutherans and Congregationalists as well, that I had flirted with Bhuddism in college, and that I was currently something of a backslider. Questions about religion always made me uneasy. One never knew if an affiliation, or lack thereof, would please or offend. But Karl seemed beyond pleasing or offending.

"Methodist?" he snorted. "All religions are a game! Hell, I was a Presbyterian until the church here closed down. Now I think I'm an unbeliever. Until I see somebody come back from *there* and say it *is* there, I won't believe."

Fair enough. I was beginning to enjoy this unconventional tour. We lurched up and down the numbered avenues which paralleled the Yukon River and then did the streets (Princess, Queen, King, York, Duke and so on) that lay perpendicular to the former. Karl identified many notable buildings and landmarks and occasionally yelled out a greeting or friendly obscenity at acquaintances on the street. "Slim! See ya later at the Flora Dora! Hey Mike! Old partner!"

"That last guy with the big black beard was old Mike Wanage, Black Mike we call him. He was here during the stampede of '98. He's over 100 years old and still going strong," Karl noted. Fantastic. Here were names and faces of potential contacts. If he were so inclined, Karl could easily package this trip as one of those ubiquitous "city tours" for sightseers. Barring the garbage and flies, of course.

"Hey, you see that young Indian fella, the one that looks like a girl?" Karl was pointing toward the boardwalk in front of the Midnight Sun Hotel. A lanky man with jet black shoulder length hair and wearing a beaded moosehide vest was standing near the door. "That's one of the Bacons. I forget his first name, maybe Vernon. Anyway, he's one of John Bacon's sons. You'll want to be talking to old John."

"What about Vernon?" I asked.

"Nah, the kids are all haywire," Karl circled his ear with a finger. "Hey, we've got some other long-haired guys here too. What do you call em, hippies? People like that used to be called bums. They're coming up from the States. Living in these old abandoned shacks around town. Creating a damn fire hazard." Interesting. That explains the young barefooted white couple I had seen on Front Street earlier in the day. Straight out of Haight-Ashbury. A gaunt man with long dirty-blond locks wrapped in a leather headband. A short woman with a shock of frizzy red hair decked out in a gingham granny dress and tattered wool coat. A hefty middle-aged Indian woman had been following them down the street, apparently troubled by their forlorn appearance. "Hey sonny, you need shoes? Blanket? Sweater? You'll get cold for sure." The couple had politely declined all offers, effecting an air of blissful nobility in their self-impoverishment. There was something incongruous, if not touching, about the scene.

Karl drove past "Indian row" and the ferry landing on the north edge of town to an isolated spot that served as the community's dumping ground. It was a small patch of ground sited precariously on a sheer rock pallisade that was crumbling into the Yukon River. A potential avalanche of unsorted tires, cans, mattresses, broken bottles, fish entrails, newspapers, and putrefying offal hovered on the cliff's rim. A cyclone of sea gulls swirled overhead. Oddly, the garbage seemed to be moving, pulsating. I squinted into the sun's glare for a better look. Immersed in the grime itself were . . . oh no, could it be? Ravens! A good dozen of my dear friends were hopping, squawking, and picking their way with gusto through the mountain of refuse. Carrion-eaters, scavengers of the North, was one thing. But feeding off the dump like common rats? If Susanne saw this she'd tease me mercilessly. I wanted to say something to my friends, call out for some restraint, a modicum of dignity. But Karl would take me for a psycho.

We dumped the day's haul and were preparing to leave when two small Indian children appeared on the far side of the clearing. Karl grimaced and waved his hand, and the two children darted back into the spruce thicket like deer spooked by a hound.

"Damn! Looks like I better set fire to this trash."

"Why? For health reasons?"

"Not really. I set fire to it every now and then. If I don't, the Indians come by and pick things out of here. Especially the kids." Karl's logic escaped me. But then he wouldn't understand my thing with the ravens.

Back on Third Avenue Karl was preparing to drop me off at my shoe shop apartment when he brought the truck to a screeching halt in front of the Occidental Hotel, a defunct three-story relic from the gold rush whose windows and doors were boarded over. On one of its sagging stoops sat an Indian couple who were now staring curiously in our direction.

"You say you're here to study the Indians, right?" Karl inquired. His tone had a sinister edge. He made it sound as if I were planning to poison the town's drinking water.

"Well, yes . . ."

"Okay, see that woman over there? That's Bessie Peterson, she's from Twelve Mile. You'll be wanting to talk to her. And the guy. That's Jimmy Stevens, originally out of Moosehide. You should talk to him too. They might know something."

"Yes, I appreciate the lead." Parked only a few yards from the people in question, and with vociferous Karl gesturing and nodding in their direction, I could see that the couple's mild curiosity had turned to suspicion as their eyes narrowed. "I'll have to contact them later."

"Oh what the hell. C'mon!" Karl flew out the door and somehow finessed me across the street and virtually shoved me on top of the poor couple. "This here is Bob Jarvenpa. He's from the States, and he wants to talk to you." Before I could utter a word, Karl was back in his truck and peeling out in a spray of gravel and dust. "Thank you, Karl!" I muttered.

Bessie, who looked fortyish in a pastel pants suit and scarf, had a nervous sickly smile on her face. "Talk? Start talking. Go ahead, start talking," she commanded. The face was still smiling, but the voice was contemptuous.

Jimmy didn't smile. He appeared downright hostile. Perhaps in his late 20s he wore workboots, jeans, a black windbreaker with the collar turned up and a '50s style ducktail. A sort of Han version of James Dean. "Hey whaddaya want? A story?" he sneered.

Wonderful! This was not my idea of how to make contacts in the native community. "I guess Karl didn't explain things. I'm here for the National Museum. We're trying to learn more about Indian history and culture in this area . . ."

"What are you? Reporter? CIA? FBI? Draft board?" Jimmy interrupted, spitting out the acronyms with palpable disgust. And he had that sneer down real good. Even curled his lip like Elvis.

"I have nothing to do with those people. Like I said I'm on a project with the museum and . . ."

"What museum? You're CIA. FBI, right? Right?" Now Jimmy and Bessie both displayed murderous smiles. Like cats playing with a mouse. Silently I cursed Karl for pushing me into this ludicrous situation. Who were these characters? At first I thought they might be drunk, but they were quite lucid. There was no telltale booze breath. Suddenly Jimmy reached out and attempted to snatch something from my rear pants pocket. Instinctively, I jumped out of range.

"What's that?" Jimmy demanded. "What are you hiding?"

"I'm not hiding anything. You mean this little knife? I've been camping on the road the past few weeks and got used to wearing it." I produced the Mora sheath knife but kept it firmly in my grip.

"Nobody in Dawson carries a knife, not even a pocket knife!" Jimmy cranked up his voice a few decibels. People waiting to get into the government liquor store up the street turned to stare at us. Bessie nodded vigorously as Jimmy assailed me for violating some obscure local taboo. "We don't carry knives here. All my friends who see you on the street don't trust you when they see that knife."

"No problem. I just won't wear it anymore." I deposited the offensive item out of view into my packsack. There was no reason to hang around this charming couple, but how to make a quick exit without giving further offense? Almost as an afterthought I asked: "Do you know any of the people at Eagle?"

"Eagle?" Bessie and Jimmy echoed in unison.

"Yeah. Eagle, Alaska. People like the Fishers? The Samms? On the way to Dawson we stopped there and met the Fishers. Let's see there was Joe, Eliza, Sarah and Mike. Also met Agnes and Norbert Samm. Real nice folks."

Bingo! Jimmy's jaw dropped. Bessie's eyes moistened. Her face softened into a radiant smile. "Gee, why didn't you say that before? Those are my relatives! Agnes is related through my mom and auntie, you know! Boy, I hope she's okay. I bet her husband treat her rough, eh?" Bessie grasped me in a friendly handshake, eyeing me expectantly.

Now Jimmy was working my other hand like a pumphandle, grinning amiably. "Hey, those are my relatives too! You shoulda said something, man. Those guys are my cousins. You shoulda said you know them." The tension visibly drained away from his face. For a few minutes we talked pleasantly of Eagle and of Jimmy and Bessie's ties in that community. I felt slightly giddy. Their intimidating pose was quickly dropped, and we were chatting like old friends. Thank god for kinship! It was difficult following the dense genealogical connections, but that could be worked on later. For the moment I felt relieved to be escaping an awkward situation.

"Look! Store's opening!" Jimmy motioned with his head up the street where a queue of customers was filing into the government liquor store. "Hey Bob, got any money? How about we go up and get us a jug of wine?" In my view, it seemed a bit early in the day to be drinking, let alone tackling a gallon of muscatel. To be sure, there were a number of bleary-eyed souls at that very moment chugging cheap red wine in the back alleys.

"Why don't we go over to my place, and we'll have a pot of tea," I countered.

"Naw, I don't drink tea. Just wine." Jimmy stood up, stretched and yawned, and then walked a few yards up the street into the beer parlor of the Westminster Hotel. Bessie trailed after him, and I waved a goodbye to my newfound companions.

Later that day I returned to the shoe shop and found Susanne in high spirits. Karl's plumber had stopped by and hooked up a waterline. We could now cook and wash with relative ease. But there was something else. "I made a fantastic contact today," Susanne announced. "Remember that old Han woman Dr. McClellan knew, Sally McCallum? Well, I went to see her today, and she's wonderful. She knows all the old folkore, and she wants to help me with history and the Han language and everything. I've got a bunch of field notes already. And guess what? Are you ready for this? She's a Wolf!"

"Way to go, Susanne!" I was genuinely happy for her. A knowledgeable elder could open up some doors for both of us, but I could not deny a certain envy. Maybe Wolves were luckier.

"So how did you make out today?"

"I didn't meet any Crows or Ravens, at least not the human kind. Let's see, I did check out the town dump. I wouldn't bother with it if I were you, it's all in my notes. And, oh yes, I made a couple of contacts, Bessie Peterson and Jimmy Stevens, who might prove useful."

"Oh, great! Who are they? What do they know?"

"They know quite a bit about Eagle people. And I think they know a lot about drinking."

Weeks drifted by. Dawson City's diurnal rhythms took on a semblance of normalcy. Some locals slept late or, otherwise, did not appreciate morning visits by inquisitive researchers. The morning lull was useful for catching up on field notes, purchasing groceries at the DCW store and handling innumerable other chores. I learned to seek out potential informants at midday when people seemed most approachable. Evening hours brought a change of mood. The streets became livelier. Tourists who had long since parked their Airstream trailers or pickup campers were out en masse strolling the boardwalks. Native children scampered through the back alleys and overgrown lots playing, what else? Cowboys and Indians. Adult Dawsonites had their own version of *passeggiata* (going for a walk) which frequently ended at one of the bars. Most nights raucous laughter and a throbbing jukebox blared from the Westminster's open doors rattling the loose wallboards of our rental place across the street.

For several weeks I resisted the temptations of the Westminster. I had been cultivating a small circle of elderly informants who were starting to open up, reveal their early lives in the Yukon, share their knowledge of native traditions. While Jimmy and Bessie were not among them, I had befriended Simon Isaac, the son of the late Chief Isaac, the leader of the Klondike band of Han during the gold rush years. And there were John and Mary Bacon, Peel River Kutchin Indians who had moved to Dawson City in the early 1930s but who still wintered in their favored hunting grounds north of the Ogilvie Mountains. I had also gotten to know John's uncle, Walter Paul who, at 90 years of age, could speak credibly about the Kutchin and Han in the late 1800s. Occasionally I would spend a pleasant afternoon with Walter in his room at St. Mary's Hospital on the south side of town where other elderly citizens were cared for in a nursing home environment. The thought that these experienced elders would even talk to a 23-year-old stranger, let alone reveal their cultural secrets, was heady stuff. I was beginning to enjoy friendships with a few non-natives as well. There was Nick Favreau, a transplanted Nova Scotian who had married one of John and Mary's daughters, a witty garrulous man with wanderlust and a fondness for drink.

I found a kindred spirit in Dick North, a journalist and fisheries warden, who embraced the Yukon's mysteries. His passion was researching the true identity and origin of the "Mad Trapper," aka

Han elder Charlie Isaac wearing a trade sash inherited from his father, the late Chief Isaac.

Albert Johnson, a Depression-era recluse and psychopath of superhuman endurance and cunning. Johnson's killing of a Mountie set off a massive manhunt through the northern Yukon in the frigid winter of 1932. Dick lugged around a bulky file of old press clippings, photographs and odds and ends of information pertaining to the case. No lead seemed too farfetched or implausible to pursue. "You know, he could've been one of Capone's men on the lam back then. Not high up in the organization but an associate. I've got some interesting stuff from Chicago you should take a look at." Dick's eyes burned with excitement as he pulled out a thick sheaf of papers. "But I'm not overlooking the northern Minnesota angle. Our boy Albert was probably a Scandinavian immigrant from those parts, most likely a Finn or a Swede. Say, you're a Finn? You've got relatives down in the Iron Range, right? Can you make a few contacts for me?" Each week Dick was pushing some new arcane and tangled theory about the Mad Trapper. I eagerly awaited these as one would savor tabloid news bulletins: "Extra! Extra! Mad Trapper now exposed as Duke of Windsor!" Or "Albert Johnson, arctic orphan, raised by grizzlies!" Whatever the truth, I admired Dick's obsession with the hunt. It was something an anthropologist needed in order to face the uncertainties and self-doubts of fieldwork.

With the possible exception of Walter Paul, who had been blinded in a hunting accident over 40 years before and who was also a deacon in the Anglican church, my newfound circle of acquaintances seemed to spend much of their leisure time in the Westminster. Yet, I studiously avoided the place. Dr. McClellan's warnings about fieldwork and drinking had hit home. Then one evening two frail Indian women I recognized from St. Mary's Hospital were slowly but surely shuffling down Third Avenue and into the Westminster. The blind woman with the cane certainly looked a lot like Rose Hansen, one of Simon Isaac's sisters. And clutching her arm, well, that other woman was a dead ringer for Rose's step-sister and frequent companion, 94-year-old Lucy Joe. Susanne had been interviewing this pair the other day at the hospital. Well, that's it, I decided. Whatever's going on in the "zoo," the "snakepit," "Moccasin Square Garden," aka the Westminster, could not be harmful to one's longevity. I stepped off the boardwalk and into the cavernous darkness within.

After adjusting my eyes to the dim light, I found myself standing in a largely empty room. There was an old mahogany bar and a western shuffleboard game and a half-dozen empty tables, save for one with a patron who had collapsed face down amid a clutter of beer bottles. Was this the infamous "snakepit?" Probably not, for a faintly muffled cacophony of laughter, shrieks, clattering glass and music welled up from an adjacent room. Pushing open a door to my right I found myself in a small anteroom. Another door led to the eye of the storm. Fifty or sixty highly vocal patrons were sandwiched into the Westminster's tiny Cabaret room. "The Jays," a local husband-wife duo belted out country-western fare from a microphone in one corner of the room while several harried waitresses ran an assembly line of drinks to the thirsty crowd. A small opening among the tables served as a dance floor, and several groggy couples were dragging themselves around to a slow ballad. The air was pungent with acrid smoke and stale beer. Squinting through the blue haze, I could not locate Rose and Lucy, but there were many familiar faces. It struck me as poetic justice that the people I had been unsuccessfully pursuing for weeks had been sitting here, a few yards from my lodging, all along.

"Hey Bob! Sit here!" I turned around to find John and Mary Bacon beckoning me from a table near the bar. I was pleased to join them. John and Mary had been very kind to me, and I enjoyed their good-natured joie de vivre. "Bob, you want three beers to start, okay?" John inquired and then tilted his head back with a piercing infectious laugh. Whenever John laughed, everyone around him seemed to break up. It was an endearing quality which, combined with a rugged whipcord physique, was remarkable for a 70-year-old man. Mary didn't have the laugh, but she had a mischievous sense of humor. Standing little more than four feet tall, she was deceptively tough. After all, Mary and John were among the few Peel River Kutchin revered locally as "real oldtimers," who spent their winters hunting caribou and trapping in the windswept alpine tundra of the Blackstone River country. Sadly, it was in this same remote fastness north of the Ogilvie Mountains that most of John's close kin, including both parents, had succumbed to the devastating flu epidemic of 1919. John and one of his male cousins were the only two survivors on the Blackstone. During that grim winter of 1919 they had dreaded each new dawn, not knowing which relatives had died during the night and would have to be buried that day.

Looking at John now with his twinkling eyes and contagious laughter, I wondered how early tragedy had shaped his personality. Few were as open and gregarious as John. Acquaintances continually walked by, patting him on the back in greeting: "Hey John! How're ya doing?!" And John would reward them with peals of laughter. I could not have been happier. I enjoyed the Bacons' company, and for a first timer the bustling Westminster had a captivating charm. The bonhomie and the buzz of activity accelerated with each beer.

I was vaguely aware of some commotion under the table. Then an excruciating pain shot through my shin. "What the hell . . .?" A heavyset middle-aged Indian woman was now seated across the table staring icily in my direction.

"Hey, did you just kick me?"

"Do you know me?" The woman replied contemptuously.

"No, but what was the kick for?"

"Well, wake up!" Her voice was filled with rage. The woman appeared sober, but her behavior was baffling. Had I unwittingly offended her in some way? Mary tugged at my arm and whispered loudly: "Don't listen to her. She's no good." Hmmm, maybe the woman was "haywire," the favorite local term for crazy. Whatever the problem, she was now staring daggers at me.

"She your wife?" The woman sneered in derision.

"Who? Mary here? You've got to be kidding. You must know Mary Bacon."

"Not her! Over there. *That* woman." My tormentor motioned with her head across the room. Billy Bacon, one of John and Mary's many sons, was cutting in on an older man, Jimmy Joe, who was dancing with . . . and in another instant Susanne's face came into view. Aha! Susanne had said she might follow me into the Westminster. And suddenly, she was a popular dance partner.

"No we're not married!" I replied. "Not even boyfriend-girlfriend. We're working up here for the National Museum." Naively, I assumed that this would clear the air, but the peculiar woman was boring holes through me with cold eyes.

"I'm Ada," she announced. "Ada Peterson."

"Hi, I'm Bob Jarvenpa."

"Are you free?" Her tone was menacing. Without warning she let loose another wicked kick to my shins. Looking up in outrage and pain I found Ada's meaty fist a few inches from my nose. "See! I got one of these." A wedding band glistened from one finger.

Now Mary was on her feet forcibly pulling me away to another chair. "Don't talk to her. She's rotten, that one." She uttered something further in Kutchin or Han to Ada who then quickly retired to another table. Bewildered, I massaged my throbbing shins, wondering what social etiquette had been breached.

"Hey Bob, have another beer. You won't feel no pain!" John shoved a Labatt's in my direction and howled with glee. The dance floor was becoming packed as the Jays launched into their version of "Your Cheatin' Heart." Mary tugged at my arm: "C'mon Sonny. You and me go round and round, huh?" I glanced at John who simply waved encouragement with his hand. It soon became apparent that if married couples came to drink together, they sought out other partners for the dance floor.

I was an awkward dancer and normally avoided such diversion, but Mary was a tough woman to resist. She grasped my arms in a powerful clinch and around we went in a shuffling improvised waltz. It was hard to believe that this slight woman in a long calico skirt, siwash (knitted wool) sweater and moosehide moccasins was 40 years my senior. She had tremendous reserves of energy. I was aghast when Mary forcefully elbowed adjacent couples out of the way, but they gave her a wide berth. As the evening wore on I was becoming her "Sonny" for every dance, at the end of which she would clap vigorously, shout "whoopee!" and then embrace me in a bear hug. "I wear you out, eh? I getting younger, you getting older," Mary teased. I soon lost track of the beers, of the time, and of my aching shins.

Although I was not aware of it at the time, there were specific historical precedents for the form and etiquette of the Klondike dance scene. Years later I would read, with great interest and an odd sense of familiarity, geologist Josiah Spurr's (1900) account of a "squaw dance" in the summer of 1896:

> The evening of our arrival in Forty Mile Post we were attracted by observing a row of miners, who were lined up in front of the saloon . . . they said there was going to be a dance, but when or how they did not know . . . The evening wore on until ten o'clock, when in the dusk a stolid Indian woman, with a baby in the blanket on her back, came cautiously around the corner . . . She was followed by a dozen others, one far behind the other, each silent and unconcerned, and each with a baby upon her back. They sidled into the log cabin and sat down on the benches, where they also deposited their babies in a row . . . The mothers sat awhile looking at the ground in some one spot and then slowly lifted their heads to look at the miners who had slouched into the cabin after them—men fresh from the diggings, spoiling for excitement of any kind. Then a man with a dilapidated fiddle struck up a swinging, sawing melody, and in the intoxication of the moment some of the most reckless of the miners grabbed an Indian woman and began furiously swinging her around in a sort of waltz, while the others crowded around and looked on. Little by little the dusk grew deeper, but candles were scarce and could not be afforded. The figures of the dancing couples grew more and more indistinct and their faces became lost to view, while the sawing of the fiddle grew more and more rapid, and the dancing more excited . . . One by one, however, the women dropped out, tired, picked up their babies and slouched off home, and the men slipped over to the saloon to have a drink before going to their cabins. Surely, this squaw dance, as they call it, was one of the most peculiar balls ever seen. (Spurr 1900:116–19)

People kept packing themselves into the Cabaret. Incredibly, patrons were doubled up, literally sitting on top of each other at the tiny tables and spilling out the doors onto the street. I wondered if this replicated some age-old expression of community, as extended families once crammed into tents at fish camps. Across the room somewhere John and a couple of the Bacon boys were doing their best to fill Susanne's dance card. At least she could manage a respectable two-step and foxtrot. I figured Mary could use a new partner, but no one was cutting in on me. Not even Jimmy Stevens. The latter was quite looped and working his way through a succession of women. He was decked out in heavy engineer boots and cutting loose in a kind of flailing rockabilly stomp. Tables tipped and drinks spilled as he careened about. At one point he screamed in mock anger at a neighboring couple: "What's wrong with you people? Dance! Move your feet!" Now here was a man who could go round for round with Mary! But she was stuck to me like glue.

"*Denek'odhere! Denek'odhere!*" Mary whispered at a neighboring couple who twirled around the dance floor with admirable agility. The middle-aged man smiled knowingly at Mary as he whisked by.

"What did you say?" I asked.

"Denek'odhere. That means 'chief.' That's the chief over there, Chief of Dawson Band, you know."

"No kidding? The chief. I've been trying to get in touch with him. I'd like to talk with him sometime."

"You want to talk with chief?"

"Sure. You probably know him well?"

"Ha ha! I know chief real well!" Mary clutched my arms in a vice-like grip. "That's my son Willy!"

Willy Bacon, of course, I thought foolishly. These Bacon sons were everywhere, even in the Indian band government. But I wondered how the local Han felt about having a Kutchin as their official leader. Well, at least he hadn't seemed put off at my dancing with his mother.

There was some commotion developing near the Jays who were taking requests from the crowd. Someone suggested "Goodnight Irene," which didn't set well with one young Indian man who felt that, at 2:00 A.M., the night was still young. He was taunting a heavyset older man who had been drinking heavily and pontificating to all who would listen: "'Goodnight Irene' is good enough for me. What's the matter with you? Smarten up, eh!" With shocking speed the older man cut his adversary down with two swift punches to the belly and then was on top of him like a lynx on a hare.

"Leave my husband alone!" screamed a tiny woman who came charging across the dance floor. With the finesse of a flamenco dancer she delivered several jolting kicks to the body of the young man who was pinned beneath her spouse's fleshy hulk. Ada Peterson had nothing on this little kicker. She was about to administer the boot again when a waitress emerged from behind the bar. "Hey, no fighting you guys. Okay?" Her weary tone suggested she'd seen it all a thousand times before. Surprisingly, the combatants quickly dispersed. I was unnerved by the sudden display of violence, but the tempo of the Westminster was barely ruffled. Mary had paid scant attention to the episode. She was noticeably drunk now and ever more eager to dance: "C'mon sonny, you and me, we win Discovery Day dance contest, okay?"

"Mary, let's take a break, alright? I'm feeling a little sick," I protested.

Fortunately, Mary was distracted by an outburst nearby. The world-weary waitress was trying to shoo away a group of underage boys who were hanging around the open Cabaret entrance laughing and cat-calling while watching the spectacle within. Without warning Mary waded into the group in a shin-kicking frenzy that sent the boys running down Third Avenue. What was this kicking thing? I made a mental note to check into it later. Maybe the Athapaskans had a whole martial arts tradition heretofore unknown. The three women I'd seen could kick their way through the roughest barroom crowds.

By the time Mary returned two waitresses had their hands full try-ing to remove a problematic customer from the premises. Throughout the evening Harry Reed, a gaunt fellow of mixed Indian-white ancestry, had been wandering into the Westminster and simply collapsing in a drunken stupor upon whatever table, customer, or patch of floor hap-pened to be available. On each occasion he was escorted to the street but somehow always managed to wander back in to create some minor chaos. He had a spectacularly crooked nose, perhaps from greeting the floor on a regular basis. The waitresses were now hauling him feet first across the floor toward the door. I was baffled that the RCMP (Royal Canadian Mounted Police) were not summoned. The man appeared to be unconscious. But Harry's limber hands had a life of their own. They grasped table legs, chairs, pant legs, door frames, anything within reach. One would have better luck prying a gibbon out of a tree. After a herculean effort, the waitresses dragged him out the door.

Sometime later I noticed that semi-comatose Harry was crawling back in the Westminster. This time the waitresses were not stopping him. The doorway was filled by the hulking figure of Lester McCallum. If the Han had sumo wrestlers Lester would certainly qualify. At six feet five inches and about 375 pounds, Lester commanded respect. He was wearing soiled green work clothes and a folded mosquito net atop his cap, probably having spent the day at his gold diggings. He appeared only mildly intoxicated, but there was a peculiar smile on his face. With hands on his hips he remained firmly planted in the doorway as he sur-veyed the crowd. Only a few steps away, his gaze stopped on me. His smile turned to a bewildered frown.

"I think we met once before over by the ferry. Hi, I'm Bob." Maybe the guy needed a reminder.

"Who? You wanna fight?" Without warning Lester reached over and grasped me around the waist with ham-sized hands. I had the sick-ening impression that without breaking a sweat he could lift me above his head and hurl me over the bar.

"Nope. Not interested in fighting. Not at all," I croaked trying to mask the terror in my voice. Without replying, Lester released me. Like a bull in Pamplona he plowed into the Cabaret crowd. Dancers tripped, drink trays flew. Thankfully, Lester was rooting out quarry on the far side of the room. My heart was pounding wildly. My head throbbed with incipient hangover. Things were deteriorating fast. It was time to get out of this place.

"Hey mister? You wanna dance?" A young Indian woman I had never seen before tapped my shoulder. Her watery eyes and mournful expression did not inspire a dancing mood. She also appeared to be quite pregnant.

"No offense, but I was just heading home."

"C'mon. One dance won't hurt nothin." So we jostled and caromed our way around the floor. I kept one eye cocked for Lester who was out of view but, no doubt, trampling somebody that very moment. The Jays were getting into a spirited rendition of "The Race Is On." The room was starting to spin. I bit my tongue to fight off my rising nausea.

"I'm Rosie Bacon," the morose woman announced.

"Oh, are you one of John and Mary's daughters?"

"No. Daughter-in-law. I'm married to their son. *He's* my husband." Rosie grimaced and pointed to Ernest Bacon who was dancing with Susanne. "We got four kids, and if *he* wants to dance with *her*, I'll dance with you." The pain and outrage in her voice were frightening. She seemed like a dam about to burst.

At the end of the number I intercepted Susanne and informed her of the developing powderkeg. We decided to make a quick and discreet departure. But as luck would have it, Mary was patrolling the doorway, and she grabbed me as I walked past.

"Sonny! Don't go yet. C'mon, we dance. Win contest." There was no reasoning with Mary now as she tugged furiously at my arms attempting to keep me in the Westminster.

"DON'T FOOL AROUND WITH MY MOTHER!" a chilling voice barked. I wheeled around and came face to face with Vernon Bacon. Haywire Bacon, as many called him behind his back. This youngest of the Bacon sons appeared quite sober, which somehow made his accusation more unsettling.

"Look, I'm not fooling around with anybody . . ."

"Just fuck off! Fuck off now!" Vernon's face was contorted in anger. I nervously watched his clenched fists. The thought that he believed I was taking liberties with his mother filled me with profound guilt and sadness. Any lingering euphoria from the evening evaporated. Mercifully, Vernon's attention span was short-lived. Before I could finish a sentence, he roughly grabbed the collar of a young ferry deckhand who had the misfortune of talking to Mary.

"Hey man, I was only kidding with her," the startled man protested.

"Just leave her alone, or I'll fight you right here." Vernon was methodically shopping for an excuse to tear into somebody. Anybody.

Finally the right moment came. Susanne and I bolted out into the darkness of Third Avenue. A few seconds later Rosie burst through the door screaming obscenities, hot on the heels of Ernest who was making his own rapid departure. The raucous din of the Cabaret quickly faded into a background hum. Shadowy recesses along the boardwalk held the staggering and slumped-over casualties of the night's excesses. Overhead the stars in the pale morning sky were already fading as the northern sun emerged above the mountains. I was completely drained but could not sleep. The evening's misadventures kept replaying in my mind. And I felt a strange glow of satisfaction, if not accomplishment. After all, I had experienced the Westminster and lived to tell about it.

After my baptism at the Westminster, the fieldwork seemed to pick up a notch. This may have been fortuitous, but more visitors were stopping by the shoe shop. Fueled by kettles of tea, pleasant social visits often evolved into formal interviews that began shedding light on questions of prime interest for our research. What was the nature of Han economy and society during the gold rush? How had the Han and the various Kutchin groups interacted through time? What was the history of Indian-European relations in the region? What about native settlement patterns and population movements over the past 70 years?

A rough picture of these dynamics began to emerge from the testimony of men like Simon Isaac who talked of their early lives, and of the lives of their parents. Simon was an enigmatic and rather worldly fellow having served in the Canadian Army during World War II. At 60 years of age he lived alone on a pension and was one of the few local Han to prefer life in his cabin in the old Moosehide settlement rather than Dawson City. He was particularly proud of his father, the widely respected Chief Isaac who had passed away in 1932. Simon often wore a colorful Hudson's Bay Company wool sash that he inherited from his late father. Thin and limber, he used animated arm and hand gestures to accent his speech. He had a wry wit and often smiled mischievously when talking. Yet, when listening to others he was serious in demeanor, and he often sat silently for long periods.

One morning Simon arrived at the shoe shop in a gregarious and somewhat nostalgic mood. He ended up visiting for much of the day. While I brewed up the first kettle of tea, he began talking about his life:

"My father Chief Isaac came from Eagle. He was *Ezan*. That's what we call the people who come from that place, you know, Ezan. Walter Benjamin, old Walter Ben, was my father's half-brother. He used to do some mission work down at Eagle in the early days when the minister was gone. And Chief Charlie was my father's uncle and the chief down at Forty Mile. When he got too old for that my father became the chief down there.

"Later my father came up here and married my mother. She was *Tronduk* or *Troncik*. That's what we call the people who live around here at the mouth of the Klondike River, Troncik. Yah, my mother's people were from around here. But my mother was born at the mouth of the Sixtymile River, you know. Right at the mouth there on Moose Island. That's a real good place to hunt moose in the spring time.

"But back before the white man and the gold rush, the Troncik stayed on the other side of the Klondike River, the south side over there, at the mouth. There was no Dawson City then. Where we're sitting now was nothing but a big muskeg swamp, eh? So the Troncik gathered on the other side for a couple months every summer for fishing. For the salmon, you know. The people built a big fence of poles and brush across the Klondike. But they left a gap in the fence where the salmon could swim through. And they had a platform right there where the men could stand and spear the salmon. The water was so clear. It was easy to spear them. But not in the Yukon. Too muddy. So people drifted along the shore in canoes with dipnets. If they see something move in the water, they just put the net in. Like a big basket on a stick. Oh, there were many ways to catch fish. And it's funny too, you know, those salmon never travel in fours, eh? They always travel in twos and threes.

"The women, they dried that fish and then put 'em in a big hole with dried willow to give a good flavor. They buried their fish to use later, you see. But they needed special ground, soft ground for that. The Troncik used to go three miles below Moosehide and then across the Yukon on the west bank over by Quebec Creek. That was named later for some Frenchmen who cut wood around there. They took out about 2,000 or 3,000 cords of wood from that place. Boy oh boy, after the gold rush started sometimes it was real hard to get enough wood and food around here. But anyway, before the whiteman came, the Troncik buried their fish in the ground by Quebec Creek. And depending on how much food they had, sometimes that fish might last the people until the real cold weather in December or January.

"In the fall time, after the fishing, the Troncik moved downriver, down the Yukon, and then up Sheep Creek for hunting. People moved all around these mountains for hunting caribou and moose in the wintertime. If somebody killed a moose, well, every family got a little hunk of that. It was divided up that way. Maybe the hunter got more of the meat if the chief decided. Ah, the breast bone is my favorite part. When it's good and fat it makes a nice soup, eh? And you can see how our language is different from the *Loucheux* (Peel River Kutchin) people, the

way we call the animals. We say *gendik* for moose, but they say *genjik*.
We say *watse* for caribou, but they say *watsai*. A little different, huh?

"The people would move back here to the mouth of the Klondike
in June. Get ready for fishing all over again. Every year, every year,

Joe Henry, a Peel River Kutchin (*Gwich'in*) man in Dawson City, prepares a
preservative stain for his newly-constructed snowshoe frames.

that was our way. Also they try to gather spruce gum and birch gum for medicine. It gets too dry in summer so they have to find it in springtime. Makes real good medicine for coughs and colds. And you can heat it up and put it on cuts and wounds, you know. After the gum dries up and falls off you're pretty much healed right up. Also the spruce and birch gum are good candies, sweet just like Buckley's Cough Syrup. And in summertime the women gathered the berries too, you know. Especially *trontil*, the high bush cranberry. The porcupines like that kind too because its so juicy. The women had to gather those berries on the islands around here, because they don't grow so well inland. And summer was the time to find spruce roots too. My mother and the other women split and dried the roots and used them for sewing their baskets.

"The Troncik traveled around quite a bit to trade in the old days. Even before the gold rush, you know, the Hudson's Bay Company had their fort downriver, Fort Yukon. That's where the 'flat country people' live. *Ucelcin Kutchin*, we call 'em. And then Hudson Bay had their fort upriver, Fort Selkirk. Up where the Stick Indians live. And then later Jack McQuesten built old Fort Rely (Reliance) just a little ways downriver from here. Yup, that's where my father got his sash, I think. From McQuesten.

"In the early days there used to be a chief down at Eagle. And he was a real 'bad man.' That's what people said, anyway. He had many many wives, that guy. He even wanted his grave to be put on a little round hill down there. There's a fence around it, you know, and people still take care of that place. But the Troncik and the Ezan people got along pretty well. No fighting with each other. And we got along pretty well with the Loucheux too. But sometimes there was fighting.

"Long time ago one of our boys was hunting in wintertime, in February, and some other Indians shot him, killed him. This was before the gold rush, you see, but people already had guns. Muzzle-loaders. It's a pretty dirty story. They hurt that boy really bad, cut him up. Tore one arm right off. Our people were angry about that and start arguing among themselves. So the chief here, *Zeig'e*, gave the order to go after those guys. Well, the Troncik could tell by the snowshoe tracks that they were different Indians all right. They could see what direction they were traveling, so they followed the tracks way far south. Took a long time too, but they went all the way over toward the Ross River. And they caught up with those Ross River Indians there and killed 14 of 'em. That took two or three months. When they got back to the Klondike here there was no snow. Yah, those were my mother's relatives, you know. Zeig'e was directly related to my mother two or three generations back."

Simon paused and gazed momentarily out the window. He seemed to be absorbed in thought. I was reluctant to interrupt but could not resist a question:

"Simon, do you remember what people, or what Indians used to live up at Chicken and Ketchumstuck?"

"Well, I never traveled there myself. Sometimes in the early days those people came down to Forty Mile to get supplies."

"Were they Troncik? Did they speak your language?"

"Oh no. They were different from us Klondike and Forty Mile people. They had a different language altogether up there. I could understand it some, but they talked more like people over at Tanana or Tanacross."

"Ah ha! Score one for McKennan," I mumbled to myself.

"Who? You mean McQuesten?"

"No, I'm just enjoying your story Simon. Here, have some more tea."

"Okay, thank you. Anyway, that's how the Troncik lived before the gold rush. I never saw all that life myself. But my step-sister, Lucy Joe, she's much older, and she lived a lot of those old ways, you know. Her parents died around 1905 when a sickness come downriver. So my parents adopted her. My father arranged a marriage for her to a man up at Fort Selkirk. So Lucy left Moosehide here around 1910, just before I was born.

"Yah, things got really tough for us after the gold rush. That started here in 1896. But the Troncik already knew about the gold long before the white man. Oh sure. We used to filet our fish on willow branches on the river gravel, you know, so people could see the yellow metal there. But the white man was really greedy for it. That's why Bishop Bompas moved our people down to Moosehide in 1898, eh? Wanted to keep us away from the whiskey and the white man. He named my dad 'Isaac' too. When Bishop Bompas started baptizing the Troncik he gave us all English names like Isaac, and Nathaniel, and Bartholomew. Like that.

"And all kinds of sickness came in with the white man. We never had measles, chicken pox and TB in the early days, eh? In July, 1925 the flu came downriver here again, and just about all the families in Moosehide were in pretty bad shape. I don't know why, but I never got sick that time.

"I've worked hard all my life. I've hunted moose, trapped beaver. In the 1930s I unloaded the steamboats here for $1.50 a day. Between 1931 and 1936 I unloaded Jack Maloi's wood rafts here at the mouth of the Klondike River. You know Jack? He's still living in Dawson. Must be in his 80s. Back around 1913 he started running those horse pack trains to the mining camps, from White River over to the Tanana. And later from the Tanana over to the copper mine at Kennicott. Then he started cutting cord wood up at Coffee Creek. He'd put 20 cords of wood on a raft and haul about 200 cords a year down here to Dawson. I used to get 75

cents an hour to unload those rafts. It was the best paying job around at
the time because the work was really hard. You had to stand around in
that cold river all day, and your arms and hands would freeze up and
ache pretty bad.

"And then I was in the army for six years. During the War, I was
over in Belgium and Italy. My unit got trapped down in this creek bottom for three days one time. We had no food. But the soldiers firing on
us looked in worse shape. They were doing all the heavy work, and they
had these sunken cheeks and eyes, you know. I guess it turned out okay.
We beat those Nazis. And I'm doing okay. I've had a pension now for five
years. But I like to keep busy doing some kind of work. I've got a partner,
a younger guy, for a little prospecting. He's supposed to meet me today,
but I don't where he is. Probably still up on the Dempster Highway. Well,
maybe I'm talking too much, huh?"

Joe Joseph (middle), Charlie Isaac (right), and Joe's grandson Michael (left),
outside Joe's home on Dawson City's north end.

"No way, Simon." By this time I was entranced by Simon's compelling narrative and did not want it to end. "This is important information. Take a break. I'll heat up some more tea."

"No, no, but I'll come back later and tell you more. I got to find my partner. Should go back to Moosehide and check my cabin too. I think there was a bushman around there last night."

"Bushman?" My mind fumbled for an image. I was vaguely aware of the widespread belief by northern Athapaskans in potentially dangerous subhuman or feral men who lurked in the forest depths. In the summer, it was thought, they approached camps and villages to capture children. "Bushman, you say?"

"Oh yeah, we had lots of 'em around here before the white man. But they still come around whistling and throwing sticks. Some kids were playing down at Moosehide a couple years ago, and a bushman came around. Scared 'em pretty bad. Well, I better go. Don't know where my partner is. Probably out chasing klooches. Girls, you know."

Simon disappeared down the dusty back alley. Eventually he would return to share more of his rich storehouse of memories. But for the moment I was ecstatic. Strands of local history and culture were beginning to weave together. I would be up late working on my field notes, and it was labor I welcomed. Despite my nagging doubts and misgivings, I was finally beginning to feel like an anthropologist.

Alcohol arrived in Han territory, along with other commodities introduced by miners and traders, in the latter half of the nineteenth century. The sale of liquor to Indians was strongly discouraged for many years, but by the early 1890s the situation was changing in ways that held grim consequences for the future. Charlotte Selina Bompas, wife of Anglican bishop William Bompas, made the following observations at Forty Mile in 1893:

> And, worse than all these, there are several distilleries where rum or whiskey is made and sold to the Indians, and they have learned to make it for themselves, and that other highly intoxicating spirit called "Hoochino" [distilled molasses]. Thus our Indians, being brought into contact with the white man, fall in only too easily with his taste for luxury, love of gambling, coarse, vile language, and for the miserable and ruthless degradation of women. (Archer 1929:138)

For better or worse, however, the Westminster was becoming a regular part of my itinerary. Perversely, I felt closest to the community when I was there. New and interesting characters were always turning up. At least some of them were agreeable to interviews later away from prying eyes. I never walked into the place "armed." Carrying a notebook or tape recorder would have been as tactful as waving a shotgun. I espe-

Annie Henry, a Peel River Kutchin (*Gwich'in*) woman, outside her home on
Dawson City's north end.

cially enjoyed running into my friends on this somewhat neutral turf. It
was a kind of time-out from the usual researcher-informant relationship. Even so, tongues were looser, and people often had morsels of
gossip to share. And while the Sturm und Drang of the Westminster
could be entertaining, I became more adept at sniffing out "haywire"
people or "haywire" situations and bailing out before the proverbial shit
hit the fan.

But the adventure and novelty of it all soon wore thin. The final straw came when friends began following me home to continue their drinking in the shoe shop. Nick Favreau, John and Mary's son-in-law, had been on a week-long drunk after an altercation with his wife. He was living from bottle to bottle on the street, often with several intoxicated companions in tow. One afternoon I spotted him in the Westminster beer parlor engaged in a heated discussion with a miner from Clinton Creek. Normally amiable, Nick was incensed about something the miner had said. Both were tall strapping fellows. Nick was in the other man's face, pressing him against the bar. Pointing down at his steel-toed, hob-nailed work boots, he growled: "Do you know what these are buddy? They're Nova Scotia boxing gloves! Wanna go a round?" The miner's eyes grew large, and he wisely withdrew to a table.

Nick smiled when he saw me coming, but his weathered face carried a heavy sadness: "Hey partner! How're ya doing? I'm not so good. This thing with Delia is tearing me up. Haven't seen my kids in three days. Whaddaya say we go to your place and talk? I've gotta sober up."

Against my better judgment, Nick's drinking buddies of the moment, Danny Bacon and Hank Hansen, accompanied us while I brewed up a pot of coffee. Once we were settled, however, bottles of wine and whiskey materialized from jackets and shirts. In a remarkably short time, Danny and Hank were loaded. Phelgmetic when they walked in, they were now sloppily gregarious. They were in high form spitting, slobbering and muttering obscure obscenities at nobody in particular when, to my chagrin, Susanne walked in the door. She shot me a perturbed look and hurried on to a back room that formed her part of the apartment. Uh oh, I thought, the Wolf is pissed! Rightfully so. Crow will eat crow over this one. I winced as Danny awkwardly attempted a pass at Susanne and then collapsed in a moaning heap under the kitchen table.

"Behave yourself. You're with people now. Watch your language," Nick cautioned Danny. Nick was chugging Seagram's whiskey straight but remained uncannily clear-headed. The coffee had long been forgotten. "Hey Danny, take five. Be a man."

"Fuck you," Danny responded from under the table. "I don't give a shit. Either way I don't give a shit." At that moment, there was no mystery why Danny was also persona non grata with his wife and family.

"You don't make any sense," Nick continued. "You're just like all Indians. You don't work, yet you're always drunk. You don't know what you're talking about. You're senseless."

I was surprised by Nick's harsh indictment of his brother-in-law, especially given his own unenviable circumstances. Eventually Hank too collapsed to the floor where both men remained prone and eerily lifeless for the next several hours. When Hank came to, he was disoriented and combative. He tried to relieve himself where he stood. By the time Hank had his fly open Nick was dragging him roughly out the door, his heels strafing grooves across Danny's puffy face. I helped Nick deposit both unwanted guests in a patch of fireweeds in a vacant backlot where they groaned, crawled and rolled about like inmates at an asylum.

"Jesus H. Christ, I'll never bring these guys visiting again." Nick remarked. "I hope I'm still welcome."

Several more hours passed. Nick kept drinking and unloading his troubles. Infuriated and humiliated at being physically barred from his own home by a welfare officer, his mood turned black. His joviality and ribald humor evaporated. I could only express my fondness for both Nick and Delia and suggest their problems might seem less serious with a new day. But before I could wean him from the Seagram's, Nick went out to collect his companions. "Danny, Hank! C'mon! Get up! Let's go get drunk!"

Bleary-eyed but smiling, Danny's bruised head rose from the fireweeds like some awful blood moon in an early autumn sky. "Get drunk? Again?" he asked. Incredibly, he was getting to his feet and lifting Hank with him. As the trio shambled across Third Avenue toward the Westminster, I felt profoundly depressed. Was this my destined role? Running a crash-pad for drunks? Should I be documenting these pitiful

Deteriorating gold rush era structures along Dawson City's 3rd Avenue.

scenes? The ravaged bodies and broken families? And did any of this qualify as "drunken comportment," the benign way that some scholars talked about uses of alcohol in other cultures? Old Joe Jacob at Burwash Landing had been trying to tell me something. His words kept surfacing in my thoughts: "Too much drinking. Too many people die."

For my own peace of mind, I vowed to get back to my original interests in ecology. It is what attracted me to the North in the first place. The immense landscape. The creativity of native adaptations to limited food supplies and the extremes and vagaries of distance, animal behavior, weather and community composition. How did people understand the environment and sustain themselves through their hunting and fishing knowledge and other institutions? But here I hit a brick wall. True, Dawson City people could talk about such things a generation or two in the past. The present was another matter. The Bacons were one of the few native families still living a nomadic bush lifestyle in the winter. Fur prices had declined enough since World War II that most commercial trappers were inactive. And only a few families even bothered operating summer "fish wheels" for catching salmon, either for sale or home consumption.

Jimmy Stevens succinctly summarized the situation one day: "Look, I had enough of that bush life when I was growing up in Moosehide. I'm gonna be a city boy from now on." Fine, but I don't want to hang around for your funeral, I mused. A few weeks earlier one of Jimmy's cousins had died of a heart attack at the tender age of 23. It was a sad day. The Anglican church was packed with mourners, including myself, for the Christian part of the funeral. Subsequently, a smaller select group of kin traveled to the Moosehide cemetery to honor the deceased in the native funerary tradition.

The more I saw of Dawson's "city boys" and their drinking ways, the more I speculated about Eagle, Alaska. Maybe the Han in that quaint log cabin community 100 miles down the Yukon River were more conservative or less swamped by contemporary "diseases of development." Perhaps they could teach me something of the age-old northern food quest. Maybe. The problem was that the summer field season was rapidly coming to a close. My finances were drying up. There was no public transport along the road to Eagle, and few people I knew ever traveled that way. I looked into hopping aboard the diesel freight barge, the Brainstorm, but its next downriver trip was a month off.

The river! Of course. I had no Huck Finn fantasies, but a few of the old-time miners were knowledgeable raftsmen who had floated the Klondike, the Yukon, the Stewart, the Pelly and other rivers in their quests for gold. Eric Larson, a Swede who had come North in the early 1930s to prospect along the Firth River near the arctic coast, overheard my plans for traveling to Eagle one day when I was sitting in Horst Scheffen's cafe.

"You say you want to go to Eagle? Build yourself a raft. Hell, with that current you'd be down there in 20 hours." Eric produced a handful of wooden kitchen matches from his shirt pocket and built a model raft on Horst's counter. "See, you just lash four or five good-sized logs to your two cross-planks. Drill a couple holes in the rear log for your two steering poles, see? They work like rudders and oars at the same time. Nail on a little box for a seat and you're in business. Just be sure you build it on a couple skids so you can push the damn thing in the water. Cheapest way to get around this country that I know of."

Eric's matchstick model was wonderfully simple and persuasive. I respected his knowledge. Eric had lived for awhile with the Eskimos on Herschel Island, and he had the hardy self-sufficient manner of Dawson's old bachelor miners. As if to boost my confidence, Eric took me to the west bank of the river to a tangle of steamboat wreckage, abandoned shacks, driftwood piles and assorted flotsam and jetsam to search for likely raft timbers. In minutes Eric spotted several candidates which he marked with an axe. His excitement mounted as he probed through the debris. I felt a twinge of guilt. Would he be disappointed if the project failed?

Eric lit a pipe and sat on a log observing the relentless current. A deceptive river, that Yukon. While it has few spectacular falls or whitewater, its steep gradient pushes a massive volume of chilled water like a great liquid runaway freight train. I threw a chunk of driftwood far upstream. In a few intimidating seconds it went racing by. "You'd be a helluva lot better off with a partner," Eric noted. "That way you could spell each other on the oars."

"Why don't you join me Eric? You could show me the ropes, and we'd have an interesting trip." At this point I hadn't considered the issue of getting back to Dawson City. That bridge would be crossed in due course.

"Hell, no, I'm too old for this. But you need a second pair of eyes to watch the river. It takes a long time to steer a raft into position. You gotta know way in advance where you want to be and where you want to land. Especially you gotta watch out for those damn sweepers."

"Sweepers?" My first thought was of the "untouchable" castes of India. What were they doing on the Yukon?

"Yah, sweepers. They can be snags, tree roots, even whole trees that fall in the river. They're stuck to the bank, but they bob up and down just under the water. Hard to see and dangerous as hell. Hit one of those head on and you'll go flying. You won't last long in that ice water either," Eric cheerfully concluded.

Maybe it was his way of educating me to danger, but Eric's ambivalence about the raft was getting on my nerves. Wouldn't it be ironic if I built a solid raft and avoided the treacherous sweepers only to overshoot my target and go floating off to oblivion. I fantasized a letter:

Dear Dr. McClellan:

As you may recall from my last message, I had intended to finish up the field season at Eagle. Events conspired to push me farther afield. Namely, it took a couple hundred extra miles to stop the bloody raft! Not to worry, the Kutchin people here at Fort Yukon are quite hospitable. I hope you will agree that a little comparative work could not hurt our project. My apologies for the rumpled and smeary appearance of the enclosed batch of field notes. The sweepers dumped my supplies on the trip down. I salvaged some items, but everything is still waterlogged. As I am nearly broke, I will appreciate any advice on getting back to the States. Bush plane fares out of Fort Yukon are astronomical.

Sincerely,

Bob Jarvenpa

Chapter Three

Crows and Sea Gulls

My glorious raft plans floundered in dry dock. Eric's sweeper stories spooked me into looking for a knowledgeable partner, but I couldn't find one in Dawson City. The seemingly idle men in the Westminster only gave me peculiar looks and polite refusals. One could hardly blame them. Jumping aboard a pile of lumber on the Yukon with a near stranger, offering little compensation and rather vague plans, was lunacy.

Depressed, I shoved thoughts of Eagle aside. Something unusual was afoot in any case. The streets were enveloped in clouds of dust. Dozens of vehicles were arriving in town by the hour, and dozens more were advancing up the gravel highway from Whitehorse. By evening pickup-campers, caravans of airstream trailers and chartered buses were prowling the vacant lots and weedy roadsides on the outskirts in search of camping space. Discovery Day was starting! I had almost forgotten about Dawson City's annual celebration, a three-day renewal ceremony which combines elements of country fair, small-town jamboree and mining camp spree in a romantic homage to the sourdoughs, or pioneer miners, who made the first major discoveries of Klondike gold.

Some of the visitors were fellow Yukoners from other communities. But many were tourists from the United States and southern Canada who had been dodging flying gravel on the Alaska Highway and decided to make a 500-mile side-trip northward to the Klondike. Discovery Day had its roots in the early post-rush years when veteran miners would parade through town bedecked with nugget chains dangling across vested suits (Berton 1954:258–67). But beginning in the early 1960s, as the mining economy continued to wither, the federal government encouraged Dawson City to promote the festival as a tourist attraction as well (Lotz 1964:125, 1970:212–19). Now, as road-weary travelers climbed out of their airstreams, they would be treated to three days of exhibits, parades, athletic contests, dances and speeches all celebrating Dawson City's legendary past. Many locals were garbed in stylized 1890s vintage clothing to create the appropriate atmosphere: prospectors' attire for men, Victorian dresses or dance-hall outfits for women.

Discovery Day had some of the dimensions of "emergent authenticity," a process in tourism identified by Eric Cohen (1988:379–82). The celebration, for example, although at one time a socially "meaningful

Dawson City's Discovery Day celebration evokes EuroCanadian frontier themes.

ritual for an internal public," also emerged as a "culturally significant
self-representation before an external public." In this sense, one might
argue that "commoditization" of the festival, including packaging and
promotion of the sourdough image, an amplified symbol of EuroCanadian and EuroAmerican achievements and gold rush history, actually
enriched rather than destroyed a field of meanings.

Indeed, one might argue that commoditization was the whole
point, the *raison d'etre* for the Klondike and its cultural landscape, an
outpost of late nineteenth-century capitalist speculation. The quest for
personal riches is at the heart of capitalist ideology, and surely this was
celebrated by many residents and visitors. The influx of tourists recre-
ated the "rush" experience which was central in the local conception of
history. The very fact that eight of every ten visitors derived from the
United States corresponded to the predominance of American miners in
the original stampede. This lent a pilgrimage-like quality to Klondike
tourism as thousands of Americans journeyed to the remote locale each
summer, in essence, to witness a re-enactment of a chapter of their own
history.

"Hell, it's just another big drunk," Karl concluded. He had stopped
by to collect our rent. As was customary, he rarely missed an opportu-

nity to provide an unflattering view of his fellow Dawsonites. "Just look at 'em! It's barely noon and the buggers are'll haywire." Karl motioned to the stretch of boardwalk between the Westminster and the Midnight Sun. Crowds of locals and visitors alike were spilling out of both establishments and milling about gregariously with open containers of beer, wine and blended whiskey. From a distance, at least, they appeared to be a cheerful lot. Their raucous bonhomie reminded me of a tailgate party at a college football game. Maybe that was optimistic. I caught a glimpse of Jimmy Stevens' trademark scowl. He was giving some poor camper the third degree about a hunting knife looped to his belt. Just then an RCMP patrol car cruised by slowly, but no one was being stopped for drinking openly on the streets this day. "You know what we call the third day?" Karl sneered. "Recovery Day!"

Spree-like hedonism aside, by the second day I was growing weary of the festivities. For one thing, it became apparent that the local Indians were as much sideline spectators as were the tourists. Discovery Day was unabashedly a celebration of gold rush history as a white male achievement. Aside from the presentation of a few token "oldtimers" who marched in the parade, the native presence, lifestyle, or historical role were ignored, just as Indians were ignored and marginalized in real life, of course. But even in the context of Dawson City, the emulation of the white sourdough as culture hero was a bit heavy handed for my taste.

Nonetheless, I was firmly planted in a crowd of tourists and Indians on that second day watching marchers and floats wind through the business district. The highway department's entry was charming in its simplicity. It featured a very large dump truck festooned with a few crepe paper streamers and a crew of hard-hatted highway workers brandishing liquor bottles in a feigned display of drunkenness. At least, I assumed it was feigned. What a great pitch for tourism it would be if the tanked-up driver hit the accelerator and mowed down a few spectators. While the procession quickly ended, a visiting Scottish pipe-and-drum band from Whitehorse was building up steam as band members continued to march through the streets. On an impulse, I followed them as they strode regimentally into the Westminster never missing a beat of their music. The place was packed like steerage in a fourth class freighter. The stench of sweat and stale beer was overpowering, but the pipers held their ground as they blasted out ear-deafening versions of "Far O'er the Sea," "Atholl Highlanders" and other stirring marches. And the crowd was quickly won over. Many patrons stood on chairs vigorously clapping in time to the music. Nick Favreau leaped upon a table, saluted the band in military style, and clomped out a rhythm with his hob-nailed boots. Trance-like, head and arms raised to the heavens, Flora Bacon whirled and twirled and whirled to the point of exhaustion. Drinks were spilling and bottles shattering. Nobody cared. This was close to a religious experience.

I noticed Eric Larson standing in the doorway, and I waved a greeting. But he was preoccupied. His hands were oddly cupped around his mouth. He almost seemed to be shouting. There was no sound. Incredibly, the fool was trying to shout at me above the infernal din of bellowing bagpipers. Apparently, hand gestures were not his forte. With great effort I extricated myself from the sweaty horde and joined Eric outside.

"Are you deaf? I've been yelling at you for ten minutes!"

"Look, Scottish music isn't the greatest background for conversation. So what's up? Change your mind? Want to take that raft trip?"

"Forget the goddamn raft. See those folks over there?" Eric nodded toward a middle-aged couple intently studying a map a few yards away. "They just got in from Michigan. They're taking a canoe downriver, and they're looking for somebody to drive their car and fetch 'em down in Eagle. I figure you're their boy."

The world dropped away dramatically on all sides as the VW bug cruised along on a high ridge of alpine tundra. The sensation was akin to flying. Somewhere in the recesses below, tributaries of the Fortymile and Sixtymile raced through forested canyons. The intense cloudless azure of the late August sky held a promise of frost and of the bone-chilling winter to come. A steady breeze streamed through the open windows, adding to the sense of release. I was an hour west of Dawson City on the old Sixtymile Road heading for the Taylor Highway that would ultimately dead-end on the Yukon River at Eagle, Alaska. There would be precious little time to dally about, for I would have to retrieve my hosts, Don and Joan Richards, and their equipment in a few days. And while I would have preferred to see the country by canoe myself, it was a blessing just to be on the road. Viewing the magnificence of the Yukon backcountry once again, even by car, reminded me of how confining the months in Dawson City had been. Like one of Jimmy Stevens' "city boys," I had faint knowledge of the bush. There were millions of square miles of it out there beckoning.

Plumes of dust announced the occasional vehicle approaching from ridge-tops still many miles away. After the international boundary and Corbett's roadhouse, the sparse traffic quickly diminished to nothingness. Apparently, most of the Discovery Day revelers were departing Dawson City via the southern route to Whitehorse. The solitude of the road invited some soul-searching. What had I really accomplished in Dawson City? Would I discover anything worthwhile in Eagle? As a novice fieldworker, I had little basis for assessing my progress except my own feelings of the moment. After a lengthy conversation with an informant I was often elated, even ecstatic. Then days might pass where absolutely nothing happened, and I felt as if the research was going down the toilet. Only much later did I come to recognize this roller-coaster as integral to the game.

My only certainty was quickly filling up spiral notebooks. Eight so far. I had become rather compulsive about taking field notes, so much so that I was falling behind in getting the infernal longhand typed up and carbon copies mailed out to Dr. McClellan. I wasn't a speedy typist, and in my view typing took precious time away from fieldwork. There was another fear. Did the cryptic field notes mean anything? Would they be of any scholarly value? That was something I preferred not to think about.

A flat tire returned me to the reality of the road. I was about 15 miles out of Eagle nearing the crest of the mountains that guarded the Yukon valley. To the north and thousands of feet below was a rich spectrum of color as umber tundra faded into blue pockets of spruce and ultimately into intense green carpets of birch and aspen. Like a necklace with jeweled facets, the Yukon shimmered and sparkled as it snaked its way through the forested valley floor. There was something oddly tropical about the scene. Maybe the ravens circling overhead were really scarlet macaws or quetzals in disguise. The land glowed in the late evening sun. Stark mountain walls did not crowd the river here as in Dawson City.

I mounted the spare but was horrified to discover that I was driving on bald tires. Gingerly, I guided the VW around wicked piles of stones and cobbles, protrusions of bedrock, ruts and washouts for the remaining miles into the outskirts of Eagle. This was the "white" part of town. Once known as Eagle City, its population had approached 800 during the frenzied gold-hunting days of the late 1890s. A vestige of its former glory, it now had barely 50 residents. The Indian section of Eagle, a separate village, was still several miles eastward and upstream on the Yukon. After a few inquiries I found a mechanic near the airstrip who promised to fix the flat the next day. Relieved, I drove a few miles back out of town to a public campsite on Mission Creek. I figured after a good night's rest I'd get a fresh start in the morning. After pitching a tent and building a fire, I noticed that the VW was tilting peculiarly.

"Another goddamn flat!" I yelled at the fading sun. Wearily I rolled defective tire number two into town where the mechanic was not at all surprised to see me. "Yup, this road'll beat shit out of any car," he quipped. I had a sudden vision of myself rolling punctured and mangled tires up and down the Taylor Highway for the next several days, frittering away my little bit of freedom. Chilled and hungry I trudged back to camp in the darkness, wolfed down a can of beans, and fell asleep instantly.

The next day I lingered in "white Eagle" just long enough to retrieve my tires and move on. The few people I met, mostly business proprietors, while amiable, seemed disappointed when they learned my destination was the "other Eagle."

"They're gettin' mean and nasty out there," the mechanic warned. "You better watch yourself. Lately, they don't seem to like us too much. Shit, I'll tell you what it is! It's all this media stuff telling about how the white man exploited the Indian and destroyed their native culture and all that. Now they're blaming us."

"You mean the Indians in Eagle are holding you personally responsible?"

"Seems that way to me. We're the only white folks for miles around. Convenient targets. Why are you going out to the village, if you don't mind my asking?"

"Well, I'm supposed to be studying native culture and history. Actually, I made a quick stop here several months ago. Do you remember Dr. McClellan? I've mostly been working with the Eagle people's relatives over in the Yukon Territory." I felt uncomfortable under the man's appraising gaze.

"You don't say!" the mechanic whistled and shook his head with disbelief. "I don't see how you people can do that."

"Do what? Study their culture?"

"No, I mean hang around with 'em. Live in their villages. Especially the way it is now with all the drinking. There's always accidents. Just the other day some young woman out there hurt her leg real bad. Lots of suicides too. It's all tied up with drinking. You don't see people going crazy on hooch in our side of town. But over there? Hell, some of those guys'll go out and earn maybe $900 fighting fires in the bush and then spend it all on booze when they hit town."

The mechanic's words were a tiresome if familiar refrain that depressed me. No doubt, some of what he said was true, but the condescending attitude, the tone of moral superiority, was hard to swallow. How many times had I heard this same sermon on the "Indian problem" from whites in Dawson City who were themselves incorrigible drunks?

My irritability lifted by early afternoon when I followed a dirt track to a dead-end on the river and came upon a spellbinding vision. In a level clearing on the south bank of the Yukon lay a small cluster of log dwellings, some with corrugated tin roofs but others with sod roofs boasting tall shocks of grass. Interspersed among the houses were raised log caches, canvas wall tents, platform racks with row upon row of drying salmon, kitchen gardens with ripening potatoes and carrots, and an assortment of outbuildings and storage sheds. It was a dead ringer for what scholars like June Helm and David Damas (1963) called a "contact-traditional all-native community," a place firmly rooted in the

Log dwellings dominate the Han village landscape at Eagle.

native past but also tied to the external world. Whatever it was, there was something touching, hauntingly exotic yet familiar about this scene which put a lump in my throat.

My mind drifted back to Klukshu the year before, a villagescape that had affected me in the same way. That place had been deserted at the time, and now as I parked the car for a closer look at Eagle village the absence of people and activity gave me pause. There was a surreal quality to the moment as if approaching a museum village frozen in time for the voyeur. Surely, eyes were upon me, but I was reluctant to approach the houses.

Walking aimlessly along the river bank, I admired the siting of the village. It was nestled upon one of the few level terraces available and only a few yards above the Yukon itself. The shoreline here appeared relatively protected from erosion. But across the river the towering grey earthen cliffs of the north bank rose as a mighty rampart straight out of the water. A flicker of movement caught my eye. Suddenly a great hunk of earth calved off the cliff face as the torrential current slammed into it. A couple of undermined willows near the cliff's crumbly edge teetered in the breeze and then joined in the plummet to the roiling waters below. It was an alarming sight. One could imagine entire encampments and villages tumbling into the void. The landscape took on a frail and lethal aspect.

Croak, creak, croak. A faint sound was audible over the seething river. Creak, croak, creak. Raven friends where are you? I scanned the treetops and cabin roofs, but the dark sentinels were nowhere to be seen. After their shameless gorging at the Dawson City dump they had been hiding from me. Just like the people here. It would be my luck to come all this way and learn that everyone had departed for a moose hunt. After all, there were only a half-dozen families here, perhaps 50 souls maximum. It wouldn't take much to vacate the place. I stopped at a small wood frame church. It offered no Anglican, Catholic or other denominational banner. Croak, creak, croak. Was it coming from the church? What ceremony could produce such a grating noise?

Creak, croak, creak. Splash! No, the commotion was definitely in the river. Peering over the bank and down at the water's edge I spotted a Rube Goldberg-like contraption fastened to the shore by two long planks. Croak, creak, croak. Splash. Two long-armed basket traps rotated on an axle with the current in an irrepressible rhythm. Creak, croak, creak. Splash. A fish wheel! I should have known. But the wheels near Dawson City were miles out of view. Here was one of the ingenious devices scooping up salmon in plain view while its owner was off somewhere tending to other matters. Just as I reached the shoreline a plump dog salmon flipped out of an upraised basket, down a chute and into a

A fish wheel scoops up salmon on the Yukon River near Eagle, Alaska.

conveniently positioned storage box. It was nearly full. Some say that European miners on the Tanana River introduced the first fish wheels around 1904 after which they quickly spread to Indian and white fishermen alike on the Yukon and Kuskokwim rivers. I wondered if the Han still used any of their older repertoire of dip nets, basket traps, weirs and spears.

"Hello, mister! Lookin' for fish?" A young Indian man was ambling down the bank. He was decked out in engineer's boots, jeans, a nylon jacket and Australian bush hat. Was the church service over? As he approached, though, I noticed he was carrying a bottle of beer and sporting a euphoric smile.

"Oh no. I was just admiring your wheel. It's the first one I've seen."

"This one belongs to George Fisher. We've got two more upriver," the man grinned amiably and then grasped my hand in a firm handshake. "I'm Johnny Samm. You know my Dad? Norbert? Hey, we're all drunk here. We've been drinking for days. C'mon. C'mon with me."

During my months in Dawson City I had never received such a straightforward invitation. As if drawn by a riptide, I followed Johnny up the hill to the home of his parents, a tidy one-room log affair that was filled with people all trying to talk at once. Apparently there was no church gathering. Rather, half the village was crammed into Norbert and Agnes Samm's place. Ironically, many of them had just returned from a trek to Dawson City for Discovery Day, some for the first time in several decades. They were now winding down after days of celebrating. There was a collective sense of euphoria and adventure as people recalled reunions with seldom-seen relatives and the excesses of open drinking in the streets of Dawson City. Oddly, there was no alcohol visible in the cabin. Yet, people seemed mildly high, still charged up from their recent experiences. Without announcements or farewells people continually walked in and out the open door. All horizontal space in the sparely furnished room was claimed. People were lounging on several small beds in the back of the room. A lone table was crowded with people eating rabbit stew ladled from a pot on the wood stove.

Norbert Samm, a man in his late '50s, gave me a warm greeting and insisted that I sit by him on one of the beds. He wore a hearing aid in his right ear connected to a battery pack on his chest. A thick wad of chewing tobacco protruded from his lower lip, and he continually leaned over to spit into a can on the floor.

"Bob, here have some stew," Norbert offered passing me a bowl. "It's nice having some meat for a change, eh? Hey Agnes, put some wood in that stove. We need more stew. Use those rabbits that Henry got. Maybe put some turnips and carrots in there too." He was smiling, but there was a stern edge to his voice. Agnes, a stout woman in a floral print dress, was in constant motion around the stove and table. She never uttered a word, and her face revealed little emotion.

I had hoped to fade into the background of this gregarious group, but everyone was eager to know which of their relatives in Dawson City I knew personally. Establishing connections was important, so I began tallying up my friends and contacts. Just hearing the names seemed to strike a responsive chord.

"You know Tom Thompson!" Norbert cried. "Hey, he's my brother-in-law. You know Sarah Black too! Well, she's my sister. I stayed at Sarah's place in Dawson. Brought her 100 pounds of dried fish too. What about Ada Peterson, do you know her? That one's my sister too." With a houseful of eager inquirers, the wealth of genealogical information became overwhelming. I would have to reconstruct the essentials later on my kinship chart. The latter I kept on a large roll of butcher shop paper. When unfolded its cryptic maze of lines, circles and triangles looked like an incredibly inefficient subway system. Nonetheless, it showed that ties of blood and marriage between Eagle and Dawson City Indians were densely interwoven.

Given the close ties, I was perplexed when people expressed hesitancy about their identity. At one point Norbert motioned to his assembled companions saying: "We're all Han here, you know. Han Kutchin. You know that?"

"Yes. Dawson City Indians are also Han, is that right?" I asked.

"No, just us Eagle people. Dawson people are different."

"Do you speak different languages then?"

"No. They talk the same as us. Well, maybe they are the same as us," Norbert replied uncertainly. "Yah, I guess they're Han Kutchin too."

Similar hesitancy had been expressed by my contacts in Dawson City, including the older folks who presumably knew the traditional ethnolinguistic boundaries and markers. In fact, few seemed to use the term "Han," except when I broached the subject. Like Simon Isaac, people identified themselves by localisms like Troncik (Klondike Indian) or Ezan (Eagle Indian). Had the gold rush eroded Han identity? Or was the whole notion of "Han" an external category imposed by neighboring Kutchin and anthropologists? There was no simple answer to such questions.

Johnny was fiddling with an expensive Japanese radio-cassette tape recorder he had recently brought back from Viet Nam. He didn't talk about his war experience, but he carried on about the radio. It was a gift for his parents. He was proud of its engineering wizardry, demonstrating all that it could do. At one point he turned to his father: "How about more beer?"

"No more beer!" Norbert's smiling face turned icy.

"Well, how about some whiskey?"

"Hey, when I went to Dawson you took my whiskey. You put water in it. There's nothing left now!" Norbert's temper flashed. "Why don't you provide for your stomach, hey? All you know is to drink. I don't give you no drink till you learn how to provide food for this family."

"Why don't you keep your fuckin' mouth shut." Johnny was visibly hurt as he stormed out the door.

I felt embarrassed for both father and son, but no one else paid much attention to the outburst nor to Norbert's prolonged muttering. Johnny had set him off. Now he complained at great length how sense-less his children were about food and drink. He lashed out at his wife for not keeping timely meals. Agnes' eyes smoldered behind the impassive face. Her fussing movements around the stove made me nervous. Norbert ought to clam up. I envisioned a kettle of hot stew flying across the room scalding all in its path.

Fumbling around in my packsack I found a faded old photograph that Dick North had given me. Its grainy image revealed a fair-haired middle-aged man, known as Arthur Nelson, standing among several Indian acquaintances in front of a log trading post some decades ago. Nelson stared pensively (or suspiciously?) over one shoulder in the direction of the photographer. In the foreground an Indian man was hauling a sack of flour up an embankment. One of Dick's current theo-ries was that Nelson and Albert Johnson and the infamous Mad Trapper were all one and the same person. A Mountie killer with a mul-tiple personality disorder? Anything was possible. All I knew was that Dick was most eager to have me circulate this photograph during my travels. Maybe it would stir some memories.

"Say, have any of you ever seen a white fellow who looks like this?" I inquired dropping the photograph on a table near the window. People crowded around for a better look. Mercifully, Norbert stopped his food harangue. As if hunched over a microscope, he solemnly peered at the blurred figure.

"Who is this guy?"

"I was sort of hoping you might know."

"Why? Is he some kind of *tse'taojin* [bushman]?" Norbert asked.

The others were snickering. Norbert was putting me on, even though the reference to "bushman" was no laughing matter.

"Probably not a bushman," I replied. "He's supposed to be some-body named Arthur Nelson."

"So are you looking for this man? Is that why you're here?"

"Not exactly. You see, the photo was taken back in 1927. At the Ross River post in the Yukon. He's probably no longer living. I was won-dering if you ever saw somebody that looked like him around here in the old days?"

"Say, you're not a BI are you?" Norbert glared at me with mock suspiciousness.

"BI? What's that?"

Charlie Jonas, a husky older man who had just entered the cabin was shaking with laughter. "BI. Norbert means FBI. He wants to know if you're one of them 'authority men'."

"Hell no. I'm no FBI." I feigned indignation.

"Hey, that's all right. I don't care if you are authority man. We tell you what we know. We'll help, but we can't go too far now!" Norbert gave me a collusive wink and shook his head. "Boy oh boy, and here I thought you was authority man."

As it turned out, no one in Eagle claimed recognition of Arthur Nelson. It made sense. The scene in the photograph was over 40 years and hundreds of miles removed. But the conversation took an unexpected turn when I mentioned Dick North's suspicions about a connection between Nelson and the Mad Trapper.

"Mad Trapper? What's that?" Charlie Jonas frowned.

"You must have heard of the Mad Trapper of Rat River? The white guy that went crazy and killed a Mountie back in the '30s. You know, the guy called Albert Johnson."

"Albert Johnson! Well, why didn't you say so!" Norbert's face light up. "Sure, we know who Albert Johnson is. He's been through our country here. Yup, killed three RCMP too, that Johnson."

"No, it was four! Albert Johnson killed four RCMP!" Joe Mayo, a burly older man with a silver grey brush cut, who had been sitting quietly in a corner of the cabin, now yelled out excitedly. He and Norbert seemed to have some kind of adversarial joking relationship. "Your wrong Norbert! Anyway, Bob, your picture there? That's Albert, hey?"

"No. That's Arthur Nelson. Although maybe he used an alias. Maybe later he became Albert Johnson. But the Johnson I know about supposedly only killed one RCMP."

"Listen Bob! You want to find out about these things, you ask *him*, he's seen Albert Johnson!" Joe pursed his lips and used them to point out Charlie Jonas who was helping himself to a bowl of stew. I could hardly believe what I was hearing. Someone with face-to-face experience with the Mad Trapper? Dick North will be green with envy. I looked inquisitively at Charlie who was gobbling down the stew like a man possessed. The room grew quiet as if awaiting a performance. After draining the bowl, he paused to catch his breath, and then rose to his feet and began his story.

"Yeah I seen Albert Johnson. That was in Circle back in 1915. I grew up in Charley River, but our people used to travel downriver to Circle." Charlie was pacing the floor, moving his hands about in an animated fashion. "It was in a bar there in Circle where I seen him. He was wearing a good wool shirt. Like yours," he gestured in my direction. "Except he had his underwear on over that shirt. And another strange thing. He had no coat on. It was real cold. Must a been 40 below. Middle of winter that time. And he just walks in there with no coat on! Had to be tough, that guy. Anyways, like I was saying, Albert Johnson he comes walking into that bar." To everyone's amusement, Charlie mimicked Johnson by striding confidently across the cabin floor and then freezing rigidly like a deer caught in the headlights. "Boy, he got scared! He sees himself in the mirror, in that big mirror they got hanging behind the bar there. He was real jumpy. Then he figured he was only looking at himself! Ha ha!" Norbert and Joe and the others were cracking up. Charlie was on a roll. He retrieved a smoking pipe from his pocket, stuck it in his mouth and finished his tale. "So then Albert Johnson asks the bartender if its okay to smoke. Bartender, he doesn't care. So Albert just sits in a corner in the back by himself. Smoking his pipe. Alone. He didn't say nothing after that. Just sits alone watching who comes in the door. Yup, that's what I remember."

I was confused. Was Charlie's story for real? Or were my hosts having some fun at my expense? Norbert's expressive face contained no hint of a put-on. Indeed, people seemed genuinely pleased by the account and all but applauded as Charlie returned to the stove to refill his stew bowl. He had the contented look of someone who had entertained his cronies well. Maybe that was the point. Charlie certainly looked old enough to have been a teenager in 1915. But would he have been hanging around a bar in Circle? More to the point, if Albert Johnson had been roaming through that country, years before he had become infamous, would anyone have noticed him? Questions raced through my mind, but I held my tongue.

Sometime later Charlie got up to leave, and he took me aside noting that his tale about Albert Johnson was only an appetizer. Could I stop by his tent over near the Fishers' place tomorrow? There we could talk "confidential," as he put it, and I could hear the "whole story" on Johnson. Yes, yes, of course I'll try to visit. I had no pressing engagements. For all I knew, there was a rich reservoir of Mad Trapper folklore just waiting to be tapped.

By the end of that first day my head was spinning with a cyclone of information on everything from Albert Johnson and local family histories to fishing technology and native vocabulary. I had met half the villagers. Little kids addressed me familiarly as "Bob" (pronounced "Bup"). Some of the young men drew me into a their jocular exchanges:

"Hey Bup, are you a hippie? Just kidding! Ha ha! You're an authority man, right? Ha ha! Just kidding! No, but you really are Albert Johnson's nephew, right? Right? Hey, everybody come over here and look

Isaac Juneby (left) and Harry David (right), two Han men from Eagle.

at this old picture. This is Bup's uncle, Albert Johnson. Looks just like him too!"

People I had scarcely met were inviting me into their homes, feeding me, entertaining me with enchanting fiddle music, sending me on my way with gifts of dried salmon and freshly snared rabbit. Late that night I lay in my tent in a pleasurable state of exhaustion. Too wound up to sleep, I pondered the irony of having one of my most rewarding days come at the end of my fieldwork. The kindness of the villagers was profoundly humbling. I had done nothing to deserve it. And what did I have to offer in return really?

That was answered the next morning. My Volkswagen! The poor Richards' Volkswagen to be exact. Vehicles were scarce in the community, and I quickly became a chauffeur of choice. The Samms needed supplies from Beiderman's store in the white section of town. The Fishers wanted to haul jugs of fresh water from a nearby spring. Somebody had to go to the post office. Somebody else wanted to sell some moosehide moccasins to the proprietor at the craft store. There was no shortage of errands to run, and I was pleased to help out.

Until talk of the "Flat" came up. It seemed that some people wanted to carry on their post-Discovery Day celebrations, but the last drop of alcohol had been drunk. Norbert was still testy about Johnny's trick with the whiskey. Some of the men dropped hints: "Hey Bup. We're thinking of making a run to the Flat. Whaddaya think?"

That meant a beer run, a 70-mile roundtrip excursion up the chuck-hole-ridden Taylor Highway to Columbia Flats, a blip on the road where alcohol could be purchased at a small lodge. Four of the village's largest men wanted me to drive them there. It would have been easier getting the front line of the Los Angeles Rams into that car. Springs would snap. Those bald tires would explode. I visualized the flaming wreckage of the Richards' VW wrapped around a spruce tree at the bottom of O'Brien Creek canyon, shards of beer bottles embedded in bodies like shrapnel.

I tried to mask my disappointment. A goddamn beer run? College fraternity stuff. If only we were heading out on a caribou hunt instead. But the die was cast. One of the main promoters of the trip was Joe's son, Victor Mayo. Victor had been particularly congenial and helpful to me. And at a mere 29 years of age, Victor was the locally elected chief of the Eagle community. How did one say no to a chief?

When departure time arrived, and after some gnashing of teeth, I managed to restrict the passenger list to Chief Mayo and Norbert Samm. We arrived at O'Brien Creek Lodge without incident where the two men purchased several cases of beer, several bottles of whiskey, and a large bag of candy bars to munch on during the return trip.

"Hey Bup?" Victor inquired as the VW bounced and lurched back toward Eagle. "You don't mind if I drink?"

"It's illegal isn't it?" I asked.

"Yah, but I got a hangover headache. I need something."

"Yah, they're darn rough if they catch you," Norbert noted. "But the cops never come up here."

Soon Norbert and Victor were slugging down beers at a furious clip. Oddly, they never finished any given bottle. Rather, they drank them down halfway, tossed them out the window, and pried open new ones. We had to make frequent roadside stops so that the men could relieve themselves, and so that Victor could restore some feeling to his aching legs. As he put it: "I got poor circulation. Froze my legs pretty bad one winter."

Invariably, during the rest stops Victor would playfully taunt Norbert by grabbing the older and smaller man's biceps. "Hey, Norbert you got any marscle?" Norbert would squirm away and assume a mock fighting pose with fists at the ready: "Ha ha! I can beat you any day. You and Joe together! You guys are too fat. Gotta be skinny like me!"

Back on the road Victor observed, "Ah Bup, you take good care of us, eh?"

"Yeah, but you shouldn't be drinking now. We'll be in deep shit if any police are around."

"Maybe you're right." And Victor threw out another half-empty. "You know Bup, I'm gonna become a minister so I can stop drinking. My girlfriend won't marry me unless I cut out the drinking. So I'm going into the ministry. That's a good idea, huh? Bup?"

"Well, it can't hurt."

"Geez, that Victor never stops talking, do you?" Norbert groaned. "Be quiet now. I want to talk to our friend here."

I slowed the VW to a crawl, and Norbert began pointing out subtleties in the landscape. A series of ridges were prime marten country. They bordered part of his trapline which ran over into the Seventymile River country. Like many local hunters, however, he had let his trapping area lie dormant for years owing to low fur prices. Norbert's geographical sense astounded me. He knew intimately every patch of willows, each bend of the river, every cliff face. All these features were infused with meaning through a lifetime of travels and bush experience. Near a particularly prominent ridge about five miles out of the village Norbert's voice betrayed a sense of urgency and excitement.

"See that notch up there? That's a special place for us. That's where the caribou cross. One time I killed seven caribou there in just three hours."

The caribou crossing? Hmmm. Yes, indeed. What Norbert was telling me now was the kind of knowledge I really coveted. Norbert's interpretation of the landscape was revelatory. Somehow it seemed like a key to understanding how Han culture was organized. How they had adapted to the northern environment for generations, if not millennia. I stopped the car and walked out a few yards to get a better view of the windswept, craggy escarpment. Victor had passed out in the back seat. Norbert joined me at the side of the road.

Crooaaawk! The sudden announcement was startling. A lone raven exploded out of the trees behind us. Riding a gentle wind current steadily upward along the mountain wall, it hovered momentarily near the caribou crossing, and then disappeared beyond the ridge. A good omen, no doubt. Oddly, a wave of sadness overwhelmed me. Would I see this place or these people again?

"Ha ha! *Tautre* [crow, raven], my friend, you know where the caribou go!" Norbert tossed me a candy bar and yanked the cap off another beer. "You know, Victor over there, he's a Crow. You can call him tautre too."

"I'm sort of a crow myself. The crows, the ravens, they've been good friends. How about you, Norbert? Are you a Crow?"

"Nope. I'm *bek'e*. I'm a Sea Gull. My mom and her family were Sea Gulls. That makes me bek'e."

"What about Wolves?"

"Sure, you'll find those people up in Dawson. We're just Crows and Sea Gulls here in Eagle. But, hey, I'm married to a Crow! Agnes is tautre. That's how it works. You can't marry your own kind."

"Crows and Sea Gulls, eh? You're sure about the Wolves?"

"Yeah. Something wrong about that?"

"Oh no. It's just that I know one Wolf up in Dawson who'll be disappointed."

"Sometimes you sure ask a lot of questions. You know, Bup, you should come back here. Live here. There's a lot more we can teach you."

"You must've read my mind, Norbert. I would like that."

A week later I was back in Minneapolis feeling emotionally drained. It was as if I had been on a theater stage for three months and was finally permitted to retire to my dressing room. Everything was a bit out of kilter. The academic routines of graduate student life seemed deadly dull, if not surreal.

Then one day returning to my apartment I walked into a confetti storm of shredded moosehide. Feral, my roommate's dog, had ripped apart my prized pair of Yukon mukluks. Strangely, that simple act snapped me out of my funk. With mounting excitement I began sorting out my pile of field notes. Vivid memories and emotions came flooding back. Any lingering innocence or naivete about looking into other people's lives was firmly shattered. I had been baptized into the complicated, exhilarating and often depressing business of fieldwork. And having survived my stint in the Yukon, I yearned for more. I wanted to see another face of the North, the one in the bush beyond the roads. Some prolonged experience with Northern natives was in order, including the challenges of facing a winter on their terms. The only questions were when, where, and with whom?

PART II

Trail of the Chipewyan

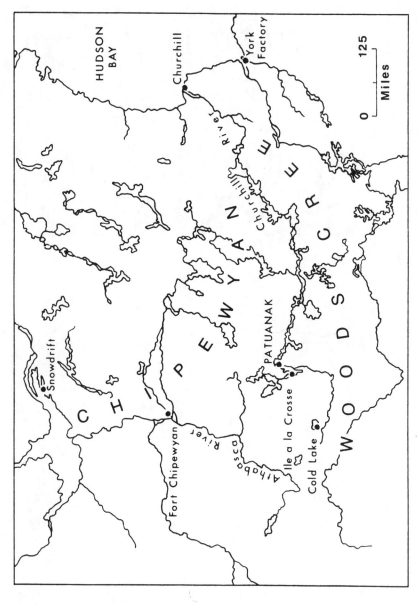

Recent territorial distribution of the Chipewyan in north-central Canada. Village of Patuanak is highlighted near the headwaters of the Churchill River. Woods Cree neighbors border to the south and east.

Chapter Four

With Reserve

The bush plane bounced around on the late afternoon thermals cruising steadily eastward over an immense crazy quilt landscape of muskeg, spruce and aspen forests, meandering streams, and glimmering lakes. Except for an occasional esker, gravel ridges formed by retreating glaciers, the terrain was washboard flat. Smoke haze from a forest fire somewhere to the west bathed the scene in an eerie refracted light. This was roadless country. And it stretched a good 600 miles east to Hudson Bay and 800 miles northward to the Arctic Ocean. To the untrained eye, the panorama was both intimidating and breathtaking. Mile after mile passed by seemingly with no trace of settlement or human presence of any kind. If the plane ditched here and we survived, how would we find our way out?

"Wanna take a look down there, eh?" the bush pilot asked. Without waiting for an answer, he quickly dropped the Cessna 180 from a thousand to a few hundred feet in altitude. Banking sharply around the bay of a small lake, he pointed toward two minute figures. Squinting through the window, I could make out a cow moose and her calf standing in weed-choked shallows. But there was something else.

"What's that break in the trees?"

"Where? Oh, that's the winter trail. Part of the main dog sled trail between Buffalo Narrows and Patuanak. Some people use snowmobiles now. Maybe you'll travel on it this winter. If you end up working around here."

If indeed. Patuanak was a remote Chipewyan Indian community near the headwaters of the Churchill River. I had never seen it. Until a few days previously I had barely heard of the place. Now, with growing apprehension, I realized a lot was riding on this obscure destination.

As the pilot climbed back up to cruising altitude, my mind wandered over the events of the preceding year. After the excitement of the Yukon I had re-acclimated to the world of seminars and colloquia and finished most of my formal graduate study at the University of Minnesota. Conducting fieldwork for the doctoral dissertation would be the next big hurdle. But this presented something of a dilemma. Since I had earned my ethnographic spurs in Han country, it seemed only natural to return there for more prolonged research. Friends and contacts in

Dawson City and Eagle would help me continue, and I had developed an acute nostalgia for those places.

Yet, my interests were crystallizing around issues of ecology, subsistence, mobility, and territoriality. Professor Robert Spencer, my adviser, encouraged me to select a field situation appropriate to the problem at hand. Spencer was not an Athapaskan specialist, but he had accumulated an impressive cross-cultural wisdom from his varied field studies in North America, the Middle East, South Asia, and East Asia. He had a speaking or reading knowledge of at least 20 languages. Moreover, his pioneering research among the North Alaskan Eskimo was a landmark in cultural ecology. Heeding Spencer's advice, I wrote to other northern scholars inquiring about Athapaskan communities where hunting, fishing and trapping livelihoods, and nomadic lifestyles, might still be important.

As the first letters arrived, I eagerly tore them open. Naively, I had hoped to find a salient nugget of information, perhaps along the following lines:

> Mr. Jarvenpa: Your search is over! Why not work with the people at Lower Trout Lake? They're located about 200 miles downriver from the Black Kettle Band who, as you know, are treated at length in my recent monograph. My sources suggest the Trout Lake folks are heavily dependent on bush food and have fairly extensive winter travel circuits. Since there have been no ethnographic studies in the area, this could be ideal for your purposes . . .

Instead, I was in for a rude awakening. The letters I received were quite cordial. But many were thin on specific suggestions and heavy on caveats. Don't expect to find much "traditional bush living" anywhere in the subarctic, they warned. Terms like "dependency," "micro-urbanization," "welfare economy," and "sedentization" peppered their language. As the spring of 1971 approached, I grew increasingly depressed about my plans.

Then, one day a letter arrived from James G. E. Smith, a curator of ethnology at the National Museums of Canada in Ottawa. He didn't mince words. Smith encouraged me to work with the Chipewyan. With about 5,000 people, and communities spread between Hudson Bay to the east, Great Slave Lake to the northwest, and the Churchill River to the south, an area roughly the size of Texas, geographically and demographically they were the largest group of northern Athapaskans. And, apparently, hunting and fishing economies were vibrant in many of the communities.

I already knew that Samuel Hearne's (1795) account of his travels with Matonnabbee and his Chipewyan relatives in the early 1770s provided one of the best historical baselines available for any Athapaskan culture. But Smith noted that contemporary ethnographic studies were just taking off. Only a few years previously, James VanStone (1965) had completed a study of culture change at Snowdrift on Great Slave Lake. Smith himself was currently working with Chipewyan at Brochet, and other young scholars, like Henry Sharp at Black Lake and David Smith at Fort Resolution, were in the field. These anthropologists were all working in northern Chipewyan country, among a loose territorial aggregation of bands known as *Ethen-eldili-dene* or "caribou eaters." These were Chipewyan who had a long historical adaptation of hunting barrenground caribou herds that migrated back and forth across the forest-tundra ecotone.

And there was something else. According to Smith, the southern Chipewyan were largely unknown to anthropologists. A regional cluster of bands known as *Thilanottine* or "those who dwell at the head of the lakes," these people were descendants of Chipewyan who had moved south into the full boreal forest with the expanding European fur trade in the late eighteenth century. Occupying the headwaters of the Churchill River, they adapted to a new environment where moose and woodland caribou were more common as food animals and where the Western Woods Cree were potentially hostile neighbors. The southern Chipewyan became the hunters par excellence in the evolving fur trade economy. Apparently, some of them now lived in and around old fur trade centers like Ile-a-la-Crosse, Buffalo Narrows and Portage La Loche while many others were scattered in smaller isolated communities.

Smith's letter ignited a torch. In the late summer of 1971 I excitedly packed up my supplies and journeyed to northwestern Saskatchewan hoping to spend a year with the southern Chipewyan. The only overland access to the region was via a rough gravel road which departed the northern prairies near Prince Albert and Meadow Lake and then punched northward through the boreal forest for 450 kilometers before terminating at La Loche.

Late eighteenth-century depiction of a Chipewyan man carrying a birch bark canoe (from Hearne, 1795).

I boarded what was euphemistically called "the bus," a battered Ford van overloaded with local Indian passengers and luggage and pulling a makeshift trailer filled with mail bags, food supplies and other cargo destined for the northern road settlements. This ungainly affair was driven at punishing speeds by a disgruntled middle-aged white man who muttered patronizing comments under his breath whenever we passed near a native community or homestead:

"Judas priest, what a sad bunch!" or "I don't believe these people. Why, my two little brothers could work harder than these bums!"

If the passengers were offended by these outbursts, they did not voice any complaints. There was little conversation in Chipewyan or English to break the jarring dust-ridden tedium of the road. But Several hours into the ride, a large wolf seemed to materialize out of nowhere. It loped gracefully in front of the van, clearing the road in a couple strides before disappearing in a spruce thicket. The other passengers were instantly alert and animated. "*Nunie*," someone said. I recognized the Chipewyan term for wolf in excited conversations around me. Outside of a zoo or museum diorama, I had never seen one of the animals before. The wolf-raven rivalry business from the previous year's fieldwork surfaced in my thoughts. Perhaps it was the sun's glare on the grimy windshield, but I could have sworn the animal looked right at me before it vanished into the bush. Was the wolf taunting me?

"Excuse me, but how do you say raven or crow in Chipewyan?" I felt ludicrous but could not resist asking a fellow traveler.

"Raven? Oh, we say *datsa* or *datsacho*."

"Datsa. Yes, thank you." I quickly scanned nearby tree tops for some sign of my long-departed comrades.

A few minutes later the van rounded a bend and entered a lengthy narrows between two formidable bodies of water. Peter Pond Lake lay out of view to the southwest. Churchill Lake emerged dramatically to the northeast. On this clear and windless day it was a glistening azure carpet that stretched far beyond the horizon. Out of these headwaters rose the Churchill River itself, a massive highway of water that flowed 1,000 miles eastward into Hudson Bay.

"Okay, you potlickers, I haven't got all day! If you're getting off in Buffalo, get out now." The driver lurched to an abrupt stop, flung open the van doors and, with an exasperated air, began throwing bags and boxes onto the road. All but a couple passengers deboarded and claimed their dusty parcels.

Buffalo Narrows was an elusive scatter of older log dwellings, weathered wood frame houses, makeshift trailers, and prefab structures hugging the southwest shore of Churchill Lake. There was little in the way of a town center, barring a Hudson's Bay Company store and an old hotel near a bend in the road. Abandoned cabins and mink ranches, as well as discarded truck hulls and machinery, loomed ghost-like from patches of second-growth timber and weedy scrub. The bleak townscape was relieved only by the shimmering expanse of the lake. Reflecting its fur trade origins, most "Buffalo" residents were Indians and Métis. Commercial fishing and mink ranching had spurred the town's growth in the 1940s and 1950s, and now it was emerging as a major transport and service hub for the region with a population approaching 1,000. Oddly, on this pleasant mid-August day, the place was quiet as a crypt.

A flutter of movement caught my eye. A flock of pelicans was lifting off the lake, gliding upward on air currents in an ever-expanding spiral. Gaining altitude, the large ungainly birds became remarkably graceful. As the aerial ballet reached its zenith, there was a distracting commotion nearby. "Croaaaaawk!" A familiar throaty metallic call broke the calm. Two dark shadows sailed overhead and landed on the peak of a roof.

"Datsa, my friends," I muttered to myself, "you're here too!" The ravens seemed jubilant as they hopped and skittered along the roofline. Seeing them after a year's absence put a lump in my throat.

"What's that, you say? You're heading on to The Crotch? I mean La Loche?" The driver gunned the van engine impatiently as he motioned for me to get in.

"Nope. I think I'll be getting off here." Impulsively, I grabbed my canvas packs and duffels and heaved them to the side of the road. Maybe the ravens were here for a reason. Besides, the driver had already mangled two tires and a wheel rim playing Mario Andretti. I had no desire to spend the night stranded in the van for lack of a decent spare.

"Suit yourself."

"Say, can you tell me what that place is over by the lake?" I pointed to a ranch-style building which the ravens had staked out. They were still up on the roof squawking, flapping and hopping out their peculiar greeting dance.

"Yeah, that's Athabasca Airways. Hank LeFleur's place."

"Is he a good bush pilot?"

"Probably the best damn pilot in this territory. He can fly this country in the dark. In a snowstorm. In his sleep. You want to fly anywhere in the bush, you see Hank."

The van driver left our small group dodging sprays of gravel and choking in plumes of dust as he made a great show of peeling out. He'd be lucky to reach La Loche in that bucket of bolts. The passengers looked immensely relieved to be on their feet and heading for their homes. I was now alone with a mountain of gear in an unfamiliar place. Walking

toward the house of the dancing ravens, however, I felt an unexpected
surge of euphoria, as if I too were going home.

"No way I'm flying you to Dillon tonight, Armand. No siree! Now,
I'm gonna grab myself some supper." The husky older white man's voice
had a menacing edge. He spun around on a counter stool to face a steam-
ing bowl of stew.

"No good. No fuckin' good for me. Gotta get back tonight. Partner's
waitin' for me, you know," countered the Indian man. The latter was
somewhat younger but of equally muscular build. With unlaced work
boots, drooping trousers, unbuttoned wool shirt, soiled nylon jacket, and
a red visored work cap twisted back at an odd angle, the man was hap-
hazardly attired, if not overdressed for the weather. He was drenched
with perspiration.

"What are you, deaf? You want to catch a ride on a mail flight? Fish
flight? Fine, come back tomorrow and I'll see what I can do."

"Bugger all, anyways, eh? Tomorrow's too late." The Indian's
slurred words betrayed his intoxication. He paused momentarily, perhaps calculating his next move. He staggered a few steps toward the
counter, laying a hand on the older man's shoulder. "Hey, you gotta . . ."

With cat-like agility, the older man sprung to his feet. He grabbed
the would-be client by his jacket collar and the seat of his trousers,
marched him across the room like a disobedient child and, unceremoni-
ously, shoved him out the door.

"He's telling me what I gotta do?" The bush pilot growled as he
returned to his stew. "Goddamn fucking warwhoopers!"

Armand was now sprawled out on the ground in front of the pilots'
house. Two younger white fellows, apparently assistant pilots, were
relaxing around a cribbage board in a corner of the room. The ruckus
had barely distracted them from their game.

"Hey, you know why old Armand there wears his politics on his
back?" Grinning slyly, the senior pilot pointed toward a campaign
sticker pinned to Armand's jacket. The printed slogan promoted a local
candidate in an upcoming election. "Hell, with his face in the gutter,
that's the only way people can read em!" The cribbage players joined
their boss in a hearty laugh at Armand's expense.

"Is that guy going to be okay?" I inquired. Dragging a couple
Duluth packs through the door, I felt awkward stumbling upon this
scene.

"Who? Old Armand there?" The pilot scoffed. "He'll just sleep it off.
In the morning he'll pole vault his way back to Dillon. Yesiree! So, what
can I do for you?"

"I'm looking for Hank LeFleur."

"You're looking at him."

In the full light of the Athabasca Airways office the older pilot, this nemesis of "warwhoopers," bore a startling resemblance to John Wayne. Fiftyish, with a receding hairline, LeFleur was a rangy muscular man well over six feet tall. Moreover, he had Wayne's stern countenance, the Wayne swagger, and the crusty no-nonsense manner. When he barked orders, underlings jumped. It was like walking in on a movie set for *Rio Bravo*. Maybe he'd cold cock me with a rifle butt. Bush pilots had a reputation as the cowboys of the North, but this really pushed the envelope. Yet, as I was to discover, some of LeFleur's bravado was tongue-in-cheek. And he had a mercurial temperament. After chewing out some hapless soul, he could quickly display an affable side and an earthy sense of humor.

"Can you get me into some of the smaller, off-road native settlements?" I quickly laid out my research plans, stressing the need to find a Chipewyan community with an active bush economy. I had no idea if LeFleur would take any of this seriously. After all, poor Armand was still rolling around in the dirt. Since arriving in Saskatchewan some weeks previously, I noted, I had sought advice and blessings from numerous quarters: the Federation of Saskatchewan Indians, Department of Indian Affairs and Northern Development, Indian and Métis Department, Department of Natural Resources, and the Royal Canadian Mounted Police, among others.

"I can tell you more than those guys," LeFleur stated flatly. "Look, I've lived in this country for many years. I fly into the bush all the time. I know who's catching fish. Who's sending fur out. If you want to live with the Chips, I'd go to Patuanak. Those people work hard, and they're the best hunters and trappers around. I know because I fly more fur out of Patuanak than any other district."

"Patuanak, you say?" The very name held a mysterious allure.

"Yup. When do you want to go?"

Heavy rains grounded all flying for several days. When the clouds finally broke, LeFleur fueled up his Cessna 180 float plane. He had mail freight destined for Patuanak. Gratefully, I was able to tag along on discount fare.

After miles of unbroken forest and bog, a roiling bank of low clouds appeared on the eastern horizon. Approaching closer, the cloud mass loomed to gigantic proportions. One had the sense of flying off the edge of the earth. As the mists swirled and disintegrated in the morning sun, a spectacular body of water emerged. The elongate Lac Ile-a-la-Crosse was actually a huge lake expansion of the Churchill River. Somewhere 40 miles to the south was the old fur trade center of Ile-a-la-Crosse, first established by French-Canadian and English traders in the 1770s–1790s. Our plane descended and then banked around an outlet at the northern end of the lake where the river roared through a narrow channel.

"Shagwenaw Rapids." LeFleur shouted over the drone of the engine. He motioned to the white water below. A short distance beyond, the river flowed into island-studded Shagwenaw Lake. On its west shore a clearing was faintly visible.

"There it is. Patuanak!" LeFleur dropped the plane in a slow circling descent. Dozens of dwellings hugged a bare patch of ground claimed from the forest. "That's the Catholic church!" LeFleur yelled as we passed over a large steepled structure near the river's confluence. "Father Moraud was the priest here. Died a few years ago. You'll be hearing about him."

"And that over there is the Bay. Hudson's Bay Company store." LeFleur pointed toward a large, white clapboard, red-roofed structure at the opposite end of the village. "They've got a new trader in here. Young guy from Scotland. You'll be meeting him."

So the Indians here were quite literally sandwiched between trader and missionary. For reasons that would become apparent later, there was something appropriately symbolic about this. I made a mental note to myself to check into the matter. As the bush plane continued its descent, it afforded one last, fleeting Gulliver-like gaze. What were those peculiar tiny log structures down there, near the houses? Where did the meandering trails into the bush lead? Why was that flotilla of boats putting ashore? Questions nagged, but my panic was fueled by more pressing concerns.

The Chipewyan village of Patuanak, Saskatchewan. Handmade wooden skiffs line the lakeshore. In the background, visitors' tents surround the Catholic church during a pilgrimage.

"You want to see the chief, right?" LeFleur asked as the plane's pontoons hit the water.

"Yes. The chief and councilors, first thing." With a growing sense of dread, I realized that many months, if not years, of preparation for this moment could go down the proverbial toilet in a few seconds. I needed to gain formal permission from the people, from their officially elected leaders, in order to conduct my research and live in their community. Patuanak was a federal Indian reserve as well as the main settlement of the English River Band of Chipewyan. These people had received registered treaty status and reserves, among other provisions, through extinguishment of land title in Treaty No. 10 in 1906. The band government was headed by a chief and three councilors elected to office every three years. Regrettably, I had no experience in obtaining *informed consent*, a precondition for any ethically responsible ethnographic research. When I worked in the Yukon, Dr. McClellan had handled these delicate matters in our behalf. What would happen here? Would the Chipewyan see any value in my research? Or would they find it preposterous and send me packing on the next bush plane out of town?

LeFleur taxied to a large wooden dock near the Hudson's Bay Company store. What had seemed to be a ghost town from 500 feet in the air was bustling with activity at ground level. The arrival of the plane itself was a worthy attraction. Dozens of people appeared. Some ambled unhurriedly toward the shoreline. Others quickly assembled on the dock, waiting for LeFleur to step out of the plane. A few yards away two young men were unloading gill nets and boxes of whitefish from a canvas freight canoe. In turn, they relayed the boxes to an older man, heavily attired in a denim jacket and rubberized pants, who was stooped over a makeshift wooden table and galvanized washtub. With rapid-fire knife cuts, he was gutting the catch and throwing the fresh fish in clean boxes. On the ground behind him several nets were spread out to dry. A woman was smoke-tanning a moose hide nearby. She poked carefully at the embers of a smudge fire while adjusting a large twirling cylinder of hide suspended above it. And beyond, faintly visible in the shadow of a log house, two elderly women were scraping the hair off a moosehide. The laughter of children punctuated the air. A half-dozen of them, stripped nearly naked, were frolicking and leaping off the end of the dock. Several odd, runty black dogs tussled and snapped at each other as they scampered along the boulder-strewn shore. The leader was dragging what appeared to be the remnants of a moldering beaver carcass. On a small rise above the lake two older men were having a leisurely smoke. They wore depression-era wool caps, and they seemed to nod and smile knowingly as they gazed in my direction. Scents of smoke, fish, shoreline muck, and gasoline commingled in a distinctive and not unpleasant aroma. Patuanak was utterly foreign to me, but I felt strangely at home and excited by its atmosphere. Getting turned away from here would be a major disappointment.

"Hey Vital! You old bastard, how're ya doin'?" LeFleur greeted a young Indian man who was grabbing the plane's pontoon.

"Pretty good Hank. Got our mail yet?"

"Is the Pope Catholic?" LeFleur began flinging heavy canvas sacks and a few other parcels to the dock. With an audience at hand, LeFleur's talents as a natural raconteur became apparent. He regaled the people with a tale of his latest flying mishap and a few off-color jokes. "You know why the Ukrainian suicide rate is so low, don't you? Have you ever tried jumping out of a basement window?"

"Hey Hank," an onlooker parried, "you know what we call a boat-load of Chipewyan fishermen? Fish and Chips!"

"That's a good one!" LeFleur chuckled. Almost as an afterthought he pointed toward me. "Say, this fellow here needs to see the chief. Is Albert around?"

"Think so. You come to band office, okay?" The young man, Vital, had a sullen no-nonsense expression. His head gestures indicated that I should follow him a few yards to a small wood frame building under construction. He deposited me inside and then trudged off somewhere across the village. Prepared for a long wait, I was startled when three figures appeared to materialize out of thin air. Had they been there all along, hidden behind a pile of lumber? Facing me from across the room were three tall, wiry middle-aged men. They had lean angular faces, and their thick shocks of black hair were trimmed in the same distinctive bowl cuts. They could have been brothers. Moreover, they all wore blue nylon jackets with "Patuanak" embroidered on the chest. Uniforms of office I thought, admiringly. Later I discovered that half the community was attired in this latest fashion sold by the local Bay store.

The men stared at me expectantly. An uncomfortable silence ensued. For all I knew the three men had nothing to do with the band government. Finally, one of the men, wearing thick glasses and a nervous smile, stepped forward and extended his hand. "Albert Stonypoint, Chief."

"Pleased to meet you. Bob Jarvenpa," I stammered with relief.

Another nerve-wracking silence. Was this a test? Not knowing the protocol, I rifled through my knapsack and produced a sheaf of documents explaining my credentials and plans. Handing them to the chief, I launched into an explanation of my mission. After several minutes, I fumbled for a suitable finale: " . . . and so if I can study how the local people here make a living hunting, trapping, and fishing, and how they move across the country, maybe I can learn important things about the Chipewyan way of life."

The men remained stone silent. Damn! I cursed myself for what must have been a confused, if not impertinent, presentation. The chief handed my papers to his cohorts. Soon they were conversing animatedly with each other. The conference went on for some time in Chipewyan. This looked bad. No doubt, they were giving me the boot.

A heavyset man wearing a carpenter's apron wandered into the room. After listening in on the palaver, he turned to me: "You know, these guys really don't know much English. Only Chip and a little Cree."

I was chagrined that my little speech had been so much babble. Apparently, most people here beyond their mid-30s spoke only Chipewyan. Younger folks who had been exposed to formal schooling had some command of English, but even for them everyday village conversation was conducted in "Chip." I felt woefully unprepared on this front. There was no crash course in conversational Chipewyan. I had studied the work of the linguist Fang-Kuei Li, an expert on Chipewyan, and while his papers were among my supplies, book knowledge went only so far. I would have to trust my ear, my tape recorder and dumb luck to pick up some rudimentary Chipewyan.

"No problem," the heavyset man was saying. "I'll talk for you. Now, what do you want to do here, and what do the people get out of it." Man, this guy cuts to the chase, I thought, as I explained my project one more time. The man started translating into Chipewyan and then paused, musing to himself in English: "I see, this man's an observer. He wants to study our culture." There it was. My whole enterprise captured in a few well-chosen words. And I was struggling with cumbersome platitudes about "adaptation" and "spatial organization."

Penetrating questions were quickly relayed to me: "Your studies? What you write? You won't write up anything *bad* about us?"

"That's not my intention. Anything I write will be given to the band." This was an enormously complex issue, and I felt my simple response was inadequate.

"You want to live *here*? For a whole *year*?" The tone was incredulous. They could have been addressing a Martian.

"Well, yes. With your permission."

"But *how* will you live?" A very good question, indeed.

After all, non-Indian outsiders were rare, save for a few transient whites who occupied familiar roles such as trader, itinerant priest, and school teacher. My role was nebulous, my means of support invisible. I muttered something about being resourceful and having a small grant to pay for basic provisions.

"Do you want to go out in the bush too? Live on the trapline?"

"Yes, definitely. If the people will accept me, I need to be in the bush, to see that way of life."

The chief and his men held a fairly long conference. When they finished, one of the councilors, a fellow named Louis Muskrat, somberly posed a question: "Do you want to study the creatures too?"

"Creatures?" I was mystified. Images from B-grade horror flicks came to mind.

"Oh yeah, the creatures," the translator clarified. "You know, like the moose, the caribou, the beaver. Do you study the creatures too."

"Well, in my work, how people interact with other species is real important," I replied cautiously. "Yes, creatures are included." To my ear, this sounded inane. It was like saying "batteries are included."

After another deliberation, the chief delivered an unexpected decision through the translator: "It's all right. They say you can stay. And we have a cabin where you can live."

After shaking hands with the chief and councilors, I departed feeling lightheaded and emotionally drained. Mercifully, long months of uncertainty were at an end. Others were only beginning.

A luminous purple-green curtain hung in the sky. Like an electromagnetic serpent, the aurora borealis undulated and shimmered, glowing with greater intensity as the temperature plummeted. A nightly chorus of sled dogs was tuning up. Yips and howls at the north end of the village were answered by shrill barks on the south end. Soon the air vibrated with plaintive wails. An eerie laughter echoed off the lake as the loons began their own concert.

Reclining on my bedroll, I savored the night sounds. The small cabin I was to rent from the band was being used as a storehouse, so I had pitched my pup tent nearby. Most villagers had retired hours ago, but I was too wound up to sleep. Relieved at having my foot in Patuanak's door, I wondered if I would catch a meaningful glimpse of life behind it. Or would it get slammed in my face? Either way, I vowed to learn from the experience. Finally, in the early morning hours, elation gave way to sleep.

"Okay, this is where you stay tonight," a distant voice announced.

Great! I'd love to stay here tonight, I thought. I was in a half-dream state, up near Shagwenaw Rapids. Villagers crowded the banks. And the river was alive. It literally overflowed with plump silvery whitefish. In kamikaze leaps, the fish were jumping to shore where people happily grabbed them.

"Here, eat this, you'll like it," an old woman said as she handed me a piece of smoke-dried whitefish. Its rich fragrance was intoxicating. I raised it to my mouth, but before I could eat there was a disturbance above. An unmistakable flapping and croaking. Several ravens were settling on top of an aspen. Wait a minute, I mused, those birds look awfully familiar. Didn't I see them at Buffalo Narrows?

As if in answer to my suspicions, one of them let out a deafening squawk and then clearly stated: "That's right! We helped you out back there. Now, it's your turn. You should give us something before you eat." I was flabbergasted, but offered my whitefish in outstretched arms and waited . . .

Heart racing, I awoke in a sweat. That same dream, with minor modifications, had haunted me in the Yukon. A dream analyst would have kicks with this stuff. Even more disturbing, there was a hulking shadowy presence outside. I felt my chest tighten. Damn! Something was pawing at my tent door. Maybe a 200-pound raven out for a night of mayhem.

"*Dliyanat'e?*" ("How are you?") a muffled voice asked. I recognized the Chipewyan greeting.

A head appeared through the door flap. It was Vital, the somber young man who had delivered me to the band office. Now he wore a solicitous grin. "You want some scotch?"

Already I had learned that Patuanak had voted itself a "dry reserve." Liquor could not be bought, sold or consumed on reserve land, at least officially. Supplies of booze still slipped in from bootleggers in Buffalo Narrows and Ile-a-la-Crosse, and some enterprising individuals cooked up batches of home brew. Nonetheless, I saw nothing to be gained from drinking with this fellow. "No thanks, I'm bushed. I think I'll call it a night."

"Remember, you're on reserve now!" Vital hissed. His breath reeked of alcohol, and his grin quickly turned to a scowl. "You want to *stay* on reserve?" Stumbling through the tent door, his bottle flew, anointing my bivouac with 80 proof Teachers scotch. Wonderful! This place will smell like a barroom for days, I thought.

"Sure, I want to stay on the reserve," I replied taking a drink from the proffered bottle.

"You're from the States, right? Right? Well, if I were chief, you know what I'd do?" Vital snarled defiantly. "Tell you to get the hell out." The man's rage alarmed me.

"You don't like people from the States?" I asked cautiously.

"Don't listen to what I say." Vital's voice suddenly softened. His manner became almost apologetic. "But you're on our reserve now. You do what the chief says. He's boss."

"Yes, I met the chief. Seems like a nice guy."

"I know I have, whaddayacallit, a drinkin' problem? But not when I'm workin', eh? Hey, how come you're not drinkin'?"

"Sorry. I'm not big on scotch." I could manage barely one swig to Vital's three. I was tempted to bring up the "dry reserve" business but feared rekindling Vital's ire.

"Don't think I'm against you," Vital said with a pained expression. "I just want to make sure you're not here to make trouble for us. That's my job, I always check up on people, you know."

"I understand. I'm a stranger here. Nobody really knows me. I would do the same thing."

"The people here will treat you good." Vital's eyes moistened with emotion. "That's our way. We'll take you out hunting, on the trapline. You'll have to get up early and work hard all day. And you'll have to eat bannock and lard!"

"I would like nothing better."

Vital paused to draw deeply from his bottle. When he finally came up for air, he was snickering "That's good! You know what the people here say? 'Bannock and lard make the Indian happy.' Yah, bannock and lard make the Indian happy." For some reason, he found this quaint sentiment hilarious, and, convulsed by fits of laughter, he collapsed on my bedroll.

When Vital dropped his tough facade, he was rather likeable. In a confessional mood, he acknowledged that his drinking might jeopardize some position he held in the band office, forcing him to run his long trapline this winter. Whenever he referred to "white people" or "the white man" in a generic sense, however, his tone was bitter. He alluded to some vague "troubles" his family had experienced with whites. Was this the real reason for his midnight visit? Or had the chief sent him to check up on me, to see if I was a troublemaker?

Thankful that Vital was finally departing in a good mood, I cheerfully joked: "Goodnight Vital! You know, when you first came here, I thought you were a raven!"

"Raven?"

"You know, datsa, the raven."

"You thought I was datsa?" Vital looked perplexed.

"Well, I guess I was just having a dream. It's not the first time that's happened."

"You know what that means, datsa? It means, shit on the mouth, or shit on the beak. Because those birds eat anything. Any kind of garbage. That's why we call 'em datsa." Vital gave me a peculiar look and stumbled out into the darkness. I was stunned. I had never given any thought to the literal meaning of the Chipewyan term for my feathered comrades. What's more, I had come precariously close to calling Vital "shit face."

I expected Vital to become a thorn in my side, but after the mysterious midnight visit he faded from view. In the first days people were overtly friendly but kept a wary distance. Moreover, it appeared that I would have to live out of my little tent for an indefinite period. While this was far from satisfactory, it had an unintended benefit. Most of my belongings remained unpacked and in storage in the "band hall," a large wood frame building in the center of the village used for public meetings and community events. Almost daily, I needed to retrieve some supplies, and a small crowd would gather to watch me open up a duffel or rearrange a pack. A few bolder individuals asked questions. I loaned out a banjo, a shotgun, and a few other items to people who admired them. These gestures were appreciated, and they gained me a small circle of acquaintances.

At the same time, I needed provisions. Pilot biscuits and tinned meat from the Bay post quickly grew tiresome. I initiated a daily pattern of walking to Shagwenaw Rapids to cast for pickerel and jackfish. This provided at least one meal per day of fresh fish. Barely beyond sight of the village, the rapids offered a serene haven, a place to collect one's thoughts. Sea gulls hovered above the roiling water scouting out dead fish and other morsels which the river coughed up. Canvas freight canoes and wooden skiffs, mounted with whining outboard motors, occasionally ran the rapids. Some were filled with families returning from a day's berry picking. Others were piloted by men carrying box loads of fresh fish to buyers in Ile-a-la-Crosse.

"Looks like a big *uldai* you got there?" A young man asked. He had been watching me struggle with the fish and had just beached his skiff.

"This jack here? Yah, it's the biggest I've caught so far. Thought I'd take it back to my tent for dinner."

"Ever try *etthai*?"

"Is it like jackfish?"

"It's whitefish. Dried whitefish. We eat it all winter. My mom's making up a big bunch right now. C'mon with me. I'll trade you some etthai for the big uldai."

That was how I met Marcel Flatstone. A thin young man with shoulder length hair and a quick wit, he was comparatively well educated having spent years outside at boarding schools. All his siblings had married or moved away. As the youngest child, he was living with his elderly parents, at least for the summer. He had been hunting and was now returning home with a few freshly killed ducks. Accepting his invitation, we ascended the rapids and traveled around the big peninsula into Lac Ile-a-la-Crosse. Marcel's family lived in an old log dwelling some distance away from the village and other families. I wondered if this reflected a kind of exile status. Yet, Marcel's parents were as outgoing and gregarious as he. It seemed that they preferred the tranquility of their solitary homestead.

I would soon discover that other Chipewyan families still occupied small log cabin communities scattered downriver at places like Dipper Lake, Primeau Lake, Knee Lake and far to the north at Cree Lake.

Indeed, until fairly recently, Patuanak itself was a seasonally occupied place containing only a few log dwellings and tents. With the arrival of government-sponsored housing and an elementary school in the mid- to late-1960s, many families gravitated to Patuanak making it the English River Band's main community with over 400 residents. Yet, the whole idea of a large permanently occupied settlement was still something novel and, perhaps, socially indigestible.

When we arrived, Marcel's mother was outside at a gutting table. Her silvery hair was drawn back in a bun, and her feet were encased in plain moosehide work moccasins tied at the ankles. She was working her way through a tub of whitefish. Wielding a large curved knife, she transformed each fish into a thin sheet, its flesh riddled with delicate cuts, suitable for smoke-drying. A few yards away at the edge of the woods stood a square log cache or *loretthe kwae*, resembling a dwarf's house. Suspended from poles inside were dozens of thin-cut whitefish absorbing the fragrance of a slow smokey fire. Marcel's father was relaying his wife's handiwork from gutting table to cache. A tall man with an eagle's beak nose, he wore fancy beaded moccasins inside low-cut rubbers, the favored footwear of older men.

Harry Gunn Jr.'s family erects a temporary sun shade at Knee Lake village.

Marcel deposited my jackfish and his ducks at his mother's feet. She continued her labors for some time, but before my visit ended she retrieved a large sheet of etthai, or dried whitefish, for me.

"Here, eat it like this," Marcel instructed as he ripped off hunks of tender dry fish and popped them into his mouth.

Remembering my recent dream, I experienced an odd sense of déjà vu as I wolfed down the succulent morsels. The fragrant, slightly oily whitefish was delightful to eat, and I told Marcel to compliment his mother for me.

"Hey, Mom! He likes it! You better get him another piece, eh? He brought us a pretty big uldai."

Marcel explained the various ways of eating etthai. In the winter, people slathered the large pieces with moose fat or lard. The fish could be pounded into fine flakes of pemmican and mixed with fat and berries, among other possibilities. Our simple exchange of fish was the start of a friendship. Marcel's parents spoke only a few words of English, but they always greeted me with warm smiles and made me feel welcome. Marcel sometimes wanted company on his daily inspection of rabbit snares and forays for ducks. I happily complied, accompanying him on trips to the small grassy bays and inlets at the north end of Lac Ile-a-la-Crosse. It was my first learning of bush ways, and I felt sharing a meal with Marcel's family was the end to a perfect day.

"Hell, I should go out girling." The young man, Jimmy Stonypoint, sighed as he threw a few sticks in the fire.

"Girling? This town is dead now, eh. All the young ones are going out to school anyhow," observed another man.

"You're right. Their mommies and daddies are too strict around here. You gotta go down to Pinehouse if you want to have fun."

"What about Verna? You tried her yet?"

"Tried her? Hey, I taught her first, you know."

"Well, maybe you should follow her to Beauval."

"Naw, but maybe I could get some love medicine."

Half a dozen young men were gathered around a late evening fire in front of my tent. Their banter was punctuated with snickers and peals of laughter. Sexual liaisons and conquests were favored topics. Despite the mirth, there was a serious and cynical undercurrent. Patuanak had a reputation and self-image as a community of hard-working, church-going "bush" Indians. Parents kept a close watch on their unmarried daughters, and if older folks wished to drink or gamble with cards they did so circumspectly. From a Chipewyan perspective, however, Cree communities like Pinehouse Lake had a liberal attitude toward sex and drink. The Cree people generally possessed powerful magical-medicinal knowledge, including such things as love medicines.

Chipewyan woman pounding moose meat into pemmican at Knee Lake on Churchill River, 1929 (courtesy of Public Archives Canada, PA-20387). In earlier times most Chipewyan lived in conical lodges covered with caribou hides or sometimes with spruce boughs. After World War I, homemade canvas wall tents, of the kind pictured here, became common, and they remain the favored portable dwelling for bush work.

Yet, the Chipewyan called the Cree *ena* or "enemy." The two groups had a long history of animosity and conflict, and it was known that powerful Cree sorcerers could facilitate misfortune, illness or death by "working medicine against" their adversaries. Therein lay the rub and a good deal of ambivalence for the Chipewyan.

In the fading twilight I had been roasting a fish for my dinner when Marcel stopped by for a visit. Deciding that we needed a "feast," he had rounded up a group of his friends, all young unmarried men like ourselves. They brought more fish, tea, bannock, lard and additional wood to stoke the fire. The camaraderie of this spontaneous meal and gathering was infectious. While I did my best to follow the nuances of the jokes and stories, I was most grateful for the fellowship and the chance to meet new people.

"Aaaarrgghh!" A bone chilling cry echoed through the village. Sled dogs never sounded quite so miserable, I mused. Could a human voice produce such wailing? The men around the fire stopped their banter to listen. In the moon-lit shadows, a figure lurched around the corner of a nearby house. "Aaaaooooooohhhh!" The figure, now plainly a large man, bellowed with pain and rage. Turning toward the house, he attacked it with uncontrolled fury, kicking at the wall as if it were an animate being. He slammed his bare fists through a window pane. The door flew open, and an elderly man peered out into the darkness. Behind him on the floor, faintly visible in dim lamp light, was a circle of elderly male and female cohorts placing one dollar bets in a deuces-wild card game. The door was quickly bolted shut again, and the bellowing assailant punched his bloodied fists through another window.

"Holy smokin'! It's John!" gasped Marcel. His voice betrayed a mix of awe and fear.

"Who's John?" I asked.

"John Lynx. He's okay when he's sober. But drunk? He's hell. Stay away from him."

"Yah. Real dangerous, that guy," Jimmy added nervously. "Let's go get him."

To my dismay, Marcel, Jimmy and the others hurried toward the bellowing Lynx, picking up weapons on the run. Stout pieces of firewood, a galvanized wash tub, and an old pail rained down upon the man's head, face and shoulders with sickening accuracy. When Lynx finally slumped to the ground, the young men continued their frenzied attack, kicking the prone man's body with pointy-toed western boots.

Lynx lay in a grimy, bloody heap, moaning obscenities. Surely the ferocity of the attack had done him serious injury. Lights went on in houses throughout the village, and dozens of people were crowding around the battle scene. "Son of a bitch!" Lynx's sudden scream sent a shudder through the crowd. As if magically renewed, he was getting to his feet. A large and powerfully built young man, his bruised, bloodied and ragged condition only made him seem more fearsome. His face contorted in a harsh grimace, Lynx moved menacingly toward the crowd. People backed away as if confronted by pure evil.

Lynx staggered toward another house and, hurling his bulk against it, crashed through the door. Screams and shouts could be heard within. A young woman ran out a rear entrance with several children in tow, shooing them into the safety of the bush beyond.

Alarmed by a situation that seemed to be spiraling out of control, I asked Jimmy: "Where's the chief?"

"He went to Dillon, I think."

"What about the councilors?"

"Shit! They're afraid of John."

Marcel, Jimmy and their crew ran into the house after the rampaging Lynx. Marcel's maternal uncle, an elderly man in poor health, lived there. Without warning, Lynx charged out the door carrying several men along with him. Like overmatched steer wrestlers, the men haltingly dragged their quarry to the ground. With growing desperation, they commenced another furious barrage of kicking. The blows seemed to subdue Lynx. Except for occasional moans and sobs, he lay motionless. Someone produced a rope, and people began to hog-tie the man.

"I'll take you all on!" Someone threatened from the edge of the bush. At first, I thought my eyes were playing tricks on me. The man looked like John Lynx himself, only a few pounds heavier and a few years older. It was really one of John's uncles, valiantly prepared to spare his nephew from further punishment. The hog-tying crew momentarily abandoned their quarry. A dozen people charged after the uncle, but he promptly vanished in the bush.

There were audible gasps as Lynx rose to his feet again, somehow restored from what appeared to be a near-lethal beating. Strangely, Marcel and the others were now backing away from further confrontation. People milled about nervously, intimidated by the formidable display of power. Lynx slipped away into the shadows, roaring in anguish and rage. The sound was both heart-rending and terrifying.

"Bob, you better come and stay with us tonight." Marcel was pulling me away from the scene. His parents were walking with us, nodding grimly. "We'll take the old portage trail. Easier that way."

"You're sure? All my stuff is here," I protested weakly.

"*Nezole, slini* [bad, evil]," Marcel's father interrupted. "Not safe here."

As we started along the trail, I glanced back toward the village. The cozy cluster of dwellings, framed by the lake's moon-lit surface, no longer appeared so serene and picturesque. My tent looked pathetically puny and vulnerable. And something sinister in the shadows was moving toward it. It was John Lynx.

In early September the aspens along the Churchill River turned a rich golden yellow. Nightly freezes were a promise of the winter ahead. Teams of fishermen took advantage of the cool weather to lay up supplies of pickerel, whitefish, lake trout and jackfish for their family larders and to raise cash or credit for winter trapping outfits. I finally moved into my small cabin. With my belongings in order under one roof, and with a tea pail and coffee pot continually brewing on the stove, I was prepared to greet visitors.

John Lynx remained a hot topic of gossip and speculation for weeks. The "Night of the Lynx," as I privately termed the episode, had touched a raw nerve. In its aftermath, many people fished for my reaction in a roundabout way: "Pretty good show the other night, eh?" or "Lot of action last night, eh?" I felt that I was being tested and that to show fear, revulsion or some other strong emotion would be unwelcome. So, I made light of the incident, and people seemed relieved.

Privately, however, I was disturbed. Marcel, Jimmy and their companions were unnerved enough by their battle with Lynx that they left the village for several days. They set up a tent camp somewhere down the Churchill River. The day after the rampage, people had been startled to see John Lynx, although bruised and battered, calmly walking about the village with no recollection of the previous night. Some blamed Lynx's behavior on a rough childhood. Recently, he had accosted his own father. And a long list of embittered villagers had suffered at John Lynx's hands. Others said he went bad on hairspray and lysol, common local substitutes for liquor. Perhaps these were surface explanations for a deeper problem, what Marcel's father and older folks called slini. Evil. In fact, Lynx had terrorized the community for years. For his troubles he had been beaten, stabbed, and shot. In the end, he always revived and seemed to grow stronger.

Momentarily, at least, the village was enjoying a reprieve. RCMP officers from Ile-a-la-Crosse had hauled Lynx outside to a court hearing. With previous prison time on his record, he was facing a long stretch in jail.

"*Notitsenowasja.*"

"What did you say?"

"I am going to go home and sleep."

"You are? You just got here?"

"No. I mean that's how you say it in Chip. Notitsenowasja."

"Oh, I see. How do you say 'Go to sleep!'"

"That's *nitits'anainda!*"

Jimmy Stonypoint had stopped by my cabin. He was helping me with my Chipewyan, patiently repeating words and phrases so that I could clumsily say them and write them phonetically. Bit by bit, as I gathered word lists from Jimmy and others, I assembled them into a kind of working dictionary for ready reference. Jimmy was particularly thorough in providing vocabulary for various animals, plants and landscape features. These could become important clues to the people's own understanding of their environment, or their *ethnoecology*.

"Yech! *Naduthi*," Jimmy made a sour face. "It looks just like the devil to me." He was pointing at a picture of a snake in one of my natural history field guides. Although most Patuanak people had never seen a snake, they regarded them with revulsion. Reptiles were a rarity in the area, as in much of the subarctic. The only known species of snake, the red-sided garter, was thought to range no farther north than Pinehouse Lake, a good 90 miles downriver from Patuanak. Fittingly, that place had been dubbed Snake Lake, Serpent Lake, or Lac Du Serpent by early English and French-Canadian traders.

"And we call that *ts'eli*." Jimmy gestured at a drawing of a wood frog. "Sometimes very big, that one."

"Really? Where I come from 'bullfrogs' grow pretty large." I held my hands apart to indicate a rat-sized amphibian. "Didn't know you had them up here."

"No, no. Big!" Jimmy corrected. His manner was utterly serious and business-like. He held his arms apart to suggest an animal of staggering dimensions, maybe the size of my cabin or larger. "Some people here seen it. Not me. I think I'm afraid to see it. Once over by Dillon people saw that big frog in the lake. And last year I met this old man from La Loche, you know. He says there's a little muddy lake back in the bush. If you throw sticks or rocks in there the lake just starts shaking and shaking, like a big tea pail boiling over. People don't go near that place anymore. They're afraid. It's the big frog's home."

The giant frog seemed to be an accepted part of the local fauna, as much as muskrats, say, or snow geese. In ensuing months I would hear similar accounts from others. Now, as I tried to comprehend the significance of Jimmy's words, he was taking his zoology into new terrain.

"Well, we have lots of different creatures around here. There's something in this lake too, and we don't like it." Jimmy turned his head west to indicate Lac Ile-a-la-Crosse.

"Another big frog?"

"No, but it's bad. People say it lives inside Big Island. My mom remembers long time ago, lots of us Chipewyan people used to camp there in the summer, eh. For fishing and trading at Ile-a-la-Crosse. Well, people found these big tracks in the sand on that island. And marks like a big tail dragging behind too. That was many years ago, before I was born."

"So the creature's no longer here?"

"Sure, it's here. People saw it swimming near the town, you know, near Ile-a-la-Crosse last summer. Right by the shore there are some big deep holes in the lake. Two people drowned at the holes. And that's where they saw the creature. Hey, I do a lot of fishing on that lake with my brother Prosper. And we found some big deep holes at the north end too. You know, we're trying to set our nets out from this reef? And here are these big deep holes in the rocky reef, like tunnels. So deep, we couldn't touch bottom with two poles tied together. We figure the creature's in the holes, eh? When we saw that we really got scared. We took off. We don't fish in that part of the lake anymore."

Creatures in tunnels beneath the lake? Giant frogs? It sounded like a Japanese sci-fi flick from the 1950s. I had to remind myself to always wear the anthropologist's hat, to try to understand the world through others' knowledge and experience. Jimmy could be a jokester, but I could tell from his grave, agitated tone that he was not pulling my leg. For the moment, I would take him at his word. Perhaps there were some nasty surprises out there in the bush waiting for the unwary.

"I have to tell you, Jimmy, the scariest thing I've ever heard was John's screaming."

"You heard *the* screaming?" Jimmy looked startled, and he nearly dropped his mug of tea.

"Yah, you were there. The night John Lynx went haywire. I'll never forget his horrible voice."

"No," Jimmy sighed and shook his head. "The screaming across the lake."

"Across what lake?" In my mind's eye John Lynx was now out in the bush somewhere wailing like a banshee. The vision made my skin crawl.

But Jimmy proceeded to educate me about another disturbing voice or sound originating from a lonely point of land on the east side of Shagwenaw Lake, a mere four miles across the water from Patuanak. Over the years a number of people who had traveled, fished, gathered berries or set up camp in that vicinity had been assailed by a high-pitched screaming voice, akin to the wordless wail of a person in agony. One of Jimmy's cousins had been cutting firewood there one summer, when a blood-curdling scream caused him to smash through a log with a single blow of his axe. He made a rapid departure, abandoning his wood supply. Indeed, the screams had terrified enough people over the years, that travelers now gave the area a wide berth.

"This screaming is like no animal or bird?" I could not resist asking.

"No!" Jimmy was adamant. "We know their cries. The loon, the owl, hawk, eagle. The wolf, coyote, lynx. We know their calls. *This* one's different."

"What do you think it is?"

"I don't know," Jimmy shrugged his shoulders. "Some people say it's *hotet'slini*. You know, bushman."

Bushman! There it was again, the widespread Athapaskan belief in a threatening feral man or sub-human lurking the forest depths. The Han called it tse'taojin. For these Chipewyan it was hotet'slini.

"So this screamer could be a bushman?"

"Yah. Or maybe *deneyune*. Ghost of a bushman. My grandpa told me about this white trapper. He hunted alone way up north, maybe 30 or 40 years ago. Not friendly, that guy, so our people don't see him much. I think he went crazy in the bush. He was hotet'slini, for sure. Then, one year before spring break-up that guy walks all the way down here to Shagwenaw Lake. He makes camp on other side of the lake there. Stays away from the village. But then our people find him dead. They say he ate some kind of poison berries. He was buried on that point of land. And that's where we hear the screaming. It could be that bushman scream-ing, you know, because he's dying from poison."

Jimmy's tale had my mind reeling. The Patuanak Chipewyan had constructed an interesting twist for the bushman complex. Here bush-men were personified as depression-era white trappers. In this sense, hotet'slini had a corporeal presence and a highly specific historical image. They were the bearded and bedraggled bachelor recluses of the 1930s, devoid of obvious ties to family, kin and community, and suscep-tible to becoming "bushed," going mad, losing all vestiges of humanness and, thereby, endangering the Indians. This explained some peculiar encounters I had had in the village. On a few occasions, adults "jokingly" referred to me as a "bushman" when I approached, a ruse which usually sent small children crying and running for cover. Apparently, a bearded white man was still something of a novelty and, unfortunately for me, resonated with a corpus of negative beliefs and images. Moreover, there was a double whammy in all this. A bushman could be a real terror when alive, but clearly a dead bushman's ghost was nothing to fool with either.

"Jimmy, did you ever hear that screaming yourself?" Dozens of questions swirled in my head, but this was all I could come up with.

"Nope. I think I would be afraid to hear it," Jimmy stated with a shudder. "Well, I better go now. Gotta go moose hunting with Victor tomorrow. It's their mating time now so we can call them, eh."

Setting my books back on a shelf, it occurred to me that I had just received some valuable natural history and ecology lessons. That is, if I wished to make cultural sense of them. Because of the giant animals,

the "creatures," the screaming bushmen, and other unpleasant surprises, the Chipewyan apparently were avoiding whole sectors of the
landscape. The world outside my door suddenly seemed much less
benign. It was growing dark. I watched Jimmy disappear along a trail
leading south out of the village. His cousin Victor lived a couple miles
down the lake. The trail skirted the community's graveyard on the south
edge of the reserve, and I knew that most people avoided that place at
night. Jimmy moved at a brisk pace until he reached the edge of the village clearing. Entering the bush, he broke into a run.

My mind was set. I wanted to live in the bush for the winter with
a team of hunter-trappers, to become what the Chipewyan call a *sits'eni*
or "partner." This was a risky proposition. Beyond an intense desire to
learn the ropes, I had no experience in such matters. Moreover, would
Chipewyan men who spent most of their time in the bush between October and April have anything to gain by accepting an untried apprentice?
And a virtual stranger?

Participant observation, the hallmark of ethnographic fieldwork,
varies considerably in the kinds and degrees of interaction and involvement between researcher and members of a host community. Efforts at
classifying role involvement typically place the orientation of the fieldworker along a simple continuum from "complete observation" to
"complete participation," or from "passive participation" to "active participation" (Spradley 1980:58–62). It was the latter end of the spectrum,
the domain of "active participation," which intrigued me. Richard Nelson (1973:8–9) provides a cogent definition of this approach:

> . . . The ethnographer attempts to replicate the behavior involved
> in the activities he is documenting and to learn each technique at
> least at a minimal level of proficiency. In other words, he partici-
> pates to the fullest extent possible; and by learning each skill he is
> able to do a far more complete job of documentation, for he learns
> not only by observing others but by observing himself as well.

By becoming an apprentice hunter-trapper-fishermen, a familiar
role for younger men in Chipewyan society, I hoped to gain a worm's-eye
view of their bush economy. Learning to work as a Chipewyan, perhaps,
would integrate me more firmly into the life of the community. Such
thoughts helped assuage my uncertainties. Would the research ever be
of any use or relevance to the people here? If I had nothing else to offer,
at least I could donate my own time and physical labor to those who
wanted it.

I put out the word. I would pay for my share of supplies, work as
an apprentice partner with a bush team, but take no share of the hunt,
that is, no profits from fur or fish sold. A waiting game ensued. Marcel,
Jimmy and the other young men I had befriended were themselves

apprentices or junior partners to their fathers, elder brothers, uncles or other older, experienced men. These teams did not need or want an extra hand. However, some older men began stopping by for coffee, perhaps to check me out. They were guarded about their plans for the approaching winter. Instead, they talked at length about their travels, hunting experiences and partnerships of past years. This was valuable historical information which I eagerly soaked up. Soon my cabin walls were covered with topographic maps and scraps of paper. Upon these, visitors made penciled markings of dog sled trails, trapping areas, base camps, locations of bygone winter settlements and trading outposts, and innumerable other features. The men showed polite interest in my plans and sometimes extended ambiguous invitations upon departing the cabin: "Well, maybe you can visit my trapline this winter, eh?" Yet, these offers eventually fizzled. As the weeks passed by I grew increasingly apprehensive.

"Psaaaw, haaaaw, psaaaw." There was an odd rasping sound, like someone cutting wet wood with a dull bucksaw. Somebody's at my woodpile, I thought groggily. It was 5:00 A.M. I was still snug in my bedroll.

"Haaaw, psaaaw, haaaw." The sound was louder. It was *in* the cabin! Out of the corner of my eye I noticed someone or something sitting near the stove. My heart raced.

"Bob, you awake?" The voice had a familiar asthmatic wheeze. "Psaaaw, haaaw, psaaaw."

"Joachim, it's you!" I stammered, nearly falling out of my cot. "You sure gave me a scare."

"Here, I brought you some dry meat."

"Thanks. Hey, I'll put on some coffee."

As was customary here, visitors would walk in unannounced and often depart without any farewells. But Joachim Deneyou had taken to showing up at my cabin at odd hours. It was disconcerting to open one's blurry eyes to an unexpected face. Joachim was a man of few words who seemed content to simply sit and pass the time. Middle-aged and unmarried, he had a slow and plodding manner which suggested mild retardation. Along with several cohorts, he occupied a niche as a water hauler. For a small fee he retrieved buckets or tubs of water from the lake, often for the elderly, widows and others in need. This service was especially in demand in the depths of winter when the mercury could plummet to minus 50°F and the lake ice could be 5 feet thick. Joachim also held a special distinction as the village "child chaser." Youngsters were expected to be in their homes before dark, and the band employed Joachim to round them up. Wielding a large stick, the mere presence of his lumbering figure was usually sufficient to send children scurrying.

"You're all spruced-up, Joachim. Something special happening today?" I admired his cowboy duds. He wore a shiny white silk shirt with brilliant crimson roses embroidered on the yoke.

"Bishop, he come. Maybe mass today." Joachim was referring to Bishop Doumachelle who oversaw the diocese from district headquarters in The Pas. Father Louis Moraud, Patuanak's long-time missionary, had died in 1965. Since that time the village had been left without a resident priest. I had attended a couple prayer services conducted by the laity and was mesmerized by the spirited singing of hymns in the Chipewyan language. A small group of older people, including Marcel's father, spearheaded the singers. I had yet to witness a formal mass, however, or speak to the clergy.

"You got trapping partner yet?" Joachim inquired.

"Nope. Got any ideas?"

"Yah, I think *Decak'ai* is good one for you."

"Who?"

"Decak'ai. He's coming right now." Joachim pointed. A large figure suddenly filled the doorway blocking out the sunlight.

"Antoine Ptarmigan." A young man stepped boldly into the cabin and extended his hand. While not tall, he had a massive torso and shoulders, like those of a weightlifter. Yet he was quick and agile on his feet. His demeanor, a compelling mix of assertiveness and nonchalance, commanded attention. And while he spoke sparingly, he chose his words carefully. "Heard you're looking for a trapping partner?"

"Sure am. At least, I'd like to be a learner." I gave my stock spiel hoping to spark interest but expecting a noncommittal reply.

"Well, I'm heading for Cache Lake next month. My trapping area starts way up there and goes into the big muskeg." Antoine traced a lengthy route with his finger across one of my maps. It was a region of labyrinthine lakes, twisting streams and very few printed place names in the rugged Precambrian shield country far to the north of the Churchill River. A trapline on the moon would have appeared no less remote. "I hunt with Frank Whitefish. We'll be in the bush till Christmas, come back here, sell our fur, then go back north again after New Year. If you want to be our partner it's okay."

I was dumbfounded. Just like that, Antoine was making me an offer. I could barely contain my excitement and, now, an unnerving realization that I would have to follow these guys into whatever unknowns lay ahead. In the bush. In winter. "Okay, Antoine. You've got yourself another partner. I'll do my best to learn your ways. But this whole thing is alright with Frank?"

"Yah. He knows. There's lots of work to do in the bush, eh? Getting wood. Making fire. Getting water. Making bannock." Antoine grinned slyly. "I didn't have much school, you know. I been trapping for my fam-

Precambrian shield, northern coniferous forest landscape north of the Churchill River. Chipewyan hunter-trappers work and travel across large expanses of such terrain.

ily since I was a kid. So maybe you can teach me some of them long words in English. And I can teach you the hard stuff in Chip."

"Great! I need the language work more than you. What supplies do I need? When should I get ready?" I was beginning to feel woefully unprepared.

"Not yet. In a few weeks. When small lakes freeze up. Gotta go check my nets now." Antoine was out the door and striding briskly toward the lake shore. He jumped into a brightly painted red and blue skiff filled with fish boxes and cranked up its outboard. The sky had turned an ugly gun metal gray. Powerful east winds were churning Shagewnaw Lake into a froth of monstrous whitecaps. Casting off, the bow of Antoine's skiff slapped violently against an onslaught of waves. The wooden vessel looked frail and puny and on the verge of swamping. But then the whining outboard motor kicked up a couple octaves. Miraculously, as if supported by an invisible hydraulic jack, the skiff lifted. Mounting the wave-tops, it shot out of sight behind a peninsula.

"Holy shit!" I gasped to myself. "And I thought Antoine was a goner."

"Hee hee!" Joachim chuckled as he drained his mug of coffee. "No problem for Decak'ai. No problem for that guy."

"What's this Decak'ai business, anyway?"

"Decak'ai, that means squirrel. Flying squirrel. That's what we call Antoine in Chip."

"Why do you call him that?"

"I don't know. Maybe when he was a baby he jump around a lot, you know, like a little squirrel. I guess his dad and mom start calling him Decak'ai, eh." Joachim paused and scanned the stormy horizon.

It seemed that almost everyone in Patuanak had colorful or humorous monikers related to some peculiarity of temperament or anatomy. One man was called "puzzle" because he enjoyed taking snowmobiles apart and fitting them back together. A man with a bristly disposition had the name *Ts'i* or "porcupine." Another with vision problems was *Neskhuze'* or "cross-eye." Some women had the ambiguous distinction of being known as "pointed" or "flat." And there were far less flattering nicknames rarely uttered in a person's presence. Since one could just as easily be called "stink shit" in Chipewyan, I figured I was fortunate to be tagged as Dastloze, that is, "bearded one" or "little bearded one."

"Hee hee!" Joachim was laughing again. "Yah, that Antoine, he's moving around all the time for any kind of work, fishing, trapping. Boy, he's fast, eh. You see him on the lake? He goes right across water like a flying squirrel, for sure. Like Decak'ai."

I couldn't argue with that.

A small crowd was assembling on the wooden steps of the Hudson's Bay Company (HBC) store. The tiny trading room inside was jammed with people. An elderly woman was cutting a swatch from a bolt of paisley-patterned cloth, perhaps to be used for a skirt or for moccasin liners. The store clerk, a local Chipewyan man, assisted a family in hefting several 50-pound bags of flour and other supplies out the door and into a waiting skiff. A long queue formed at a counter near the back of the room where people were settling debts, cashing government checks, obtaining credit advances for winter trapping ventures, and making other requests. Behind the counter stood the new post manager, David McLeod, a thin sandy-haired, energetic young man from Scotland. McLeod had served the Bay as a laborer and clerk at various small posts in northern Canada for several years. Patuanak was his first manager's position, however, and he was determined to run an efficient operation. On this unusually busy day, his wife Velma, a young Cree woman from northern Manitoba, was temporarily helping out behind the counter.

It was one of the ironies of the northern trade that a man barely 23 years of age could wield considerable power. McLeod controlled the flow of goods and credit in the settlement's largest store. In addition, he managed the post office for the community and operated one of two radiophones which served as a communication link to bush pilots, medical and welfare workers, conservation officials, and others in the outside world. As a primary distributor of goods and information, this man was in a position to reward those in his favor, or, to withhold resources from those not meeting his approval. Most Patuanak residents were concerned about maintaining harmonious relations with any reigning HBC manager. Even the church tipped its collective hat toward the old trading institution. A visiting priest, only partly in jest, once remarked: "You know what *HBC* really stands for don't you? 'Here before Christ!'"

Indeed, the priest's joke rang true. In the period between the 1770s and 1790s posts of independent peddlers and those of the major fur-trading companies were established near the headwaters of the Churchill River. The region soon became part of the contact zone between the Dene or Athapaskan-speaking Chipewyan and the Algonquian-speaking Cree. A rivalry between Montreal-based companies and the English-controlled Hudson's Bay Company was responsible for drawing some Chipewyan groups from their forest-tundra environment southward into the full boreal forest (Gillespie 1975:368–74; Smith 1975:413). Some of these southern Chipewyan became known as Kesyehot'ine ("aspen house people") in reference to their major trading fort at Ile-a-la-Crosse.

Through the nineteenth century, both the Chipewyan and Cree developed intimate economic relations with a growing class of EuroCanadian fur trade personnel at the HBC's Ile-a-la-Crosse fort and its network of secondary outposts. While the bush-oriented bands of Chipewyan and Cree served as the hunters or "primary producers" of the mercantile system, an increasingly visible mixed-blood or Métis population was occupying a niche as fur company servants and laborers. These Métis were largely descendants of unions between French-Canadian voyagers and local Cree women.

The complexity of social life increased in the last half of the nineteenth century with the arrival of French-speaking Oblate priests who established a Roman Catholic mission at Ile-a-la-Crosse in 1846. The impact of the church on the Indians was initially negligible. By the 1890s, however, the Chipewyan regularly appeared in Ile-a-la-Crosse for the Catholic mission's Christmas and Easter services, as well as summer religious instructional gatherings. The fact that their important trading-provisioning periods at the HBC post were in September and June, therefore, meant that the Chipewyan had to stage at least *four* major annual gatherings in Ile-a-la-Crosse. This was possible only by withdrawing southward from the winter range of the barren-ground caribou, a major food resource, and by shortening their annual travel circuits.

By the last decade of the nineteenth century, the HBC was enmeshed in a tangle of economic adversities that complicated its relationship with the Chipewyan, the Métis and the Catholic church. Traders in the Ile-a-la-Crosse district began strongly advocating treaty negotiations between local natives and the federal government. Although Treaty No. 10 was not implemented until 1906, the HBC was hopeful that the potential cash flow from treaty payments to Indians and scrip payments to Métis would revitalize its sagging trade and reduce indebtedness among its clientele. Also, the HBC was hopeful that federal involvement in native affairs would reduce what it perceived as a growing dependency of Indian customers and Métis servants.

Immobilizing epidemics of influenza and other illnesses killed Indians and Métis alike during the late 1880s and early 1890s. The toll of adult male Chipewyan was especially high, slowing the conduct of the fur trade. It was this turbulent atmosphere that set the stage for a growing conflict between the HBC and the Catholic priests at Ile-a-la-Crosse regarding their relationship with and control over the Chipewyan. Well into the 1900s, HBC staff suspected that the Mission was conducting a successful sub rosa fur trade in addition to its ecclesiastical functions. Church officials believed HBC trade policies were jeopardizing the physical and spiritual health of the Chipewyan. Although the Chipewyan had the advantage of cultural distance and geographical mobility to keep the competing factions from completely overwhelming them, the pushing and pulling by traders and missionaries introduced unwelcome contradictions to Chipewyan life.

Ile-a-la-Crosse's importance declined in the early 1900s as both the HBC and the Catholic church began decentralizing their operations. In the period approaching World War I, the combined factors of field-oriented missionization, seasonal trading outposts, dispensation of Treaty rights, and an embryonic commercial fishing industry spurred aggregations of Chipewyan families into summer tent and log cabin communities of gradually increasing size and permanence. One of these communities was the Chipewyan reserve at Patuanak, situated at an old summer fishing site and HBC outpost 40 miles north of Ile-a-la-Crosse. Patuanak would become one of the major strongholds of the Kesyehot'ine.

Perhaps it was fitting that Patuanak's HBC or "Bay store" should also become the community's social epicenter. It was a place to visit friends, catch up on news and simply enjoy the spectacle of others conducting business. Who was selling a nice collection of beaver pelts, or who was purchasing a new outboard motor, was soon public knowledge. Bush planes landing at the dock out front brought visitors and sojourners with news from the outside. On this cool September afternoon the large crowd on the Bay steps was in an anxious, expectant mood. A Norcanair Beaver had landed and was taxiing laboriously over the choppy water toward the dock.

"Oh no," someone groaned. "It's Ted Merck."

"You mean Ted Jerk," another hissed.

A tall blond-haired middle-aged man lugging an old leather brief-case stepped off the plane. Ted Merck worked for the Department of Natural Resources (DNR), the provincial agency which managed wildlife conservation policy. Recently put in charge of the Ile-a-la-Crosse district, Merck was now responsible for enforcing hunting, trapping and fishing laws and regulations over a huge territory which included the Patuanak area. As I was beginning to discover, however, the relationship between the Chipewyan and the DNR was complicated and delicate and marked by considerable distrust and acrimony. Following Merck off the plane was an elderly assistant conservation officer. And taking up the rear in a miniparade formation were three uniformed RCMP officers, all beefy young white men wearing prominent revolvers and gunbelts.

"Damut'a fuckin' ta'gai!" An old man on the Bay steps muttered an obscenity. "Why do those DNR guys always have to bring cops along?"

"I'll tell you why!" A companion stood on the steps and bellowed. "Because they're scared. They're scared of the people here. That's why!"

The platoon of visitors kept their eyes averted from the taunts and commotion on the Bay steps and, without a word of greeting or acknowl-edgement, walked briskly away. Soon the crowd was on their heels. Dozens of others were converging near the center of the village.

"Bob, you better come in too." Jimmy Stonypoint was motioning from inside the door of the band hall.

"Are you sure? What's going on?"

"Trappers' meeting. People might want to ask you questions."

Questions? Trappers' meeting? I had just returned to the village with Antoine Ptarmigan and one of his first cousins, Victor Whitehead. We had spent several days at the small seasonal village of Dipper Lake 60 miles down the Churchill River. I had assisted Antoine and Victor in setting out gill nets and picking up some of their trapping supplies for the approaching winter. Privately, I figured that this was Antoine's way of testing me, to see if I was bushworthy. But how could I have forgotten something as important as the trappers' meeting?

The annual trappers' meeting had become a major forum for the Chipewyan to acquire information from and express concerns to conser-vation officials on a wide range of resource issues. Its origins lay in the depression years of the 1930s when intensive trapping had created seri-ous depletions of wildlife throughout northern Saskatchewan (Calder 1957:43; Valentine 1954:90). This was not only a catalyst for the growth of commercial fishing but it also gave rise to the Northern Fur Conservation Program. The latter was initiated in 1944 by the Saskatchewan provincial government to reserve trapping rights for local residents by establishing fixed "fur blocks" (or territories) for particular communities (Department of Natural Resources 1950).

Accordingly, the Patuanak Chipewyan and their relatives at Cree Lake were assigned to fur blocks N-16 and N-18, an area of about 12,800 square miles. While this was the region within which local residents could legally trap for commercial purposes, it became by default the area where virtually all their hunting occurred. In some of the southern fur blocks that served Cree Indian communities, individual hunters were establishing fixed registered traplines. Thus far, the Chipewyan had rejected the registered trapline system. A common hunting territory open to all was more in keeping with their highly mobile lifestyle and traditions. The program also created fur block councils elected by local trappers to represent their interests to conservation officials and other external parties.

About 50 villagers were seated in the small wood frame band hall. It was the largest gathering of people I had seen since my arrival in Patuanak. The many unfamiliar faces underscored how limited my circle of acquaintances still was. While largely a male audience, a few middle-aged and older women were in attendance. One of Joachim's aunts, Rose Deneyou, gave me a smile and a nod. She was one of the few women I had managed to speak with at any length. Others kept a polite distance and let their men do the talking. Rose had promised to make me a couple pair of moosehide work moccasins for the winter. I used that gambit as an excuse to visit her and hear stories about her childhood at Sandy Lake, a small seasonal trading post community far to the north. The place had been destroyed by a forest fire in the late 1930s.

Since almost everyone smoked or chewed tobacco the dimly-lit band hall was shrouded in a dense blue fog. Curious passersby continually walked in and out of the building or lingered around the open doorway. Small children with a sled dog pup in tow scampered around the aisles. I grabbed one of the few empty chairs near the back of the hall. Nearby the trio of RCMP officers stood impassively in a sentry pose.

"Okay, we're calling this meeting to order," Ted Merck yelled. He stood at the front of the room appearing apprehensive and fatigued. At a nearby table his assistant was nervously flipping through a pile of documents. "We've got a long day ahead of us. Gregoire, can you read last year's minutes?"

Gregoire Flatstone, a small wiry middle-aged man and the locally elected chairman of the fur block, took a position at the front of the room and quickly delivered a summary of the previous year's meeting in

Chipewyan. Since he would serve as the meeting's Chipewyan-English interpreter, he remained standing throughout the proceedings. He had barely completed his summary when Jacob Stonypoint, one of Jimmy's uncles, stood up and angrily confronted Merck.

"How come DNR won't give us permits for moose?"

"Oh, you'll get those permits. Don't worry. There was some kind of mix-up in radio messages at my office in July," Merck replied.

"We been hunting moose all summer and now in falltime. And still no permits!" Jacob bristled. "You must be against the people here."

This was a sore point. Moose constituted a major portion of the local food supply. By treaty law the Chipewyan could hunt for moose and most other game at any time for subsistence purposes. However, the DNR had instituted a permit system, in part, so that its biologists could construct a census for moose population management. This was an argument that Merck's assistant now offered, but it seemed to carry little weight among local hunters. Their agitation grew until Gregoire Flatstone angrily issued his own accusation: "Well, if everything is okay, how come the DNR tried to pinch me this summer for hunting moose over at Jack Pine Lake? Yah, they try to pinch me even after I explained to the DNR about not getting permits up here. First they told me it was okay to go ahead without the permits, then the DNR still tries to pinch me on that."

Once again Merck was forced to acknowledge a DNR error and assume an apologetic stance: "Now, I'll tell you Gregoire, no one from our office was trying to pinch you. Believe me, that was some kind of misunderstanding. No hard feelings, okay?"

Hoping to avert further rancor, Merck and his assistant requested each hunter to verbally report his year's take of moose. A total harvest of 128 animals was estimated for the fur block. Allowing for apparent increases, Merck recommended a quota of 150 moose for the community for the following year along with a promise for a more timely delivery of permits. This news restored the meeting to a more collegial mood. Merck seized the moment to request an informal straw poll on the status of a dozen fur-bearing species in the area over the previous two years.

While all but two fur-bearing animals (fisher and marten) were viewed by locals as "increasing" in numbers, Merck and his assistant recorded these impressions in their notebooks with little comment or expression. A more systematic census of the beaver population, based on local hunters' counts of 500 active beaver lodges, was offered by Gregoire Flatstone as a basis for calculating a fur block quota for beaver.

Anticipating more confusion and acrimony over the issue of quotas, Merck cautiously explained the DNR's position on beaver management. However, Flatstone interrupted him with a conciliatory message: "Yah, yah, we explained that to our trappers. If they don't turn in beaver census, no beaver seals (permits), and no beaver hunting next year. It's their own fault if they don't get beaver. Not the DNR's fault."

The tension ebbed further as the hunters turned their attention to electing a new fur block chairman and four new councilors. Despite his stated desire to avoid repeating the time-consuming chairmanship, Gregoire Flatstone and the previous councilors were easily elected to repeat terms by a constituency hoping for some continuity in their dealings with the DNR. Neither surprised nor delighted, Flatstone resumed his control of the meeting and asked the registered trappers to evaluate eight young and new trappers for one-year or apprenticeship positions. Among these were Jimmy Stonypoint and several other young men I knew, and they were all accepted with little discussion. If they worked well as apprentices, they could become formally registered and start their own independent trapping operations in future years.

My head began to throb with the onset of a wicked headache. I had not eaten that day, and the meeting was grinding into its third hour with no end in sight. In the smoke-filled dimness I had been jotting occasional shorthand remarks into a tiny notebook I kept tucked away in a jacket pocket. With luck, my memory would help amplify the scribblings later. Somehow the meeting had deteriorated. A garbled roar filled the room as dozens of people talked at once. I was vaguely aware of my name surfacing in conversations around me. It was "Dastloze this," and "Dastloze that." People were turning around to look at me. Some made cryptic hand gestures as if I should stand or walk to the front of the room.

"Hey, we got another guy who wants to trap with us. Do we vote on him too?" Flatstone pointed me out.

"Everybody, quiet down!" The older conservation officer shouted. His patience was crumbling and he shot me a peeved look. "Okay fella, what's your business here?"

"I cleared my plans with the band a couple months ago," I replied hoping that Chief Albert Stonypoint might be present to vouch for me. But the chief and councilors were nowhere in sight. "I don't want to earn a living hunting or become a professional trapper. I'm here to learn about the hunting and trapping way of life. Do I need to be licensed or registered for that?"

"No, he doesn't have to be registered. He's been to my office. He's doing research up here," Merck interjected. Indeed, I had been to Ile-a-la-Crosse briefly to apprise the DNR of my plans. I needed to be sure that the resource people, the RCMP and other government agencies were not confused about my presence and purpose in this remote corner. Yet, Merck's sullen colleague seemed unconvinced.

"You better come up here so we can ask you some questions?" Gregoire Flatstone motioned for me to stand near him at the front of the room. He wasted no time getting to the crux of the matter. "I heard about you, but I never met you before, eh? Lots of people ask why you're here. So you tell us."

After so many weeks in the community, I was dispirited that my credibility was on the line. A chilling thought crossed my mind. What if I was still trying to justify myself to the community six months from now? What then? Dozens of pairs of eyes were upon me, waiting expectantly. Don't blow this, I chided myself. Was there anything I could say now that would really make a difference? Anxiously, I stated my goal of becoming an active sits'eni, to learn the Chipewyan hunting way of life, to understand Chipewyan culture. It was beginning to sound like a mantra. As Flatstone put my words into Chipewyan, however, there were some knowing smiles and nods in the crowd. Was my message getting through?

"You can't do that!" Merck's cantankerous colleague was the first to respond. "You can't go out in the bush with these people! You'll be a burden to 'em. It's hard enough for 'em to make a living as it is. Hauling all their supplies around, finding food, and all that. It makes no sense for you to get in the way."

The meddlesome man knew my own misgivings perfectly. But who was he to throw a monkey wrench into my project? I directed my comments to Flatstone: "As I told the chief and many of the people here already, I am prepared to do my share of all the work involved in running a trapline. And I will be paying for my share of all the expenses as well. That's part of the deal." I scanned the room for Antoine Ptarmigan. Surely he could verify our imminent partnership. But, like the chief, Antoine was nowhere to be seen.

"Oh well, then that's no problem for us. If you want to work too, there are many trappers who need someone to help them." Flatstone's words elicited approving nods and murmurs from the crowd. Merck's taciturn colleague was back flipping furiously through a thick sheath of papers. I imagined he was searching for some obscure statute that would get me banned from Saskatchewan.

"But Dastloze, I mean Bob, I want to ask you one more question." Flatstone eyed me suspiciously. His gaze shifted repeatedly toward Merck as if the latter were colluding with me in some nefarious plot. "Are you from the government of Canada or what?"

"I don't work for any government, Canada or U.S. I'm here on my own project but supported by the University of Minnesota. You can check my letters in the band office."

"So, you're no *spy* then?"

There it was. Spy! The "cry wolf" word that all anthropologists dreaded. The mere suggestion of "spy" would have rumor mills churning overtime. There were a few titters in the crowd, but Flatstone wasn't laughing. He skewered me with a deadly serious expression, anticipating my response.

"No, I'm no spy," I chuckled nervously. "The chief and councilors have checked my plans. Ask them. Any more questions?"

"Nope. That's all." The corners of Flatstone's mouth flinched, almost imperceptibly, into a tight grimace or smile. It was hard to say which.

I walked to the back of the room expecting some other shoe to drop. Joachim caught my arm as I passed. He whispered: "Holy smokin' anyways, Bob. You done real good." As I slumped wearily into my chair, the local crowd applauded. Several older men turned my way and greeted me jocularly with hearty laughter. The sudden display of acceptance stunned me. What was my accomplishment really? Claiming not to be a spy? Offering to chop wood on somebody's trapline? It was mystifying and gratifying. If only one could relive such fleeting moments.

"Pssst, Bob! Decak'ai wants to see you," Joachim whispered hoarsely and pointed toward the open door where a shadow lurked in the fading twilight. I walked outside to find Antoine Ptarmigan leaning against the building and peering furtively through a half-open window.

"Hey Decak'ai! You're not at the meeting? I could've used you a few minutes ago. Did you hear the way that DNR guy was raking me over the coals?"

"I can't go inside. Don't want those guys to see me."

"Who? The DNR?"

"No. *Those* guys." Antoine casually thrust one arm through the window and pointed at the RCMP officers still standing impassively against the back wall. I cringed when Antoine's hand brushed within inches of the nearest officer's service revolver.

"The RCMP? What's their problem?"

"Crazy! Crazy, crazy story," Antoine muttered as he shook his head. "Look! My uncle talks now. Maybe he explains everything."

Jeremy Montgrand, Antoine's maternal uncle, was standing prominently in the center of the crowd trying to get Merck's attention. "There's something else DNR needs to know. Very important, if you can help us." An outspoken man, Jeremy had been the band's chief prior to Albert Stonypoint. He had reigned during a tumultuous period when the appearance of snowmobiles, a school, government housing projects, increased transfer payments and other changes began to transform the community in unforeseen ways. At that time, numerous families left their smaller seasonal log cabin communities, such as Dipper Lake, to live in Patuanak on a more or less permanent basis. Indeed, the emergence of a central settlement was still creating much confusion and ambivalence. Jeremy was also one of Antoine's former trapping partners in the Cache Lake area.

Merck appeared tired and bored as Jeremy related a convoluted tale involving a nonlocal entrepreneur, Steve Jackson, a businessman from the United States, who had established a remote fly-in summer sport fishing camp two year's previously in the very center of one of the Chipewyans' trapping areas. Apparently, the man had promised to hire fishing guides only from Patuanak, since the waters lay within the community's fur block. But the man reneged on his promise and was bringing in outside guides.

Jeremy finished his attack with unconcealed bitterness: "That Jackson is no good. He's a liar. He's been going around telling lies about us and our trappers at Cache Lake. He says we are using things and breaking things at his camp at Cache Lake in the winter. Even sends the RCMP after my nephew!" Jeremy paused to let this information sink in. Antoine nudged me with an elbow, but the message was clear. "Jackson knows he's lying, because *he's* the one wrecking our stuff. In the summer, when our trappers are not around, Jackson breaks into our camps. That's right! He lets his tourist fishermen use our stuff. He makes money off that, and he never asks us for permission. That guy's a liar for sure."

Jeremy's impassioned accusations kindled an indignant mood in the crowd. The room was filled with the din of dozens of people talking at once. Merck and his colleague huddled momentarily. When they emerged they shifted responsibility for the matter by announcing that such allegations should be presented to the RCMP. Jeremy turned toward the back of the room, attempting to rehash his complaints. But one of the young officers held up his hand in protest and issued a curt statement: "This is a personal matter between individuals which cannot be resolved at a trappers' meeting. The people involved can talk to me at RCMP headquarters in Ile-a-la-Crosse."

"Hey, we have a right to speak out," Jeremy protested. He knew that Antoine had been grilled by the cops in Ile-a-la- Crosse. For whatever reason, he figured, they were trying to force a false confession from his favorite nephew.

"You heard what I said." The officer's tone was cold and ominous. "The people involved can talk to me in Ile-a-la-Crosse."

"Well then," Merck asked with palpable relief. "Any more business?"

An old man stood up and was angrily shaking his fist at Merck. He delivered the final word before walking out of the hall: "Yah, the DNR can stop pressing the people around here so hard." Since his fellow trappers were now following him out the door into the early evening darkness, any official adjournment of the meeting was pointless. Merck and his colleague looked like they had barely endured a ten round prize fight.

"So how do you think now?" Antoine asked as we walked toward his skiff. "Still wanna go trapping? Up to Cache Lake?"

"You bet," I lied. "I can hardly wait."

By mid-October nightly freezes and light snows announced a rapidly approaching winter. A few men already were departing Patuanak for their trapping grounds. I knew that Antoine Ptarmigan had wanted to get an early start as well. Oddly, he had not been around my place for many days. Figuring that he was preoccupied with last-minute preparations, I set out on an aimless walk around the village.

A few yards from my cabin, Johnny Whitefish was tinkering with the carburetor on his battered Skidoo. The engine whined and shrieked like an animate creature as he gunned the throttle, sending a cloud of exhaust fumes in my direction. Snowmobiles had been in the village for only a few years, but they were rapidly eclipsing dog teams as the preferred form of winter transportation. Owing to the popularity of the brand, "Skidoo" had become the local generic term for snowmobile. Even so, there were ardent defenders of Arctic Cat and Snow Cruiser, among other makes. On this otherwise dreary morning, Patuanak seemed alive with whirring, whining, revving engines. A faint crust of snow was reason enough for many villagers to dust off their long-dormant machinery and make a few test runs.

Beyond Johnny's place a black wall of spruce marked the edge of the village landscape where a flicker of movement erupted from a small forest trail. Wind-blown trees? Or a moose, perhaps? A murky outline of prancing shapes soon materialized into four dark sled dogs in tandem harness. An old man crouched at the rear of a birch-plank toboggan encouraging his team homeward with a load of freshly-cut firewood. The size of the dogs astounded me. These were not the giant Malemiuts of a Jack London novel. Rather, they were scrappy, scrawny black mongrels of eclectic origin. Like jackals, these very same dogs and their scruffy cohorts slinked around the village in the warm months searching for discarded bone fragments, scraps of offal and other oddments. Now, pulling together in harness, they seemed remarkably dignified.

The team trotted smartly past Johnny who was now performing major surgery on his Skidoo's gummed-up innards. Gaskets, bolts and springs littered the ground. There was something wonderfully symbolic in the scene, as if the past was having a big laugh at the excesses of the modern era. I had to remind myself, however, that dog traction itself was a comparatively recent idea. Prior to borrowing sled dog technology from European fur traders in the late nineteenth century, the Chipewyan, like most subarctic Athapaskans, did the bulk of their traveling on foot. The "snowmobile revolution," as Pertti Pelto (1973) termed the phenomenon among Finnish Lapps, was really a second-wave revolution in Chipewyan country.

The old man and his team disappeared behind a log storage cache on the far side of the village. I was tempted to follow them when a woman's voice called out.

"Dastloze, they're ready!"

An old woman in a floral print dress, with silvery hair tied back in a bun, stood on the stoop of a nearby cabin. She looked intently in my direction, waving a strange object over her head.

"Rose, is that you?"

"Yah, Dastloze. Work moccasins' are ready. I make 'em for you." Rose Deneyou, Joachim Deneyou's favorite aunt, handed me a bundle tightly wrapped in brown paper. "You try em, eh? Go inside for tea, okay?"

Inside the Deneyou's snug house, Rose's husband Armand sat next to a roaring cast iron wood stove at a small table covered with a glistening red oil cloth. A dozen stretched muskrat pelts hung from a taut rope above the stove. Whole carcasses from a couple of the skinned "rats" lay in a shallow pan ready for roasting. Freshly baked loaves of bannock were piled on the table. Commingled aromas of wood smoke, muskrat, bannock, tea, and moosehide formed a wonderful incense. As if reading my mind, Armand offered me a hunk of bannock. He was a man of few words, but he nodded and smiled approvingly as Rose served us mugs of tea and unwrapped the moccasins. Armand always wore a woolen depression cap and chain-smoked Black Cats. If he was in a nostalgic mood, he might favor me with a story of his early days wintering in the remote country up around Cree Lake. In my mind's eye, I pictured Armand and Rose as a spirited young couple in the 1930s ascending the Mudjatik River with other families in their heavily laden freight canoes.

"Look. Moccasins fit good, eh." Rose commented as I tried on her handiwork. The smoke-tanned hide had a luxurious velvety texture and smelled like a thousand campfires. The thick moosehide had a reputation for reviving from dampness, resisting rips and punctures, and enduring all kinds of abuse. After securing the ties around the ankle flaps, both pairs of work moccasins fit me perfectly. One pair was designed to be worn over many pairs of socks and with snowshoes during the coldest weather. The other pair was to be worn inside rubber boots or other footgear at virtually anytime. Bit by bit, my outfit for winter trapping was taking shape. To complete my wardrobe, all I needed was a pair of low-cut fancy beaded moccasins for village wear, like the delicate floral beadwork gracing Armand's feet.

"These are great Rose! You'll have to let me know what I owe you." Already I had learned that direct inquiries about costs or dollar values could produce extreme discomfort among some people. Being indirect on such matters was part of the transaction ritual.

"Oh, I don't know," Rose muttered as she threw a log into the stove. "No problem for that."

"Well, I have the money right here. I can pay you now if you like."

"Bob, I think the chief is looking for you." Armand interrupted. His smiling face turned to a somber frown.

"The chief wants me? Do you know why?" What a clever diversion from the moccasin business, I thought.

Armand and Rose exchanged knowing glances. There was an uncomfortable silence, and when Rose finally spoke her voice was barely audible. "Dastloze, chief wants to see you. Some old people say you walk around at night. Going from house to house." Rose cupped her hands above her eyes to suggest a furtive character peeping through windows. "You know, like whaddaya call em, a spy?"

Spy! Naively, I had assumed that any lingering spy rumors had been neatly quashed at the trappers' meeting. A new wave of gossip could be my undoing.

"I guess I'd better go look for Albert, eh?"

"Yah, yah." Armand rose to his feet and placed the bundle of moccasins in my arms. "You see chief now."

Gloomily I stalked across the village toward the band office, fearing what awaited me. The small unfinished building was open, and Chief Albert Stonypoint was standing alone amidst carpenter's horses and stacks of lumber. I cursed myself for not bringing an interpreter, but Albert caught me offguard.

"Hi Bob. When you leaving?"

"Hello Chief." I was perplexed both by the query and Albert's sudden English ability. "Leaving?"

"You trapping with Decak'ai? When you leave?"

"Oh that! We're leaving soon, I hope. Say, I was just visiting Armand and Rose Deneyou, and they say you were looking for me."

"Yah, I know. I know." Albert stared at the floor and sounded vaguely apologetic.

"Something about people talking about me. I just want to let you know that I never go walking around here at night. I usually work in my cabin at night. Sometimes I have visitors over, but . . ."

"Yah, it's okay to visit anywhere here." Albert waved his hand in a dismissive manner. "And I see you around in daytime. Never nighttime, eh. I think it's a bullshit story."

As we talked, an elderly couple entered the office and stood in a far corner waiting to see Albert. Maybe these were rumormongers coming to fill the chief's head with unseemly tales about me. My paranoia grew as they glanced furtively in my direction. Using his pursed lips as a pointer, Albert guided us out a back door and out of hearing range.

"Well, I just hope people don't believe these stories. I'm not here to make trouble. I'm not some kind of a bushman."

Albert's eyes grew wide at the latter reference. I winced and inwardly kicked myself for suggesting the image.

"Yah, yah. Thanks a lot Bob." Albert was polite but plainly anxious to deal with the elderly couple inside. "I just try to find out what people say. It's a bullshit story anyhow."

Albert returned to the band office, and I trudged back to my cabin. I felt gratified by the chief's support. But I had a new worry. How much "bullshit" was flying around, and would any of it stick on me?

The forest trail hugged the west shore of Shagwenaw Lake, occasionally looping inland to avoid patches of bog and muskeg. Near a large windfallen birch an old woman was emerging from a side trail. She stopped to adjust the canvas pack sack on her back. It was heavily laden with snowshoe rabbits. Following a few steps behind her was a young girl carrying a hatchet and a tea pail. The woman was a dead ringer for Rose Deneyou, but she proved to be one of her older sisters running a snareline with a granddaughter. Many women were active on a daily basis snaring rabbits, trapping muskrats, and hunting squirrels and other small game on foot trails within a modest distance of the village. Such efforts provided a continuous flow into family larders and a complement to the more sporadic but farflung hunting and fishing activities of men.

Grandmother and granddaughter shyly nodded as I waved a greeting and continued down the trail. After two miles the trail ended at a clearing on the lake containing a small cluster of houses known locally as "La Ronge." It was a satellite village to Patuanak. Located just south of the reserve boundary, La Ronge was a community of non-Treaty or non-status Chipewyan. Due to a variety of oversights, they had not been included by provisions of Treaty No. 10 in 1906, and thus were not federally registered members of the English River Band. Since these Chipewyan did not have access to housing programs, social welfare, and other benefits administered through the Canadian Department of Indian Affairs, it was generally acknowledged that they had to work harder to make ends meet. This produced a certain tension between the Treaty and non-Treaty communities. Yet, both peoples were equally Chipewyan in a historical and cultural sense. Indeed, many siblings and other close relatives were separated by the legal distinction. A patriarchal facet of the law allowed a non-Treaty woman to gain registered status by marrying a Treaty man, and a Treaty woman to lose her

Josette Maurice constructs a birch bark basket, sewn together with split and dyed spruce roots. Such containers are used by Chipewyan women to store berries and pemmican, among other items (courtesy of Saskatchewan Archives Board, B5613[6]).

status by marrying a non-Treaty man. Treaty men kept their status regardless of marital history.

Antoine Ptarmigan was non-Treaty. He was the oldest of eleven children still living at home with their parents, Joe and Mary. Two older brothers had married and started their own households in La Ronge. Antoine's widowed paternal grandfather, Jacob, and his widowed maternal grandmother, Sarah, lived with other relatives nearby. The network of blood and affinal ties among the twelve households here was densely interwoven. Indeed, both in physical layout and social composition, La Ronge was reminiscent of the small log cabin communities which prevailed among the Chipewyan in former years.

Prior to the 1960s, clusters of five to ten interrelated families (or about 20–50 people) typically spent the bulk of the year together in "winter staging communities" or *eyana'de*. These were distributed over a vast region and served as points for further dispersal by winter hunting teams. *Bilateral* kinship ties, that is, tracing descent from both father's and mother's relatives, were important in the formation of such communities. For example, the families frequently were linked to one another by

sibling relationships (often brother-sister ties) and by parent-child relationships (often parent-daughter bonds). Parent-daughter bonds in
particular were reinforced by a tendency toward short-term *matrilocal
residence* and *bride service*. Thus, a young groom sometimes lived with
and worked for his new wife's family for a year or more before moving
on. Such arrangements also encouraged hunting partnerships between
brothers-in-law and between father-in-law and son-in-law.

At the same time, most people had some close relatives in their
silot'ine, or "personal bilateral kindred," distributed across a number of
eyana'de or winter settlements in the region. Activating such ties was a
means of gaining access and residency in these other communities.
While the winter staging communities had faded away, ties of silot'ine
continued to be an important form of social and economic insurance for
the Chipewyan. One expected to help and be helped by members of one's
kindred. The Ptarmigan family seemed to be surrounded by silot'ine in
the little village of La Ronge.

Several Chipewyan families traveling from Patuanak to Beauval stop for a meal
and rest.

Mary Ptarmigan was working outside near her square log smoking cache, or loretthe kwae, when I arrived.

"Hello Mary. Looks like you've got fresh meat."

"Yah, Joe just got a moose over by Drum Rapids." Mary was fiftyish and of a stout muscular build like her son Antoine. Kneeling on a bed of spruce bows she made deft knife cuts in a section of hindquarters so that the meat fell away in thin sheets, as if unfolding a scroll. A young daughter, Therese, was arranging the sheets over the cache fire. In a few hours they would become dry meat.

"Is Antoine around? I haven't seen him in awhile."

"Decak'ai? Could be he's looking for you, eh. Maybe over there at Norbert's place." Mary pursed and pointed her lips in the direction of her oldest son's house. "Hey, come back later, and I give you dry meat."

Norbert Ptarmigan's house appeared to be empty, but there was movement in the little log warehouse nearby. Just as women had their special outdoor work stations, men stored and repaired a lot of their hunting equipment in separate warehouses or t'asi thelaikoe. Norbert and Antoine were inside sorting through piles of traps, snares, fur stretchers, gill nets, gas cans, canvas tarps, and other supplies. I had heard that Norbert and his two partners were leaving for their trapping grounds the next day. Pretty soon there would be no more adult males left in the village. Where did that leave Antoine and me? The two men seemed a little on edge as I entered the warehouse. As I had suspected, Antoine had been hunting with his father at Dipper Lake for the past week and moving some supplies to Patuanak.

"So what do you think about heading up to Cache Lake? It's almost October 20th, eh."

"Yah, I know." Antoine sighed deeply. He reached into a burlap sack and produced a forty-ounce bottle of blended whiskey. After a few hard swallows he passed the bottle to me. "Here Bob, try some of this."

What the hell, I thought, taking a couple chugs. I sensed bad news in the air. "Where'd you get this stuff?"

"Bootlegger. Ile-a-la-Crosse. Twenty-five dollars."

"You need this for trapping?" I jested.

"No, no! We never use kontue [liquor] in the bush. Bush is for working. Town is for drinking, eh." Antoine feigned annoyance and passed the bottle to Norbert.

The bottle traveled around our little circle a few times. An ugly back cloud drifted across the sun, darkening the afternoon. A gust of wind blew spirals of snow through the open warehouse door. Then, a harsh metallic noise sent a shudder up my spine. Peering out the door, I spotted the trio of ravens. Diving out of the sky, they sailed over the warehouse and into the bush behind us, initiating their own conversation of shrill cackles and caws. Okay fellows, I mused, something's up and it doesn't feel good.

"Dastloze, I have to ask you something." Antoine paused for another deep swig. "You're my partner, sits'eni, you know. But there's lots of talk going around. Lots of talk about you. Some people say I shouldn't go trapping with you. They think you're a spy."

"A spy?" I nearly choked on my mouthful of whiskey.

"Yah. I was visiting this old guy down at Primeau Lake, one of our oldest people, you know. And he told me, he says: 'Decak'ai, Don't go with that *Beschokdene* [American]. He's a spy. He might kill you up north at Cache Lake.' That's what he told me."

"Kill you?" I felt idiotic repeating Antoine's phrases. I also felt an immense sadness. What kinds of horrible pressures had I unleashed on this poor man?

"But I think it's just a bullshit story. People are afraid of strangers. We don't get many white guys up here, eh."

"Bullshit for sure, but I don't want to cause you any trouble, Antoine."

"People like to talk. There's lots of stories around here about me too. Just ask Norbert." Norbert smiled and nodded as he chugged more whiskey. "I'm still single, and I do a lot of girling. So people make up all kinds of bullshit stories about me. You know, like I'm fooling around with women down at Pinehouse and Ile-a-la-Crosse when I'm really out fishing."

"Yah, I see what you mean. But spying? Killing? That's something else."

"Say, Dastloze, let me ask you something." The normally quiet Norbert handed me the bottle and moved a few inches closer. It was the first time I had heard him speak any English. In his early 30s, Norbert was taller and thinner than his younger brother but formidably constructed nonetheless. It was said that he could carry nine 100-pound bags of flour on a tumpline. I noticed that his amiable smile was gone. "Do you know what it's like in the bush?"

"Not really," I muttered. "I'm here to learn."

"Well, a trapper's life is hard. Real hard! Not easy. Some days you don't eat. Hard work everyday. It's a job. You might get lonesome. And it gets real cold. Not too many guys I know can take the cold up there in the winter, eh. Decak'ai here is one of the few guys I know who can take that life. And we've been working this way since we were boys." Norbert's voice was urgent, and his piercing eyes were on me.

"I believe you, Norbert."

"I'm not against you. Decak'ai here, he's the boss of his team. I just want to know who you are, eh. You're going into the bush with my own brother."

I could think of nothing to say to assuage Norbert's fears. I barely knew him. He had not seen me working with Antoine at Dipper Lake. With the drink loosening everyones' tongues, at least the air was being cleared. The brothers talked softly in Chipewyan for a few minutes, and I strolled outside. The ravens had departed for some other roost.

"Okay Bob!" Antoine announced as he joined me outside, "We leave for Cache Lake in two days. We'd better go see the Bay manager today. We still need some more traps and other stuff."

Immensely relieved and excited, I prepared to hike back to my cabin and start packing. Antoine walked across the village clearing with me. Something was nagging at him. "We need one more thing," he said hesitantly. "A new partner."

"Partner? What happened to Frank Whitefish?"

"He quit. Told me this morning."

"Because of me, I'll bet." My elation faded. "Probably all this spy bullshit scared him off." It struck me as peculiar that I had barely exchanged a word with Frank, a man I might have to work with for months in the bush. Yet, he had been a trapping partner with Antoine for several years and was his maternal first cousin to boot.

"No, no. Partners change around a lot, you know. Frank's going back to trap with his Dad." Perhaps Antoine was sparing my feelings. Frank's timing was certainly lousy. But then Antoine related a complicated tale about difficulties on last winter's trapline. The partners had relied solely on Frank's dogs for transportation, unfamiliar animals which Antoine found hard to control. Even so, Antoine's fur hunt had proven considerably more productive than Frank's, and that became a sore point between the men.

Spy rumors might be running rampant, but I figured fate was pushing me to Cache Lake. Now we had just two days to find another trapping partner.

Chapter Five

Bush Apprenticeship

The old De Havilland Beaver buzzed over the Churchill River like a colossal bumblebee. Its ample cargo hold was stuffed with boxes of traps and snares, barrels of gasoline, canvas tarps, duck feather sleeping robes, rifles, shotguns, boxes of ammunition, gill nets, duffels crammed with spare clothing, snowshoes, skinning knives, hatchets, files, chisels and other assorted tools, kettles, skillets, tea pails, a canvas wall tent, a sheet metal wood stove, a small outboard motor, and packsacks filled with flour, lard, baking powder, and other food staples. The pilot Billy Yarmchuk was one of Hank LeFleur's trainees. His diminutive stature, boyish looks and diffident manner were that of a 12-year-old school kid flying into the bush. He kept glancing out the window and then down at his feet, which he shook with agitated annoyance, as if he had dog manure stuck to his shoes. None of this put me at ease.

Hundreds of feet below was an endless panorama of forest and water. We caught fleeting glimpses of the Churchill River's treacherous Drum Rapids and the mouth of the meandering Mudjatik or Deer River. But familiar landmarks quickly faded from view as the Beaver droned steadily northward into an immense unknown.

Dense stands of aspen, birch and white spruce trees soon gave way to stark conifer forests of scraggly black spruce and jack pine. We were entering Precambrian shield country. Its ancient granitic rock outcrops formed rugged ranges of hills that protruded hundreds of feet above surrounding lakes and bogs. Their jagged crowns were often barren of all vegetation save a few scabrous patches of lichens. The foliation of these rocks created a bewildering drainage pattern of twisting labyrinthine lakes and rivers. From above, the country looked like a fiendish rat maze filled with water. Even with map and compass, one might well disappear in such terrain.

Antoine Ptarmigan and I were wedged in amongst the supplies in the cargo hold. Each time the plane hit a pocket of turbulence, somebody's leg or arm was pinched, slammed or crushed by the shifting load. How would we lug this mountain of gear around in the bush on a remote trapline, I wondered. And where, pray tell, was our third partner? Antoine had been uncharacteristically evasive on this point. As it

127

was, we were getting a late start, too late in the year to travel to Cache
Lake by canoe before freeze-up. I agreed to pay for half of the bush
plane fee. As an active trapper of good reputation, Antoine would try to
get his half reimbursed by conservation officials through the provincial
government.

"*Thaitil*," Antoine suddenly remarked. His pursed lips pointed
through a fogged-up window.

"Cache Lake? Are we there already?"

"No, no. Thaitil, in Chip that means 'sandy blanket'. It's what we
call those beautiful places. Nice trees, flat ground. Beautiful." Antoine's
voice had a dreamy, almost reverent tone.

From the window I spotted exposed sandbanks along a meandering stream. The extensive floodplain here was covered by a thin forest
of widely-spaced jack pines, and there was little underbrush to obscure
a mattress-like groundcover of moss and lichens. The visual effect was
that of a manicured park in the midst of trackless wilderness. "I see
what you mean, Decak'ai. This sandy blanket looks nice."

"Oh yah. Thaitil, real nice. Good for traveling. Good place for a
camp. Sometimes good for hunting wood caribou too. Beautiful."

Many miles later I awoke from a fitful doze. Antoine was nudging
my arm and gesturing toward the window again.

"More thaitil?"

"No. *Sask'athatwe*. My hunting territory's down there, eh."

"But I thought you hunted out of Cache Lake."

"Yah, that's Cache Lake down there," Antoine laughed patiently.
"But in Chip we call it Sask'athatwe. That means 'lake where the bear
goes to eat fish in the springtime.' Or pretty close to that anyway."

My heart raced as I scrambled for a view through the window. A
layer of low-lying misty clouds enveloped the terrain. The Beaver had
dropped in altitude and was barely clearing the rocky hills that girdled
the lake. Looming up on the horizon was an angular, serpentine body of
water with narrow arms, channels and complicated island-studded bays
which radiated out in all directions like tentacles on a monstrous squid.
Mirroring the gun-metal gray sky, the lake's surface looked cold, metallic and forbidding on this day. By crow's flight, it was perhaps 20 miles
between the southern and northern extremities of Cache Lake. By
water, however, there appeared to be no direct route anywhere. I took all
this in with grim amusement, realizing that the place would be my
home for the next few months.

A peculiar low-pitched moan, like a baying coonhound, was suddenly audible above the Beaver's rackety engine. The cabin began to
vibrate and shimmy. Soon there was a loud knocking sound accompanied by a rather violent shaking of the entire plane.

"Son of a biscuit!" Yarmchuk yelped from up front. "That stupid canoe is gonna take us down!"

I had forgotten about Antoine's canoe. The ancient Hudson's Bay Company canvas freight model was a 19-foot, 300-pound monstrosity. It was strapped precariously to one of the plane's pontoons. Antoine had inherited the craft from his late maternal grandfather, a man he idolized. Unfortunately, the big canoe was plowing air and creating dangerous turbulence. Abruptly, our pilot turned the Beaver around in a sharp stomach-wrenching bank.

Antoine shrugged and shook his head. I knew he wanted to begin his trapping operations at the north end of the lake where he had cached some supplies the previous spring. Starting at the south end would be a setback. Within minutes, however, the nerve-wracking vibrations subsided. "Okay boys, let's try her again!" Yarmchuk shouted as he banked sharply once more and flew without incident to Cache Lake's north end.

Twenty minutes later we were perched on a tiny barren island in the middle of a deep bay. Our pilot had avoided the main shore where submerged rocks and sand bars might have snagged his heavy plane. "I guess you boys will be finding your own way out of this place, eh?" Yarmchuk yelled giddily as he gunned the Beaver's throttle. "Maybe we can split a 40-ouncer when you get back."

"Damn right!" Antoine laughed. "First we got to get some fur."

With a deafening drone the Beaver made a long lurching taxi across the bay. At the last possible instant it lifted off the water like a bloated pelican, barely clearing a wooded peninsula to the south.

"That Billy's a crazy little devil." Antoine mused as he rustled up a fire from driftwood scraps. "Well, Dastloze, time for us to work, eh?"

We enjoyed hot mugs of tea while sorting and loading supplies into the freight canoe. On our little rock I had the sensation of being stranded in a lifeboat at sea. The overpowering silence of the place intruded between our feeble snatches of conversation. If I had been seeking isolation, surely this was it. And it stretched mercifully (or mercilessly) for hundreds of miles in every direction.

"What you think? We go now," Antoine suddenly announced as he shoved the canoe into the water.

"For hunting?"

"No. We make our first camp. Over there," Antoine gestured with his head toward a spot several miles across the bay. "Nice place there by that sand point, eh. A little river comes in there. Comes down many miles through *nitilcho*, the 'big muskeg,' we call it. We'll hunt for beaver up there in that 'big muskeg,' eh."

Staring hard, my eyes detected no points, rivers or muskeg. The north shore appeared as a blurry undifferentiated mass of black trees.

Nonetheless, we took to the water, ferrying the first of several loads of supplies from island to mainland. Even heavily laden and riding low in the water, the big canoe proved remarkably stabile and responded well to the paddle.

In the fading light of afternoon, we hurried to collect firewood and stockpile our provisions inside a canvas wall tent which Antoine put up single-handedly in mere minutes. "Watch me. Next time you can do it," he instructed. It was a nine-foot-square, home-made affair. Anchor stakes and interior ridge poles were quickly cut from saplings at the site. Bottoms of the walls were rolled beneath heavy logs to block the wind. And the floor was covered with freshly cut spruce boughs to create a clean, dry, aromatic living space. A simple rectangular sheet metal stove was suspended upon four vertical wooden stakes near the entrance, its stove pipe protruding through a tin-rimmed hole in the roof. Within minutes a small fire heated the interior to sweltering temperatures.

This kind of portable wall tent was the favored home for Chipewyan men traveling in the bush. It was the focal point of their temporary encampments or *nothi*. Indeed, prior to the recent era of village nucleation, most Chipewyan families had lived in such tents for the bulk of the year as they moved around their farflung territories on annual cycles of hunting, trapping, fishing and trading. The mere thought of six, seven or more individuals crammed into a tent over the winter astounded me. How did people manage their lives in such cramped quarters?

Antoine continued sorting out supplies piled near the shore. But now he was in the canoe and pushing it off into the lake. He caught my quizzical glance.

"Forgot something at the island," he explained.

"Need any help?"

"Naw, stay here and get more wood. Make fire for tea." Antoine seemed on edge. Had I offended him in some way? Would he abandon me out here on our first day? Brandishing a hand-carved birch paddle, Antoine attacked the water with short powerful strokes. Soon the lumbering craft was halfway across the bay. When it finally faded to a tiny speck, I went to search for dead, dried out trees in a nearby windblown thicket.

The late afternoon sun slipped behind a flank of hills to the southwest. Fragments of hazy cloud quickly dispersed to reveal deep sapphire-blue heavens already twinkling with the first evening stars. The lake turned dead calm. A gathering blanket of mist on the water was a promise of sub-zero temperatures. Surely the smaller streams and ponds would freeze over that night.

Hours seemed to pass. Where the hell was Antoine? If he had encountered difficulty, I was of no use to him now. I paced along the shoreline, occasionally peering into the nothingness of the lake. The fog had grown to a thick pea soup. But something faintly audible was out there. A pair of loons, perhaps? No, the faint sounds seemed to be a dialogue in Chipewyan. Was Antoine talking to himself? The thought embarrassed me. Maybe he was upbraiding himself for going into the bush with an outsider.

Without warning the canoe emerged from the mists like a phantom ship. It beached nearly on top of me. Excitedly I began pulling it ashore. "Decak'ai! You know, I was beginning to worry..."

Then I was struck speechless. An unfamiliar young man, tall and slender, with a mop of thick black hair, rose up from the bow of the canoe and leaped nimbly to the ground before me. The stranger was silent and sullen, and he kept his eyes averted from me as he busied himself unloading new parcels from the canoe.

"Dastloze! Hey Bob!" Antoine called from the shadows of the stern. "This here is our new partner!"

"He is?" My mind was reeling. "Where did he come from? Gave me one helluva scare."

"He's my brother, August. I had to go back to the island to get him. He's kind of shy. Well, we never had a white man up here before, you know, living in the bush like this."

As his brother kept a safe distance in the shadows, Antoine filled me in on a rather involved story. I was amazed to learn that August had managed to hide from me among our piles of gear during the flight into Cache Lake. Either this was a supremely cagey fellow or I was a rather poor observer. After Frank Whitefish's untimely defection, August had been recruited for trapping duty at the last possible moment by his father, Joe. This meant pulling him out of his senior year of boarding high school down south. Shy or not, at 21 years of age August was only a few years younger than Antoine. He was the only member of the Ptarmigan family, indeed one of the few in the village, to achieve such advanced schooling.

By contrast, Antoine left school at the tender age of 12 to help his family. Now, as the eldest unmarried son, he was, in effect, the main hunter and breadwinner for his parents and numerous younger siblings. While Antoine's father was still a knowledgeable hunter and provider, health problems restricted his movements. It had been a good seven years since Antoine had last teamed-up with Joe on a winter trapline, and that had been a frightening experience for both of them. Joe had developed a severe case of tonsillitis complicated by a heart condition. After bundling his weakened father into a toboggan, Antoine had driven their dogteam relentlessly for four days through a blizzard to reach their home base at the Dipper Lake village. "It was close. Real close for my father that time," Antoine recalled with a shudder.

As we walked to the tent for mugs of tea, I felt profound admiration and sadness for my new friends and partners. Antoine, it seemed, was shouldering an awesome responsibility. Did he really need *two* green-horns screwing things up? Certainly, August knew more than I could ever learn. After all, he was local. He was Chipewyan. Yet he had never spent a winter on a trapline. Years of boarding school had deprived him of training in many of the bush living skills known to his parents and older siblings.

Before retiring, we reorganized some of our gear into smaller packs and boxes for easier handling. There was barely enough room to lay out our bedrolls. August kept a wary distance from me in the far corner of the tent. "Sits'eni," Antoine called out, gamely trying to break the ice. "We're all partners, eh. But I guess I've got *two* beginners now!"

August saw little humor in the situation. Occasionally, he engaged Antoine in muted conversation in Chipewyan. "Why did you bring me here? Who is this stranger, anyway? Everybody says he's a spy," or so I imagined him saying to his older brother.

I was filling my pipe for a smoke, when I distinctly overheard Antoine pleading in urgent whispers to August. "Why don't you say something to our friend there? He's sits'eni. He's our partner now."

"But I don't know what to say," August replied in an anguished whisper.

"Ask him where he got that tobacco."

Sometime later August stoked the stove fire and ventured toward my side of the tent. "Say, I was wondering where you got that tobacco." His eyes remained firmly fixed on the fire as his voice trailed off to a barely audible murmur.

"Oh, this here?" I held the round tin out for his inspection. "I bought it in Meadow Lake. Go ahead and take some if you like."

But August quickly retreated to his corner. Later I heard him reporting to his brother, "He said he got in Meadow Lake."

Antoine nodded. Then he looked in my direction with a knowing smile.

The big canoe moved sluggishly against the stiff current of the little river. Antoine paddled from the bow where he sat at the ready with several burlap sacks filled with steel traps and snare wire. August poled and steered from the stern, while I worked a paddle from the middle. We were moving up one of the coffee-colored streams that drained the "big muskeg." Like innumerable other bodies of water, this stream was unnamed on any modern map, but the Chipewyan called it *nitildeze*, or "muskeg river." The "big muskeg" itself was an immense waterlogged bog largely devoid of forest except for thin stands of alders, willows and birches lining the stream banks. Antoine's plan was to travel for several days up into this beaver-rich country, setting out traps before floating back toward Cache Lake.

Active beaver lodges and fresh cuttings were in evidence everywhere. The brothers were in a somber mood, however, reflecting our poor progress upstream. Antoine had hoped to use his late grandfather's outboard motor, a small 1950s model, to ferry us around. But the freezing temperatures had fouled the old machine's water pump. We had put ashore several times that morning to build fires while Antoine patiently disassembled and repaired the pump, only to have it break down again. Eventually we gave up on the outboard and took to the paddles.

"Let's stop here. Good place for beaver," Antoine commanded. A subtle jerk of his head indicated a spot on the opposite bank where fresh birch cuttings littered a muddy slide into the water. August anchored the canoe while I handed materials to Antoine. Crouching in the bow of the canoe, Antoine took scrupulous care to avoid leaving human scent on the landscape. He began by scooping out a shallow depression in the stream bottom with the back of a hatchet. Into this depression, and positioned several inches below the water's surface, he gingerly placed a double longspring steel jaw trap with the axis of the jaws set perpendicular to the bank. A thick cord anchored the trap chain to a wooden stake set in deep water. Another cord linked the trap base to a flat rock meant as a drowning anchor. Additional stakes set in deep water would entangle the trap rigging and further facilitate quick drowning.

Antoine completed the important finishing touches by baiting the set. For this he cut two small birch stakes, slicing off a section of bark on each to expose the inner tissues. Upon the wood he smeared a bit of fluid from beaver castor glands, a powerful attractant. Then he thrust the stakes in the shoreline mud behind the trap. The set was completed by placing a few twigs near the margins of the trap to guide an approaching beaver's movements. All of this was accomplished in a few minutes. Then we were off repeating the process again and again on remote bends of the little river.

Jagged crusts of ice already lined some of the banks, posing something of a hazard to our canoe's canvas hide. The advancing cold would soon dictate a change to under-ice snare-pole sets at beaver lodges. In the days ahead I would be exposed to a large repertoire of hunting methods including the different kinds of beaver sets. There were also pen sets for lynx, rock den sets for mink, and specialized trap sets for fisher, fox, and otter, among other fur-bearers. The successful use of these required a delicate orchestration of knowledge about animal behaviors, changeable weather conditions, and the hunting technology itself. "This is the way my father showed me," Antoine often remarked after fashioning a particularly pleasing set. How well would Antoine impart this knowledge to his two apprentices?

Altogether we had packed in 130 steel jaw traps, mostly large no. 3s intended for beaver, lynx and otter. There were also some smaller no. 1-1/2s for mink and muskrat. In addition, we were carrying four coils of heavy wire for constructing snares for large quarry and five coils of lightweight wire for smaller animals, including the snowshoe rabbits destined solely for our meals. Our object was to set out most of these traps and snares before the heavy freeze-up period in early November. This would become our functioning trapline, or *it'suzitonlue*, to be monitored and maintained over the rest of the winter. But setting it up was no small task. It would mean constructing sets while traveling across a rugged 215-mile network of streams, ponds and game trails in a scant two week's time. In my blissful ignorance, I had no idea what all this really entailed.

"Okay, we make camp here," Antoine announced as he pointed his paddle toward a small sandbank. "August, you get the tent. Make fire."

"Yes, *gothare* [boss]," his brother replied with mock servility.

"You don't have to call me gothare."

"You're right. I'll call *you gotharechalas* [ragged boss] instead!" August replied with a sly grin.

"You want me to whip you here?"

"Okay, okay, I'll call you *gotharechalaze* [little ragged boss]! How's that?"

In a heartbeat the two brothers were out of the canoe and rolling about on the muddy bank, engaged in a fierce struggle. In their denim coveralls and rubber knee boots they looked like dairy farmers gone berserk. Locking arms Greco-Roman style, they pushed and heaved each other about for several minutes until they crashed into a patch of alders. There was a sickening thwack as the back of August's head struck a tree. In the next instant Antoine flipped August hard on his back and pinned him decisively to the ground. By this time both men were trembling with exhaustion and taking in huge gulps of air. "Shit, don't freak out on me here boys," I muttered to myself.

Antoine staggered to his feet. August sat up grinning like a Cheshire cat. "Okay, Decak'ai, You're still the boss. Just making sure, that's all."

This little drama reminded me that Antoine was indeed the leader of our crew. We called each other "partner" or sits'eni, but this was something of a social fiction that masked the essential teacher-apprentice relationship. By addressing Antoine as "little ragged boss," August was affectionately teasing his older brother but also highlighting the difference in power and status between them.

Later I would discover that about one-third of Chipewyan hunting-trapping teams were characterized by the boss-apprentice structure. It was the primary means for socializing young men in bush knowledge and livelihood. The teacher-bosses were generally close kinsmen, such as fathers, uncles or older brothers, who often derived from the same households as their apprentices. After several years as an apprentice, a young man might strike out on his own and form new partnerships with other men. Another third of the trapping teams were composed of experienced partners, generally two or three middle-aged men all having roughly equivalent skills and decision-making power. Such men tended to be distant kin deriving from different village households. Yet another third of the workforce was comprised of rather large teams of four to seven men. The latter partnerships combined elements of the first two team types.

The expression sits'eni could be used in other contexts as well. Two women teaming up to hunt muskrats or to make moosehide, for example, could refer to one another as sits'eni. As a social identity and form of address, however, "partner" conveyed special shades of meaning whenever team members derived from different family-households and when kinship connections were distant or obscure. In such cases, "partner" could imply friendship and reciprocal bonds which extended far beyond the domain of hunting and work.

Even after a few days on the trapline, the roles of the boss-apprentice relationship were becoming fairly routine. Antoine did the hunting. Firmly, and sometimes with good humor, he delegated tasks to his crew. August and I were expected to accompany and assist Antoine, to make his work more efficient, but to learn a hunter's job simply by observing our boss. In addition, August and I were responsible for a large share of the unremitting domestic chores: setting up camps, finding wood, building fires, hauling water, and cooking meals. Since August was already expert in most of the domestic skills, I felt a bit marginalized. In essence, I was an apprentice's apprentice.

"Bob, you're next. You try Antoine. He's a hard one to beat, eh?" August laughed mischievously. It was the first time he addressed me in a familiar way. The barrier between us magically lifted. I saw the tension drain away from August's face, and I felt immense relief.

"Naw. Maybe later. I've got to get some food in my stomach, August."

We had been pushing hard for the past two days and had eaten little beyond tea and some bannock. Much of our food and other supplies had been left behind in a tree cache on the north end of the lake. Even a netfull of fish, destined to become rotting trap bait, was left behind. In our struggles to get up the river, we had neglected our own needs.

"Dastloze, you're right. We'll fight later," Antoine laughed as he brushed mud and burrs from his coveralls. "August, get the tent and fire now! C'mon, Bob, we're going for beaver."

Antoine was off tramping across the margins of the big muskeg near an expanse of spruce forest. The awkward, lumpy mounds of vegetation and partially frozen ground made walking a torturous ordeal. Yet, Antoine seemed to move effortlessly. Like the "flying squirrel" for which he was named, Decak'ai was soon hundreds of yards ahead and out of view. In the fading twilight I had fears of losing my way in the boggy maze. After a mile or so I encountered Antoine's faint tracks near a frozen pond. For several miles more I followed his intermittent trail along a stream linking two more ponds and, eventually, a small lake that was still free of ice in the center. Like a moat-encircled castle, a substantial beaver lodge graced the open water. But where was Antoine?

"*Tsa* [beaver]," someone whispered suddenly. I flinched in surprise and practically fell on top of Antoine who was concealed in a thicket of rushes at my feet.

"Man, I'm glad to see you! Are we walking all the way to Cree Lake tonight or what? I thought I'd never catch up to you."

"We eat now, for sure." Antoine pursed his lips toward a dark speck cruising through the luminous water.

The crack of Antoine's .22 rifle echoed in the still air. The speck thrashed briefly in the water and disappeared. A few seconds later it bobbed to the surface and lay motionless. What now, I wondered. The prize was floating a good 20 yards beyond safe ice in deep water. What might be needed to retrieve our meal made me shudder.

"Bob, your boots!"

"You're kidding right? It's way over my head out there."

"No. I mean your laces. Give me your boot laces."

Antoine had been busy before my arrival cutting slender spruce poles and lashing them together end to end. His own moccasin laces, belt and a handkerchief had been put to service tying up four of the poles. My laces were needed to attach a fifth. When completed, Antoine wielded a 60-foot floating probe. It was heavy and cumbersome but serviceable enough to finesse the floating beaver to our shore.

"Ah, it's just a young one," Antoine observed hoisting the carcass from the water. He whipped the animal briskly back and forth against the rushes, much like a paint brush, to remove water from its fur.

"Too small to sell, you mean?"

"Nope. Just big enough to sell the fur. My mother will sew up the hole from my bullet, eh. It will be a good pelt for sure." Antoine concluded. "But he was just a kid beaver."

"How old?"

"Probably born two springs ago. Sometimes these young beavers fool around too much, you know. They're not afraid, and that's why they get caught. This guy here? Well, his parents were giving him hell for playing around. Why, they were just slapping him with their tails when I showed up. That's how they punish their children."

"You saw his parents?"

"Yah, many times. But they're too smart to get caught. I try for years now. Big old smart ones, eh. They're brother and sister too, you know. A brother and sister married each other and started their family two years ago. These little lakes have only one house and one family. The young kid here was getting ready to move away, start his own family at that next pond down there. You walked right by it." Antoine expounded at length on the sociological mysteries of the beaver. The excitement in his voice suggested that he was just warming to the subject. Inwardly I cursed myself for not packing a little notebook along to make some jottings. Hopefully, I would remember some fragments to write up later at the tent.

"You make the beaver seem like people," I jested.

Antoine gave me a quizzical look as he placed the "kid" into a small packsack. "Well, I guess that's right. Beaver were once people," he replied wistfully.

Several hours later we staggered into camp. I was not surprised to find that my pocket pedometer registered ten miles for our trek. My muskeg-battered feet registered twenty. August had a roaring fire prepared and some fresh bannock loaves cooling by the door. These we slathered with lard and quickly devoured as an appetizer. The piece de resistance was the beaver. After August boiled the butchered sections lightly in a large kettle, we polished off the entire offering, gnawing and licking the bones clean. It was my first taste of the rich fatty meat. My partners were openly pleased by my appetite for this ubiquitous bush food. Privately, I could not shake the strange sensation that we were eating "people."

"I think my luck will change now," Antoine observed cheerfully as he scraped the last shreds of meat from the beaver's skull. With a sheath knife he scooped out delicate morsels of brain matter and ate them. "This will make me think like a beaver. And maybe I'll dream tonight. Then we'll catch more animals for sure."

"Yah, I'll dream too Decak'ai," August replied. "We need some bigger beavers than this little kid, eh!"

I had heard references to "dreaming" before and knew it was somehow connected to personal power and hunting prowess. Men dreamt about the animals they wished to pursue, or even about sexual liaisons with women, as a prelude to successful hunts. One's power, or *inkonze*,

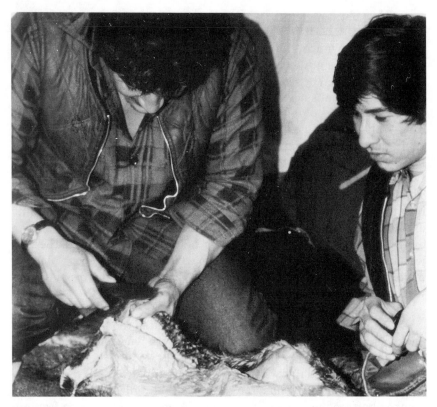

Apprentice Rene Janvier (right) receives a lesson in beaver skinning and butchering from his older partner Joe Black (left). In a trapping camp, the day's fur catch is often the evening meal.

was intimately interwoven with dreaming, divinatory acts, rituals of respect to slain animals, and the act of hunting itself. Even as we spoke, Antoine bundled up the bone fragments of the beaver we had eaten and delicately placed them in the crotch of a small tree outside our tent. I desperately wanted to learn more about these matters but was almost delirious from exhaustion. "I don't think I can dream tonight. How big do beavers get anyway?" I inquired.

"Some beavers are very big!" August replied.

"Sixty, seventy pounds maybe?"

"That's nothing. Nothing for a giant beaver."

"Yah, tell him about the beavers in the Churchill," Antoine suggested as he re-entered the tent. The brothers exchanged knowing glances.

"Well, the village, Patuanak, there sits on top of an old beaver dam. That's why we call that place *banichari* in Chip. It means 'where something broke through,' you know, where the river broke through that old beaver dam," August explained.

"So this dam must be huge?"

"Yah, its underneath the whole village. And then it crosses way over to the other side of the river."

"And the beavers that made it, where are they?"

"They're in the Churchill," August interrupted with an irritated edge. "And in Lac Ile-a-la-Crosse. You know Big Island down there, eh? That used to be an old beaver lodge. That's what I'm telling you, Bob, these are *giant* beavers."

I had been expecting a joke at my expense or some charming bit of folklore, but August was offering neither. My mind flickered back to Jimmy Stonypoint's fear of giant frogs and his allusion to the large nasty things inhabiting Lac Ile-a-la-Crosse. Was there a connection with the giant beavers?

Belying my prediction, I dreamt vividly that night. But these were not visions welcome to a Chipewyan hunter. I was back in the village snug in my little tent. It was night, and the sled dog chorus was in fine form. Suddenly pandemonium broke loose. Shrill screams and agonized shouts echoed across the village as people ran from their homes. Above the fray was a more fearsome sound, an eerie mind-numbing wail. Where had I heard that sound before? The awful wail was getting closer. I fled from my tent and joined a crowd hurrying toward the lake. But it was a trap. John Lynx rose like a horrible phoenix from the dark water. The demons that possessed him were in full fury. With his bloody mangled face contorted in rage, he advanced on the terrified crowd. As I turned to run, a loud liquid rush from a breaking wave was audible behind me. I turned once more. John Lynx had vanished. In his place an ominous shape broke the lake's surface. Something very large and unspeakably dreadful was emerging . . .

Day by day our team enlarged the trapline. We traveled over a circuit of valleys and small lakes radiating outward from the northern arms and bays of Cache Lake. This was accomplished entirely on foot as the smaller waters were rapidly freezing. Antoine always walked in the lead. Over doubtful patches he swung his ever-present hatchet into the ice ahead like a farrier beating an anvil. "Two or three hits and no water, it's safe. Two inches of ice for sure. We keep going," Antoine explained. "One hit and water comes up, we turn back. Try different way."

The "two-hit" method left little margin for error in my view, but I was grateful to be walking on ice. It was a reprieve from the infernal muskeg and tangled windfalls. While I could not match my partners' agility or stamina, I was heartened that my capacity for walking in the bush steadily improved. Moreover, I shared Antoine's and August's eager anticipation to be always on the move, to explore new terrain each day. After a week it was time to relocate our base camp and extend the trapline into the country around the south end of Cache Lake and beyond.

Cache Lake itself was still open but shrouded in icy fogs that threatened an imminent freeze. Antoine and August chatted happily as we paddled the lumbering canoe southward. Two problems tempered their optimism, however. Food was surprisingly scarce, especially fresh meat. Since all our efforts were geared to getting the trapline up and running, there was little time to hunt for food per se. Like all trappers, the brothers hoped to kill a moose or wood caribou along the way and to cache a substantial supply of meat. But there were no guarantees. Eventually the trapline itself would start producing meat as well as furs. In the meantime, we ate what we could grab on the run, a spruce grouse shot here, a whitefish netted there, or a rabbit snared near camp.

The other problem was snow. A lot of it was falling. To my neophyte's eyes, the heavy wet flakes imparted a magical quality to the landscape. Like icing on a spectacular cake, the white mantle transformed the stark conifers to glistening beacons. But Antoine was not thrilled with the situation. "Don't like this kind of sky," he announced. "Will snow many days for sure. Too early for big snow, eh. No good." Heavy snows usually arrived well after a hard freeze of Cache Lake, but the implications of being "too early" were lost on me.

"Maybe I still have bad luck," Antoine sighed.

"Yah, bad luck for sure, Antoine. You should be like Dastloze here," August gestured teasingly in my direction. "White men are lucky, eh!"

"You can't be serious, August," I protested.

"Sure! Look, you have that fancy camera there. Nice sleeping blanket too, with goose feathers. Lots of things, eh. Yah, I think white men are lucky!"

"Things!," I snorted. "Only you and Decak'ai have caught any beavers. I think Chips are lucky."

August and I were developing a joking relationship. This was profoundly pleasing to me. August had a wry sense of humor, and Antoine frequently became the target of his jests and taunts. The brothers often kidded each other at length in Chipewyan metaphors which I could not follow. To be included in this exchange at any level reassured me of my place in the team. It helped solidify our working relationship as well.

"I think we're all gonna be lucky here," Antoine interrupted as he directed the canoe ashore. "Good place for lynx."

We put ashore ten miles down one of the lake's western bays and hiked inland through a chain of small lakes. Antoine's two-hit method guided us safely across a narrow body of water called *tanatwaze* or "little long lake," and then across a circular pond called *t'obetwas* or "hay-around lake." Not all the place names had a fixed or timeless quality. We passed by a small lake called *da'idanecultwe* or "pants lake" because, as Antoine explained, "somebody hung a pair of pants in a tree over there." Another lake was known as *tuketwe* or "rubber boots lake" because 15 years before some other hunter lost his boots at that vicinity. Yet other names reflected more distant and dramatic events. The rapids on a nearby river were called *ena'ikwazeni'i* or "enemy stole the little boy rapids." The name recalled a tragic episode in the nineteenth century when a Cree man abducted a Chipewyan boy named *ikwaze* (literally "warble fly") and escaped upriver never to be seen again. The land beyond the little lakes rose steadily into a steep-sided birch-lined valley, a type of landscape the Chipewyan call *xul'ai* and known to be a favored habitat of lynx.

Antoine dropped his packsack near what appeared to be a jumble of brush. Gingerly he whisked away the fallen snow to reveal a small circular pen or corral formed from logs and sticks placed between upright tree trunks. The pen or *iyuse* had been built a number of years before by one of Antoine's uncles and, with minor touch-ups, was still in serviceable condition. There were dozens of others in the territory which could be put to use with simple repairs.

At the entrance to the pen Antoine quickly scooped out a small depression in the snow, lined it with spruce bows, and gently set down a jaw trap. The latter was sprinkled with crushed dried-out grass to conceal the trap visually and protect it from the elements. After a thick anchor stake was driven into the ground outside the pen, Antoine completed the lynx set by splitting the top of a small bait stake with his hatchet. Into the crack he inserted a tight bundle of grass that had been soaked in beaver castor.

With bait stake in hand, Antoine paused for a few seconds seemingly lost in thought. Suddenly he raised the stake to touch an overhanging tree branch. Then he waved the stake in the air, tracing a broad arc, before sticking it emphatically in the ground near the back of the pen. "That's how we do it," Antoine remarked with satisfaction. "That's how our old magicians did it too. For good luck."

"Magicians?" I asked. My mind conjured a dark bearded fellow in top hat and tails, pulling scarves out of his mouth at some carnival.

"Yah, guys who know something, *inkonzedene*," Antoine replied quietly as he hefted his pack. "We better move fast now!"

We trudged onward into the intensifying snowstorm. I wanted to learn more about the magicians or inkonzedene but would have to wait for a more opportune moment. In varying contexts, inkonze could mean "shadow" as well as the power or knowledge people obtained through dreaming. Who, then, were the inkonzedene or "shadow people?" The magicians? As we approached the next lake I felt a violent cramping in my bowels. Perhaps this was revenge for talking or even thinking about sensitive matters such as inkonze, I thought nervously. Most likely our morning meal of boiled rabbit was not agreeing with me.

"I'll catch up. You guys go ahead," I yelled as I darted behind a shoreline screen of stunted spruce. No doubt, my need for privacy struck my companions as most peculiar. Like other men traveling in the bush, my partners displayed little modesty in "bathroom" behavior. Around camp they would walk only a few yards from the tent at anytime of day and in anyone's presence to purge their bowels. If nature called on the trail, a man might squat down in the snow almost anywhere, drop his coveralls while his partners waited a few feet away, and do his duty. Try as I might, I could not "take a shit" in public.

The situation was worse than I had thought. I had a full-blown case of diarrhea. And I was carrying no toilet paper, a luxury item in short supply. Scanning the snowy waste around me, I could find no moss, a conventional bush "toilet paper" and the traditional baby diapering material among the Chipewyan. Antoine and August already had disappeared into the whiteout of swirling snows on the opposite side of the lake. Miserable, soiled, and out of sorts, I hobbled after my partners fearful of losing their trail.

After crossing the lake and stumbling up a steep stream canyon, I was relieved to spot Antoine and August at the outlet of another lake. They were busy setting a snare pole at a large beaver lodge. A hole had been chopped through the ice nearby. With a long curved stick or *naitthi*, cut from a poplar branch, Antoine had probed beneath the ice to determine the precise location of the lodge entrance. In front of this passageway, the brothers were now inserting a long pole affixed with four wire snares.

"Holy smokin' anyways, Bob," Antoine shouted. "You don't look too good."

"I was just starting to come back for you," August added. "We thought you got lost. Or maybe a bushman got you."

"You guys got any moss or paper? I'm in bad shape here."

August fumbled through his pack but could find nothing but an old greasy rag. "Here, take this. Maybe you can find some moss over there, eh." August pursed his lips and motioned toward a shoreline stand of jack pines.

As I trudged off, the brothers gamely tried to conceal their laughter. They were snickering and whispering softly. The one word I understood was *san* for feces or "shit." I was mortified.

Hours later we were back in the canoe confronting a new dilemma. Like the middle of an hourglass, the halfway point on Cache Lake was a constricted channel. It was only a few hundred yards wide but several miles in length. The Chipewyan aptly called this place *njudinka* or the "narrows." To our dismay, however, the entire channel was frozen over. The gateway to Antoine's southern hunting territory was blocked.

"We work like dogs now," Antoine declared gravely.

I had assumed Antoine was speaking figuratively. Within an hour, however, he had the three of us hitched up in sled dog fashion with ropes around our waists and chests. By bending over and pumping our legs furiously we were able to drag the heavily-laden canoe short distances over the ice. With our gear aboard, the awkward canoe probably weighed 800 pounds. But our real enemy was the wet snow that coated the top of the ice. The slushy material acted as a brake, readily sticking and freezing to the canoe bottom after a few yards of pulling. The frozen crust had to be delicately chiseled off the fragile canvas countless times to allow any forward progress. In the midst of all this Antoine periodically ventured forth alone with his hatchet testing the ice. It had to be a good four hatchet "hits" thick to prevent our load from breaking through prematurely.

After three hours of dragging, we appeared to be no closer to open water. Perhaps my perception was distorted by exhaustion. I felt dizzy. My leg muscles trembled. I was fully capable of collapsing if we should risk stopping to rest. I began to detest our miserable zeppelin of a canoe. It was a malevolent being set on doing us harm, or so it seemed. Maybe Antoine's talk of bad luck was not far fetched.

"Decak'ai, there's not much sun left," I groaned wearily, wondering if we would have to spend a second day on the troublesome narrows.

"You don't like being a dog, Dastloze?"

"Hell no. The way I'm pulling we'll never reach open water."

"Never?!" Antoine laughed at the absurdity of my statement. "We're already halfway across the ice. No problem for that. Anyhow, I always follow what my father told me."

"Your father?"

"Yah. He told me: 'Never turn back.'"

Never turn back. The phrase stuck in my mind. It seemed like a key to Antoine's personality, or at least a fitting motto for this ambitious young Chipewyan man who moved fast and took chances. Indeed, both Antoine and August accepted our grueling work cheerfully, without uttering a complaint or obscenity. I was shamed by their example.

Two hours later, panting like over-worked sled dogs, we struggled toward the edge of the ice. Evening darkness was quickly descending.

"Bob, do you know how to run with the canoe?" August asked as we cast off our rope harnesses.

"Run with the canoe?"

"Yah, we have to get across that thin ice first," August gestured to the wet slippery surface ahead that led to the open water beyond. "We start pushing the canoe. Then go a little bit faster. Pretty soon we're running, eh. When you hear the ice start to break, that's when you jump in the canoe."

It sounded simple enough. On the slick wet surface the bulky canoe glissaded along with startling speed. The three of us pushed and trotted briskly beside it. Warning cracks from the buckling ice shot out. We kept running. For a scant second I lost my concentration and looked toward my partners for some cue. It was a costly second. Already they were leaping nimbly into the canoe. I plummeted through the ice and up to my neck in the frigid water.

Oh shit, I thought. An image flashed through my mind. It was a grave marker with my name on it at the bottom of Cache Lake. Fortunately the canoe was nearby. I grabbed August's outstretched paddle and clambered aboard. I looked and felt like a drowned rat. My heavy clothes were sodden lumps which began to freeze with exposure to the air. I dreaded thinking about the miles ahead to the south end and the condition I might be in.

The brothers were nonplussed. They had seen and experienced it all before. One of Antoine's former trapping partners had flipped his canoe in deep water the previous fall. With a heavy snowmobile suit on the man had sunk like a rock. Miraculously, he landed on a submerged tree where he remained in chin-deep water until rescued sometime later.

Antoine and August wasted little time in putting ashore and building a massive fire. It was only a stopover to help me dry out. We would have to keep moving toward the south end. The entire lake could freeze over that very night, leaving us stranded miles from our destination. I felt immensely grateful but ludicrous hopping about naked, searching for dry clothes while Antoine and August patiently suspended my waterlogged trousers, boots and parka on poles near the fire. They murmured softly in Chipewyan as they appraised my antics. Suddenly the two brothers were convulsed with peals of barely suppressed laughter.

"I know I must look like an asshole out here," I said. "But don't worry, I'll know how to run with the canoe next time."

"No, no Dastloze, you don't understand," August giggled hysterically. "We're laughing about those two little lakes!"

"What lakes?"

"Where we put the lynx traps this morning."

"Okay, I remember."

"Well, we named those lakes for you, Bob."

"How do you mean?"

"In Chip we're calling that first lake *Setsanismatwe*. You know, 'Didn't Wipe Ass Lake.' And the second lake, we're calling that one 'Ass Wiped Lake.' Like I told you, white men are lucky!" August paused to let the message sink in.

I could only marvel at my partners' capacity for humor, even if it was at my expense. After seeing my quizzical expression they rolled about in a delirium of laughter nearly singeing themselves on the flaming logs. I would have laughed even louder had I known that henceforth those two landmarks would indeed become memorialized in the local language as Didn't Wipe Ass Lake and Ass Wiped Lake.

The daily grind was taking its toll. While I was learning valuable lessons about Chipewyan bush ways every day, documenting them was another matter. Most waking hours were consumed with life on the trail. By the time our evening meal was finished, I had little enthusiasm for writing up field notes. Our cramped tent offered no privacy, and I felt conspicuous, if not impertinent, doing paperwork, especially if my partners were baking bannock or skinning beavers.

One evening at our south end camp, Antoine offered an obvious but brilliant solution to my dilemma: "Bob, why don't you tell us our story."

"What kind of story?"

"No. Our story. What you're writing about us in your little book, eh. Read it to us."

And thus began an enjoyable evening ritual. I was expected to write a faithful account of each day's itinerary, adventures, and mishaps, replete with conversations, pedometer readings, trails covered, sets constructed, animals trapped, meals eaten, and any other items that might come to mind. Then I would read the account aloud and await the brothers' judgments.

"That's good, but you're forgetting the snares we put over by Muskeg Lake," Antoine observed one evening.

"Yah, and you should write what we told you about that old bushman Crazy Louis," August added. "How he killed his partner up here many years ago? Remember?"

With this editorial process in place, my field notes soon doubled in length and became richer in content and perspective. I was ecstatic. But caution was needed. I could not afford to abuse the privilege by betraying my hosts' confidences or revealing some of my own inner thoughts.

On a subsequent evening we had finished reviewing my notes when August offered another suggestion: "Dastloze, why don't you tell us a story?"

"But we just covered it," I replied waving the notebook.

"Not that one. I mean a made-up story."

We were all relaxing on our bedrolls waiting for the stove fire to ebb away before turning in. Antoine had prepared a pile of finely shaved spruce kindling to be used in starting the next morning's fire. The brothers looked at me expectantly. Racking my brain for a suitable tale, I remembered some grisly horror dramas from the old *Inner Sanctum* radio program. Perhaps one of those would do. With all the suspense I could muster, I related the story of a mad scientist who took revenge on his enemies by having them swallow capsules filled with tiny fish hooks. Eventually the capsules dissolved. After securing the victims in his laboratory, the ghoulish scientist turned on an electromagnet to torture confessions out of them.

"And nobody's seen that old scientist to this day," I concluded.

"That's a real good story," August smiled approvingly. "Tell us another one, Bob."

"Maybe I'd better save some for other nights. Now it's your turn. You guys tell one."

"But I don't know any stories. What can I tell?" August replied sheepishly.

"Anything you want. What about your magicians, the shadow people. How do you call them, inkonzedene?"

"You mean like *Eredk'ali*?" Antoine asked.

"Who's that?"

"He was powerful, that guy. Lived to be 300 years old. For the first 100 years he was a wolf. Then he became a man. Eredk'ali could fly south with the geese too. That's really what his name means, 'to go flying across.'"

"He's Chipewyan?"

"Yah, a lot of the people around here are related to him. The Cree were always after him, but he was too smart and too fast. They could never beat him. My late grandfather knew him. Knew his whole life story too. I remember when I was a boy and my grandfather started talking about Eredk'ali. It would take two or three days to tell that story, eh. I could never stay awake to hear about his whole life." Antoine shook his head wistfully.

"Well, go ahead Decak'ai. Tell us a small piece of the story."

"No, I wouldn't say it right," Antoine was almost apologetic. "But your story about the fish hooks reminds me, you know, we had another guy around here. Maybe I'll tell about him."

"A magician?"

"Yah. We call him *Labidsas*. He had strong medicine. In the old days some of the Chip men around here used to go up and down the Churchill on those big boats, the Hudson's Bay Company barges or york boats, bringing supplies to the villages. Every time they stopped at this one village an old Cree woman would come to the boat and hold out a pan to the men. That old woman was a powerful medicine woman, a magician. And usually the men would put something in the pan, like flour or lard. They were afraid she might work magic against them, eh." Antoine paused to scoop himself a mug of tea.

"Well, Labidsas was the most powerful Chipewyan medicine man and curer around here. He went with those men on their next trip, and the old Cree woman came down and held out her pan. This time Labidsas beat her away with a stick and said, 'I will give you nothing.' The Cree woman was very angry. She told Labidsas and the men: 'Three bad things will happen to you before you get home.' Soon the men were back on the river, and sure enough, Labidsas could feel something bad was coming. And he knew what it was too. A big wind and big waves were going to wreck their boat. But Labidsas stopped it with his power.

"Before getting home, the men had to make an overnight camp. Labidsas had a tent with two other guys, just like we are here," Antoine looked wryly at August and me. "That night he could feel something bad was coming again. He knew what it was. He told his partners to stay in the tent. Labidsas lay down outside. Soon two wolves came for him. But before they got him, he killed them right on the spot with his magic.

"The next day the men came to their own village. Another big wind blew up. Something bad was coming for sure. But this time Labidsas could not tell what it was. Just like that a fish hook stuck inside his 'thing,' you know," Antoine made an awful grimace as he pointed down at his crotch. "He was in a great pain. He asked the people to put up his little tent. Inside the tent he had hanging all the skins of his animal helpers. He could talk to them and ask for their help, you know. Labidsas called out to the weasel and the marten, but they couldn't get that hook out. He called all the different animals, but they couldn't help. Labidsas knew he was dying. Then he remembered the wolverine. He called him, and the wolverine got that fish hook out."

"That's a great story, Decak'ai," I commented.

"Not done yet," Antoine replied as he drained his mug. "Then Labidsas sent the hook back to the old Cree woman. But he made it of two fish hooks tied together, like this," Antoine demonstrated with curled forefingers pulling in opposite directions for a more lethal hold. "The old woman was sitting on the ground fixing her fish nets. The fish hook traveled through the earth. It came up beneath and stuck right into her 'thing'. The old Cree woman screamed out in pain: 'aiyayei!,' and fell backwards on the ground and died right away. Okay, now I'm done."

I had never seen Antoine so animated and voluble as when narrating this tale. He became a different person. I now knew a bit more about the shadowy "magicians." I was beginning to appreciate the complex and often troubled relationships between Chipewyan and Cree peoples as well. There was much to ponder.

"Thanks for telling me about Labidsas, Antoine," I mumbled as I drifted off to sleep.

"Well, I figured you liked fish hooks. So, Bob, what kind of story you telling us tomorrow night?"

One afternoon Antoine had gone off alone to inspect a nearby line of traps. I was hauling dead spruce trees to camp and chopping them up for firewood. Approaching the tent with a fresh load of wood, I was startled by muffled voices and heart-wrenching sobs. Was August sick or hurt? Who or what could be making such distressing sounds?

I peered furtively through the tent flap. A couple rabbits were simmering in the big kettle on the stove. Toward the rear of the tent August was hunched over in a peculiar position.

"August, are you okay?"

"Shhh!" August put his finger to his lips. He gripped something in his hands. "It's almost time. Maybe we'll get a message."

I had not seen the rabbit snare wire antenna that ran out the back of our tent and up a nearby jack pine. It was connected to a small battery-powered transistor radio which August now tuned and adjusted. "Almost time for *Northern News*. Sky is clear. We should hear something."

The idea of a radio link to the outside world seemed nothing less than miraculous. As August fiddled with the dials, the sobbing soap opera voice faded out. Now country singer Freddy Hart was belting out his latest hit "Easy Lovin," currently a popular tune among young folks in Patuanak.

Then, *Northern News* was on. It was fifteen minutes of nonstop greetings and announcements, relayed by radio deejays in Prince Albert, to native families, kin and friends scattered throughout northern Saskatchewan. In the fall and early winter months especially, *Northern News* became a means for families to send information and supportive messages to their men in the remote trapping camps.

Antoine had joined us in the tent. The three of us struggled to hear through waves of static. A woman in the Ile-a-la-Crosse hospital was announcing the birth of a baby girl to relatives in Portage La Loche. Birthday greetings and the promise of a visit by grandparents at Montreal Lake were sent to a grandson at Green Lake.

"Hey listen," August cried, "somebody from Patuanak!"

The message was terse and to the point: "Okay, this goes out from Clementine Muskrat of Patuanak to her husband Ovid Muskrat at Red Sucker Lake. She says 'Kids are all sick and we're out of wood. Come home right away.'"

"Poor Ovid," Antoine muttered. "Looks like a tough winter for his family."

It struck me that a few short years before, when most families were still seasonally nomadic, isolation and fragmentation were rare problems. The rise of a central settlement and the all-male bush economy carried unforeseen social and emotional costs. As *Northern News* drew to a close, my partners seemed disappointed.

"Were you expecting a message?" I asked.

"Yah, from my dad." Antoine noted. "He and my uncle might try to meet us up here, near the south end. Help us bring our furs back to the village around Christmastime. But I don't know what day. Or what week. It's okay, we'll listen again when sky is clear."

"Wait, Decak'ai!" August exclaimed. "Another message from Patuanak, I think!"

We huddled around the radio as the announcer stated: "And our last news today goes out from John in Prince Albert to Agnes Lynx at Patuanak. He says 'I'm doing alright. Will work at Hudson Bay for awhile and be home around Christmas.'"

Antoine's expression turned dark and sullen. He grabbed a shotgun and stalked off into the darkness.

"Hah! Just like I thought," August sneered. "A few months in jail, that's all. Then the bastard'll be back in Patuanak making trouble again."

"This 'bastard'? Are you talking about John Lynx?" I shuddered at the thought but could not resist asking.

"Yah. You know him?"

"Sort of." How could I forget a man who kept an entire community in terror.

"Well, he's no good. He's no friend to my family. Always trying to fight Antoine too."

"What's his problem?"

"I don't know. But sometimes he comes after Antoine with his brothers too. They beat him up real bad one time down in Ile-a-la-Crosse. None of those Lynx brothers are any good."

"What's *their* problem?" A whole gang of maniacal Lynx brothers was almost beyond my comprehension.

"I don't know!" August shrugged his shoulders and looked deeply pained. "Jealous maybe. Antoine has many things, you know. A nice skiff. New Snow Cruiser. Many guns."

"But didn't he earn those?"

"Sure! My brother works very hard in the bush. Works hard for what he has. But some people don't see that. And they get jealous."

Intellectually, I tried rationalizing all this as an example of the "limited good" principle. Some anthropologists like George Foster (1955) argued that peasant communities and other small-scale egalitarian societies viewed their world and its resources as sharply delimited. People tended to share what little they had. Individuals with inappropriate wealth might be sanctioned in various ways to make them expend their wealth or distribute their possessions. Perhaps Antoine was a hoarder, and the Lynx brothers were trying to "level" him to some acceptable community standard.

On an emotional level, however, this argument carried little weight. John Lynx in the flesh was a terrifying bully. People shrunk from him like evil incarnate. It hurt me to think that my partners had suffered at his hands. And now this man was returning to the village. What did that mean for my friends? Indeed, now that I had been so generously accepted by the Ptarmigan family, what did it mean for me?

Cache Lake finally froze over on November 9th. It was the earliest freeze-up in Antoine's memory and time for us to move back to the northern part of the trapping territory. We broke camp around 5:00 A.M. I dreaded the long day ahead. Once again we assumed the roles of "dogs," this time harnessed single file in front of a heavy birch freight toboggan loaded with our supplies. Real sled dogs might start the day chowing down on a whitefish or two, I thought ruefully. Our stomachs were empty and growling.

Thankfully, the big canoe was now stashed at the south end where it would remain until spring breakup. Antoine wanted to push nonstop for our north end base camp in one day, a 25-mile trek. This was a demanding task under ideal conditions. But persistent snows promised to obscure pockets of weak ice, slush and other hazards.

As we marched into the white void I reflected on our progress. In little more than two weeks our team had set out 104 traps and 41 snares. Judging from my pedometer and maps, we had traveled over 280 miles, 114 miles of which had involved tramping through rugged bush. Given our various setbacks and mishaps, these were hard-won miles indeed. The trapline was effectively up and running. This should have been cause for celebration.

But we were barely one step ahead of Antoine's "bad luck." He referred to it often, and John Lynx's untimely message did nothing to boost his spirits. The simple truth was that the trapline had not started producing yet. Each day our hunger grew. The few beavers and rabbits we managed to catch were not replacing the thousands of calories we burned off in each day's toil. Would we be reduced to eating minks and fishers? Like other members of the weasel family, these animals were considered starvation food by the Chipewyan and rarely eaten.

The former slush-hell of the "narrows" was now a frozen crust. We crossed it with relative ease. By midday we had stopped several times to build small fires, boil up tea and conserve our waning strength. The toboggan seemed to get heavier as the day wore on, but Antoine was reluctant to stop and make camp.

Dusk approached in late afternoon when we stopped in a small inlet on the west shore. "Make fire here!" Antoine commanded abruptly. He stalked off on a short trail to inspect a few lynx snares. August and I set to work immediately in what was now a familiar routine. Fire building was one of the most important responsibilities entrusted to an apprentice by his boss. An experienced trapper expected periodic fires on the trail to warm and sustain himself and his team. It was also a test of one's manhood. The ability to construct suitable fires quickly under varying conditions required extensive knowledge in selecting sites, wood and tinder. And fire was often the difference between life and death.

We were both exhausted, but I followed August's lead in grabbing tufts of beard-like moss tinder off nearby spruce trees. August used one of our snowshoes to shovel out a big bowl-like depression in the snow. This we lined with spruce boughs to create a dry sitting area. As August ignited the flaming moss and a delicate cluster of spruce shavings, I clambered about the bush searching for large logs that would fuel the massive fire which Antoine preferred for drying out damp clothing and taking off the chill.

August was preparing a stake for the tea pail when a noise in the bush startled us. Antoine was back. He had run the trail in record time. His grave expression told us that the snares were empty. We would stay hungry.

Antoine glanced at our modest fire and then exploded in a stream of Chipewyan expletives. August made a feeble retort and then backed off in stony silence as Antoine continued his harangue in English: "I give you all this time, and look! Just a little fire, and there's no tea! What've you been doing?"

August had no answer for his brother. Indeed, he was expected to give none. Antoine's ire was directed squarely at August. I felt awful. I was responsible for the fire too. Moreover, I knew that August idolized his older brother and would go to almost any length to please him. He had once confided to me: "I respect Antoine, and I want to show him I am a man too. Like he is."

But on this gloomy day August and I failed the manhood test. We hurriedly drank our tea and returned to our harnesses. Out of anger or humiliation, we pulled with renewed determination. We would reach the north end out of spite. Up front in the lead harness Antoine's face was out of view. I imagined he was having a private laugh at the outcome of his lesson.

Several hours later we arrived at the end of one the lake's northern bays. A partial moon illuminated the early evening sky. Our intended base camp was still another four or five miles on the opposite shore. However, we were now at the site of one of our earlier camps, a place with a small tree cache. Here I found one of my packsacks which contained an almost forgotten treasure. Hidden at the bottom were a bag of dried apricots and a bottle of Hudson's Bay Company brandy.

We wolfed down the apricots, but I hesitated in revealing the brandy. The Chipewyan had strong proscriptions against bringing liquor in the bush, no matter how much people might drink in the village. Similarly, there were strong feelings about observing the Sabbath in the bush. Except for the barest of domestic camp chores, hunting, long-distance travel and other arduous work were avoided on Sunday. I was reluctant to violate local protocol.

"Dastloze, what's in that bottle?" Antoine asked suspiciously. It was the first word anyone had spoken since the embarrassing fire fiasco.

"I can't lie to my boss. It's kontue [liquor]."

"Let me try it." Antoine swallowed deeply and passed the bottle around. "It's okay to have a little, eh? We worked hard today."

After sharing a few swigs, our outlook brightened considerably. August was soon trading playful jabs with Antoine as an invitation to a serious wrestling bout.

"Say Bob," August suddenly inquired. "Isn't it your turn to fight Decak'ai?"

"I can't fight if I'm drinking brandy." Drunk or not I envisioned the powerful Antoine hurling me about like a rag doll. "How about a Russian dance contest? Whoever falls first buys another bottle of brandy back in Patuanak."

Crouching on the lake ice with arms folded tightly against my chest, I did my best impression of a Russian or Ukrainian folk dancer with legs kicking out furiously. Soon the three of us were step-kicking about in a competitive frenzy. We repeatedly kicked, slipped and collapsed. Our absurd appearance set off fits of hysterical laughter. Everyone was claiming the victor's bottle.

"Shh, Decak'ai," August suddenly whispered and gestured with his head toward the lake. "Nunie!"

A rangy wolf, silhouetted against the moonlit snow, was loping across the bay. For a fraction of a second it stopped and looked back in our direction. I was struck by a haunting sense of déjà vu. The wolf near Buffalo Narrows last summer had glanced back in the same questioning manner. But that was a different wolf. Wasn't it? August reached for the rifle lashed to our toboggan.

"No! Not this one," Antoine whispered harshly. "See, he's going our way."

In a heartbeat we were back in harness pulling across the ice. The wolf was moving toward our destined camp, or so it seemed. Yet I puzzled over Antoine's statement, "he's going our way." Did it hold some hidden meaning? Antoine had great respect for Eredk'ali, the wolf-turned-man, someone his beloved grandfather had known personally. But Antoine also respected Labidsas, the magician who killed wolves. Were these powerful fellows connected in some way? In their own origin myth, the Chipewyan were borne of a union between a woman and a dog-like creature, offering a dense tangle of symbolic associations. For the moment, at least, Antoine was ebullient, and this lifted the mood of the team.

"I think my luck will change now," Antoine remarked excitedly. It was the last thing he said before pulling into camp that night.

For several nights the mercury plummeted into the sub-zero range. The still night air was shattered by unearthly groans, an eerie metallic ringing, and occasional sharp explosions, like echoing gunshots. These were not sounds of the imagination. Cache Lake's ice was merely thickening. Indeed, the noises were comforting. Thick ice over the large, deep bays would make travel safer.

One morning I accompanied Antoine a few dozen yards into the bush behind our camp. A huge mound of snow betrayed a makeshift ground cache assembled many months before. After removing the snow and a layer of heavy logs and boulders designed to discourage bears and wolverines, a large canvas tarpaulin remained.

"Dastloze, what you think's under here?" Antoine teased.

"I don't know, Decak'ai. Home brew? Maybe you've been holding out on me."

"Ha ha! No. What do we really need?"

"Well, a hindquarter of moose would help. Or a fine dog team to get around with. Am I close?"

"Dogs? Pretty good guess. We don't have to be 'dogs' no more."

Antoine grinned slyly and threw back the tarp with a dramatic flourish to reveal a large snowmobile. Its polished white and red fiberglass shell glistened in the morning sun. I was dumbstruck. The brothers had revealed nothing about such wonders. Antoine had alluded to his previous winter's troubles with Frank Whitefish's dogteam. I had assumed that the Ptarmigan family was simply retiring its dogs as well, and that our team would be forced to hoof it in the bush.

After a few tugs on the starter cord, the engine roared to life. Antoine repeatedly gunned the throttle, coaxing the machine to a high-pitched whine. The air was quickly filled with a dense pall of gas fumes as Antoine tore out for the lake. He circled around the small inlet in front of our camp in a series of test runs. After making some adjustments on the carburetor, he hitched up the freight toboggan. August and I assisted in rigging up the side boards, backboard, and canvas cradle that converted the toboggan into a true cariole capable of holding hundreds of pounds of cargo.

"How do you like our *klicho* [big dog], Bob?" August yelled as Antoine drove us around the inlet.

"A real beauty! Does it have a name?"

"Snow Cruiser. Twenty-four horsepower. Real strong, this one. Not like those little Skidoos, you know."

"But how did it get here?"

"Antoine bought it last spring. Drove it up here just before break-up. Yah, this'll be our first year without real dogs. First winter with Snow Cruiser."

First winter with Snow Cruiser.

That gave me pause. If my partners had any misgivings about converting to the iron dog they did not express them. Local traders wanted anywhere from $850 to $1200 for the latest models, a costly investment that matched the annual income of many hunters. A poor year on the trapline, or a sudden downturn in fur and fish prices, could quickly put one behind in payments. And traders were not shy about repossessing iron dogs.

Yet, most local Chipewyan hunters were phasing out dogs in favor of Skidoos or Snow Cruisers. More than 60 machines were now owned by families in the Patuanak area. Speed was the obvious attraction. Under the right trail conditions, a snowmobile could cover in 12 hours a route that might require four or five days by dog team. Dogs had to be carefully fed and rested. With adequate feed, however, a sound dogteam could travel for unlimited distances in the bush. By contrast, a snowmobile's outward limit of travel was sharply defined by the gas supply a trapping team could haul.

Our outfit contained only three 12-gallon drums of gas. This appeared outrageously insufficient to my untrained eyes. But I was overlooking the fact that snowmobiles and dogteams alike were only a means

A race on Shagwenaw Lake, testimony to changes of the late 1960s and early 1970s when snowmobiles eclipsed sled dogs for winter transportation.

of travel between base camps, or between base camp and village. Much of the tedious day-to-day off-trail travel in the bush would continue to be on foot, a pattern that had not changed for generations of Chipewyan hunters.

It was a Sunday, a day of rest. A good day to take stock of our situation. The unveiling of the Cruiser was an occasion to celebrate. August replaced the old soiled layer of spruce boughs in our tent with fresh ones. "Changing the rug," the Chipewyan called it, a simple act of bush hygiene which elevated everyone's spirits. I spent a leisurely afternoon catching up on my field notes while Antoine continued tinkering on the Cruiser's engine.

"A lynx, a beaver, and an otter," Antoine announced as he entered the tent for a tea break.

"What?"

"Write that in your little book Dastloze," Antoine smiled cryptically. "A lynx, a beaver, and an otter."

"But what should I say about them?" I was perplexed.

"I had trouble sleeping last night again. I'm catching animals for sure. That's why."

Since arriving at the north-end camp Antoine's dreams had become more frequent and intense. He usually referred to this circumspectly as "trouble sleeping." This was a highly desirable kind of trouble, however. It came as no surprise that Antoine decided to bend the proscription on hunting on the Sabbath. After finishing his tea, he trudged off alone to check a short snare line on a nearby stream while August and I hauled wood.

It was dark when Antoine returned. August began making apologies in Chipewyan for not starting the evening meal, but Antoine waved him off. From his bulging packsack he retrieved a large male lynx. Its huge paws and feathery ear tufts were still caked with snow. "It's okay. I'll be the cook tonight," Antoine announced. After skinning and butchering the animal, he fried the fat hindquarters in lard. We spent the rest of the evening savoring our windfall of food and swapping stories. It was my first meal of lynx. It was the only carnivore, aside from bears, that the Chipewyan ate with any regularity. It tasted remarkably similar to its chief prey, the snowshoe rabbit.

"We're not finished yet," Antoine observed as he grabbed one of the lynx's pelvic bones, a large hatchet-shaped piece, from a heap of scraps and offal. Antoine closed his eyes as the divinatory ritual began. He raised the bone high above his head with one hand. His other hand, with index finger extended, slowly approached from the opposite direction. After a momentary hesitation, Antoine thrust his finger cleanly through the pelvic bone's hole, or obturator foramen, on the first attempt. "This will bring me more luck for sure. More luck hunting lynx," Antoine smiled as he passed the bone around the tent. But neither August nor I could repeat the performance. For the moment, at least, we would have to ride on the coattails of our mentor's luck.

Antoine gathered the remains of the lynx carcass and placed them in the crotch of a nearby tree which already held the decayed remnants of several other sacrificed animals. This gesture of respect, like divinatory rituals and dreaming, was part of the delicate process of actually obtaining power from animals, what the Chipewyan called *biu'aze.* Inkonze referred to knowledge and power generally.

Antoine returned to the tent with a second packsack which had been leaning against our woodpile. He made a show of emptying its contents. A large beaver tumbled out followed by an otter with dark sleek fur. With smoking pipe clenched firmly in his teeth, Antoine seemed supremely contented as he set about skinning the catch. August and I praised his success. Questions loomed in my mind, but I was reluctant to break the special atmosphere.

Sensing my curiosity, Antoine encouraged: "Go ahead, Bob, show August your little book."

I flipped my notebook open to the page written earlier that day. August read the notation loudly with great gusto as if it were a lottery ticket he had been expecting to win: "'A lynx, a beaver, and an otter!' Holy smokin', anyway!"

For a time Antoine's luck seemed to hold. The trapline started producing with regularity. Our pressing hunger abated. The Cruiser did its job in hauling us from camp to camp. True, the engine occasionally lost power, but Antoine and August could perform minor mechanical miracles with nothing more than a filed-down spoon, a tube of ambroid glue, and fragments of snare wire.

"Dirty gas" was a recurrent problem. Filters and pumps had to be removed frequently to locate impurities blocking the fuel line. Sometimes this was accomplished on the open lake in the midst of a driving blizzard. On one occasion, the Cruiser's right ski was sheared in half when Antoine struck a snow-covered boulder many miles out of camp. It seemed to be an insoluble predicament. "Dogs don't break down," August noted wistfully as I helped him build a fire. Antoine chopped down a nearby birch tree. With skinning knife and axe he fashioned a graceful wooden ski which was bolted to the bottom of the old metal appendage. In less than half an hour our team was back on the move.

Our omnipresent nemesis was the snow. The heavy leaden skies unleashed new storms every few days. Snow was waist deep in some parts of the bush. Cache Lake was not freezing fast enough to support the accumulating burden. The lake ice cracked and buckled. Water then spilled over the surface, mixing with new snow to create dangerous hidden pools of ice-water that were resistant to freezing. Chipewyan called the wretched stuff *takatwe* or "slush." There were few things in the environment abhorred more than "slush." Travelers often were unaware of the hazard in their midst until they were mired in it. All forward progress came to a halt. Equipment had to be tipped on end. The exposed fast-freezing slush was then laboriously chiseled away from toboggan runners, snowmobile drive tracks and skis. With luck, 20 or 30 yards could be gained before miring down once again.

The situation had deteriorated rapidly by mid-December. One day our team spent 12 agonizing hours moving camp a mere four miles across one of the lake's northern channels. Most of that time had been spent literally pushing machine and toboggan through a slush hell. Even with the Cruiser tied down on full throttle, one man had to run ahead on snowshoes clearing a path while the other two ran beside the machine, lifting the skis out of the slush and shoving it along just to gain a few yards. It seemed incongruous that we were reduced to breaking trail for a snowmobile.

Our strength was quickly sapped. At day's end we were alarmed to find that six gallons of the precious gas supply had been expended in the effort. Would we have enough fuel to reach the south end, let alone the village? The rendezvous time with Joe Ptarmigan was quickly approaching. To make matters worse, a major storm pinned us down for several days at the new camp.

As the storm subsided we busied ourselves with preparations for another move. But the normal good-natured banter between the brothers also waned. Perhaps they were dreading what lay ahead. I took this as a bad sign but kept my feelings hidden. Hauling in a load of dead timbers and cutting them up with a bucksaw kept my mind occupied. I was beginning to take some pride in my handling of firewood.

"What's this?" Antoine inquired suspiciously. He was pointing toward the stove. He had just arrived back from inspecting a long line which produced little beyond snow-covered traps.

"We're having rabbits," August replied matter-of-factly as he stirred the kettle.

"No, I mean *in* the stove." Antoine was impatient and on edge.

August switched to Chipewyan, and the two spoke rapidly and stridently for a few minutes. I knew they were discussing the firewood. Something was amiss. Antoine was a real demon on fires, and I was reluctant to interrupt. Suddenly, Antoine grabbed his packsack and stormed out of the tent. August was embarrassed. We sat for some time in uncomfortable silence.

"Did I screw up?" I finally asked.

"Well, Antoine didn't like the kind of wood you got today."

"What kind is that?" I was mystified.

"You got the kind that goes 'snap' and 'pop' like a rifle shot, eh. It could burn a hole in the tent."

A greenhorn's mistake, I thought ruefully. In my haste I had grabbed some dead jack pine timbers, rich in sap and ready to explode when burned. Dead spruce was always the preferred choice.

"But why didn't Antoine talk to *me*? It's not your mistake." I felt guilty about August catching my flak.

"Maybe he's shy. Anyhow, I told him you worked real hard getting this wood. It's okay to use it for one day."

"Thanks, August, but I don't want to burn down our only tent! And what's this 'shy' business? Antoine's my boss!"

"Maybe he feels bad about burning your blanket."

Everyone's nerves were raw. True enough, the previous morning Antoine had dropped the red-hot stove lid on my bedroll. It's Dacron cover burst into flames. I awoke to find a fire licking at my head. Goose feathers and down swirled around us like fake snow. We all had a big laugh at the gaping hole in my bedroll. But the ravaged bag was a serious problem. Temperatures had dropped as low as −35°F in recent mornings. January could bring readings in the −55°F range. Would I end up like Antoine and August's beloved grandfather? As an orphaned youth he had no blanket. Each night found him hugging the dying embers of some adoptive family's fire. The thought sent a chill through me. Eventually, we devised a serviceable patch for my bag from a discarded flour sack. But apparently Antoine harbored guilty feelings about the incident.

The sun was already setting at 3:30 P.M. when a shrill hawk-like whistle broke the silence. Antoine was announcing his return and perhaps a change in mood.

"I could smell that fresh bannock way out in the bush!" Antoine said cheerfully as he entered the tent. He tore off a piece from a loaf cooling near the stove and popped it in his mouth.

"Why are you eating that *new* bannock?" August suddenly snapped. "There's still some old bannock in the grub box."

"What do you mean?" Antoine sounded surprised and hurt. "*You* always try the new bannock first."

August's dander was up. He had spent the afternoon brooding and baking fresh loaves for the long trip ahead. Antoine's indiscretion with the food was now a major affront. To make matters worse, August hurled an insult in Chipewyan. In an eye-blink, Antoine was on top of his brother, dragging him roughly out of the tent by one leg. In the struggle, the stove was knocked over. Flaming cinders and boiling water flew everywhere. As I fumbled to upright the stove, a brief but intense scuffle ensued outside.

When August re-entered the tent, his face was contorted in a mask of rage and pain. Hastily he donned his parka and a packsack. After loading our .30-30 rifle, he stormed out into the darkness. Now Antoine and I were left alone in embarrassing silence. Something in August's expression had alarmed me. If he decided to leave us, we would be in a precarious situation. But where would he go? In my mind's eye, I saw August angrily tramping mile after mile across desolate muskeg toward some unreachable destination. Should we go after him? But I could not approach Antoine. He withdrew deeply into a private shell. This troubled me as much as August's departure. I winced every time a jack pine knot exploded in the stove.

"Maybe we should turn in," Antoine muttered hours later. It was nearly midnight. The certainty of slush hell awaited us in the morning.

KA-BLAAM!!! A deafening rifle shot rang out within feet of the tent. Antoine caught my eye for a fleeting second. A lifetime of fear and hope seemed to be etched on his face.

Then August strolled nonchalantly into the tent. He looked fatigued but was smiling and swaggering with exaggerated bravado as if to hide or purge former bad feelings. "Almost shot a wolf out there," he said gesturing with the .30-30. "No, not that other wolf, Decak'ai. This was a different one."

The difficulties of reaching Cache Lake's south end surpassed even our worst fears. After a torturous day of pushing the Cruiser and toboggan through hidden pools of freezing slush we arrived at the halfway point at njudinka. Our gas supply was almost gone. There was grim speculation about having to ditch the machine. We were on the brink of exhaustion. It had been dark for several hours, and a temporary camp at the narrows seemed the only recourse. But Antoine kept staring at something on the southern horizon.

"That big bay there?" Antoine pursed his lips in the direction of the south end. "I think it's freezing faster, eh. Not so much slush now."

Soon we were furiously shoving the whining Cruiser toward the bay. There was a subtle lurch in the machine's drive track. Suddenly the machine was moving forward on its own steam.

"Quick! Get on!" Antoine yelled. "If it stops here, it'll never go again!"

August leaped on the seat behind his brother. Miraculously, Cruiser and toboggan were still moving forward, buoyed above the slush by a perilously thin layer of ice. I made a leaping grab for the toboggan but then let go. My extra weight was dragging the outfit into the slush.

August yelled something at me before the brothers disappeared into the darkness. "White men are lucky!" I thought he had jeered cynically. Was that possible? Had my partners found an opportune moment to abandon me? Perhaps I had brought them enough misfortune. In my delirious state, I imagined the brothers laughing giddily as they cruised across the ice toward a reunion with their father, Joe Ptarmigan. "The old people were right Dad," Antoine was saying. "That Dastloze was bad, but he can't hurt us now."

I staggered after my partners. Our south-end base camp was out there somewhere in a maze of islands and peninsulas 15 miles away. I doubted my ability to find it, let alone cover the distance, on this cloudy moonless night. Somehow I had ended up carrying a heavy packsack which acted as a piledriver punching my boots deep into the slush. My feet were quickly soaked. Each step became excruciating. Nearsighted, and with glasses fogged and iced over, I soon wandered off the faint snowmobile track.

"You're in deep shit now," I muttered to myself. Should I stop and build a fire and wait for morning? Or would that be a mistake, like a casualty in a Jack London short story? A flicker of movement on the ice ahead caught my eye. A shadow was moving among the shadowy snow drifts.

"The wolf, is it you?," I whispered hopefully. "Eredk'ali, I need some help here."

"Crooaaawk!" The raspy cry startled me. A familiar flapping and fluttering of wings carried the dark bird overhead, sailing from one side of the channel to the other. I felt oddly embarrassed. Why was I addressing wolves? Had I forgotten my other comrades?

"Datsa, it's good to see you," I mumbled apologetically. "I hardly ever see you around at night." Like the whiskey jacks, ravens sometimes hung around our camps in the daytime filching the odd scrap of offal.

The raven circled the channel croaking and squawking furiously. Then it flew south across the big bay. Perhaps this was a sign. I locked the bird's flight path in my mind and trudged on hoping to catch a second wind. I was also terrified by Antoine's last words. A paraphrased version kept replaying in my head: "If you stop here, you'll never go again!"

Eventually the three of us reached the south end, but at some cost. Antoine and August used up the last of the gas bulling through a final barrier of slush. A valuable hatchet was lost. August partially disabled himself after slicing his right hand open on a skinning knife while fumbling through our grub box in the dark. Antoine's wrists were sprained and swollen after a fall on the ice. My leg muscles cramped up, and I ran a high fever that sidelined me in camp for several days. We were a bloodied and bedraggled team, but we were still together.

One evening a long-anticipated *Northern News* message came through on the radio: "To Antoine Ptarmigan on Cache Lake from Joe

Ptarmigan. Tried to make it up on December 17th, but had to turn back. Snow and slush real bad. Will try again in a few days."

"December 17th?" Antoine asked glumly. "That was yesterday. Well, maybe we won't make it to Patuanak for Christmas this year."

Trail and travel conditions were wretched throughout the country. Trappers were mired down in camps everywhere. A lull in the snow and super-cold temperatures would be needed to freeze up the perilous slush. And, as if the spirits were listening, that is exactly what happened.

Several days later a faint, quavery, high-pitched whine was barely audible above the moaning wind. "Listen!" Antoine commanded. "Two Skidoos, old ones! It's my Dad, and my uncle Jeremy for sure!" To my ears, the sound was like a lethargic mosquito buzzing somewhere in another room.

Several hours later two battered yellow and black, 10-horsepower Skidoos pulling freight toboggans arrived at our camp. Joe Ptarmigan and Jeremy Montgrand, my partners' mother's brother, entered the tent without formal greetings or fanfare and helped themselves to mugs of tea. They were the first people we had seen in two months! Yet the occasion was treated casually, as if these men had been with us all along.

Joe and Jeremy were both hefty, good-humored men in their mid-50s. They nearly filled our little tent. August was quiet and deferential in his father's presence. Antoine became our spokesman, engaging the men in a lengthy conversation. My comprehension of Chipewyan had improved enough so that I could follow much of the discussion about our travel difficulties, the fur harvest, Joe and Jeremy's hunting efforts, and news from the village.

When the visitors' eyes shifted toward me, I sensed what the next topic would be. Was Dastloze really a partner? A sits'eni? Had he worked out? I quickly busied myself near the stove following August's lead as a deferential apprentice. Luck was with me on this day. Two of my snares held rabbits which I now prepared for a meal. Antoine was offering the men some bannock I had baked that morning. Maybe I would pass muster yet.

Joe and Jeremy reminisced a bit about their past. As children and as young married men in the 1930s and 1940s, they had spent many winters with their families traveling and hunting in the Cache Lake area, and over a vast region that extended north to Cree lake. Colossal herds of wintering barren-ground caribou migrated into the area in those years providing an abundant source of food, skins for clothing, and bone and antler for implements.

"But the last time those *hotetthena* [north caribou] came this far south was 1950," Jeremy noted. "It's kinda funny too, you know, because the old people always said that when those caribous crossed the Churchill River, they would never come back here again. And it's true!

They crossed the Churchill in 1950, and they never come this far south anymore. All we have now is moose and *etthun* [wood caribou]."

Jeremy's observation was not "funny" in a comical sense. It referred to a profoundly serious dilemma. The Chipewyan interpreted major historical changes in animal distributions as withdrawals or withholdings due to flagrant "disrespect" by hunters. Periodic shortages of moose in some areas were explained in these terms. Failure to observe the normal gestures of respect, including excessive hunting in the 1930s, were thought to have offended the barren-ground caribou and triggered their precipitous decline in later years. This constituted a breach of the natural order which was not easily rectified.

"Hey Jeremy?" Joe asked. "Remember that time we killed a bunch of fat caribou on the north end here? At those little lakes? We were just young fellas then, eh."

"Which lakes you mean, Dad?" Antoine inquired.

Joe described the terrain in some detail.

"Oh yah. Ass Wiped Lake," Antoine replied in complete seriousness. "We had good luck with lynx there. But not so good at Didn't Wipe Ass Lake."

When we broke camp the following morning, my thermometer registered −40°F. Burlap sacks stuffed with our rough-skinned furs were packed into Joe and Jeremy's toboggans along with some of our other gear. The final stages of cleaning, stretching and drying of the pelts, preparatory to marketing, would be handled by Mary Ptarmigan back in Patuanak. Women generally managed all the fine-handling of furs as well as the fine-butchering and processing of most food animals. We traveled south caravan style. The trail which Jeremy and Joe had laboriously broken over several days had finally frozen into a hard surface. For the first time in many weeks we were able to travel with relative ease.

After numerous stops to repair broken toboggan hitches and iced-up carburetors, we arrived at the little settlement on Dipper Lake. Only a few families lived on this isolated section of the Churchill River. Jeremy's brother, Edward Montgrand, and his family kindly treated us to a meal of rabbit stew. Then we were off on the final leg of the journey on an old dogsled trail which cut westward across a series of small lakes toward Patuanak.

"Dastloze, how does it look to you?" Antoine asked excitedly. We had stopped on the east side of Shagwenaw Lake where Jeremy was adjusting the load in his toboggan. Patuanak was visible as a cluster of twinkling lights four miles away on the opposite shore.

"It looks beautiful," I replied without conviction. In truth, the sight was jarring. A place which seemed like a wilderness outpost several months before, now appeared as Los Angeles to my eyes. Returning to the village suddenly scared me.

Mary Bernard (left) and Jeanne D'Arc Bernard (right) cooperate in scraping the flesh and hair from a moosehide. Hide making is an arduous, complex process that may require 40 hours of labor spread over three or four days. Chipewyan women also generally handle the fine butchering and dry meat making operations.

"Hey Bob, you never did fight Antoine," August taunted. "How about now?"

The older men were occupied with Jeremy's toboggan. Antoine grinned as he struck a boxer's pose, circling steadily and landing light jabs on my shoulders and chest. What the hell, I thought. It was still 40°F below zero. A stiff wind was blowing off the lake. And I was finally fighting my trapping partner.

On Christmas eve the Patuanak Catholic church was packed for midnight mass. Returning trappers and boarding school children home for the holidays joined their families in an overflow crowd in the plain white building. The bishop of the district flew in specially for the occasion. Before administering the sacrament of communion, he delivered a short sermon on the significance of Christ's birth. He also admonished the congregation: "The Lord's house is not a restaurant." Special mass or not, candy wrappers and soda bottles were a sore point for the bishop.

The community was gearing up for a festive period of family reunions, Church activity, band hall dances and drinking which would culminate on New Year's eve. Visiting relatives from Buffalo Narrows, and settlements as distant as Stoney Rapids, were arriving daily by snowmobile and bush plane. Bootleggers from Ile-a-la-Crosse were doing a brisk business. A few bold individuals made their own batches of home brew, a potent concoction of fermenting water, malt and yeast known locally as "gazoochpooch." But such operations were difficult to conceal from the prying eyes of the chief and his councilors, dry-reserve advocates, and one's enemies.

Despite my trepidations, I quickly readjusted to village life. A new pile of field notebooks, some of them quite ragged and stained with grease, blood and tea awaited me in my cabin. I began the tedious process of converting them to typed format. Reliving the events of the past months through the notes forced upon me a nagging question. What did it all mean? Did my apprenticeship reveal anything of significance about Chipewyan society?

For the moment I took comfort in a new level of acceptance in the community. People who had shied away from me before, now seemed approachable and sometimes curious to hear about my experiences. Returning from the bush, with no apparent harm done to myself or my partners, represented passage through a kind of threshold. I had passed from marginal stranger to legitimate sits'eni. I was invited for meals at the Ptarmigan household and became better acquainted with Joe and Mary and their large extended network of relatives. All of this was immensely heartening.

But there was another reason for feeling optimistic. Despite all the setbacks and difficulties, our team had actually fared well in the hunt. Our harvest of 15 beaver, 17 lynx, 12 mink, 2 fox, a fisher, an otter, a weasel, and a muskrat was sold to the local Hudson's Bay Company trader for nearly $700. While that was several hundred dollars below Antoine's expectations, it was among the highest pre-Christmas sales of fur in the community. Other hunters had been frustrated by the crippling weather as we were. Many who had delayed their departures for distant traplines became captives of the slush. Others had been forced to relocate their hunts closer to the village.

Late one night August appeared at my door with a bottle of rum. He was mildly intoxicated, having spent much of the day celebrating with cousins visiting from Cree Lake. He was in a confessional mood. We spent several hours reliving our time on Cache Lake.

"Dastloze, you probably think I'm crazy right now, eh?"

"A little high but not crazy."

"I got something I want to tell you. You won't get mad at me?"

"Now you're making me nervous."

"Okay. We're good friends now. Sits'eni. I don't think of you as a white man anymore. You're a Chip."

At a log warehouse or *t'asi thelaikoe* in Patuanak, Joe Black (left) and Rene Janvier (right) assemble their early winter catch of fur for marketing. Snowshoes, stretching boards and hoops, snowmobile, freight toboggan, and other essential equipment are ready for use.

"Thanks August."

"There were times out in the bush when I was real angry at you." August confided.

"I guess we had some tough times."

"Yah. Like when we're building those fires. Antoine wanted everything fast and just right. And we were so slow. I wasn't really mad at you. I just wanted to please my brother."

"I wanted to please him too."

"And there were times when I was really angry at Antoine, too. You know, I could've walked all the way to the south end that night he took my bannock. But I respect my brother too much." August's eyes moistened as he recalled that night.

With his conscience salved August became jovial again. We joked and talked into the early morning hours. Before departing the cabin, however, August unloaded one additional burden.

"Bob, you remember those little pills you always gave us?"

"Oh sure. You mean the vitamins?" At most evening meals I had made it a habit to swallow vitamin C as well as multivitamin tablets. The brothers had been curious about them, and soon they were taking them as well.

"We really didn't eat ours."

"You didn't?"

"We pretended to eat them. Then we hid them under our bedrolls, eh."

"Why?"

"Dastloze, now don't get mad at me," August said sheepishly as he staggered out the door. "We're friends now. But we thought you might kill us out in the bush. The pills might be poison. So we hid them. Remember, that's what the old people told us, that you were a spy. You'd try to kill us."

Chapter Six

Forests Aflame

The mid-winter months passed remarkably quickly. Antoine renewed an old partnership with his uncle Jeremy Montgrand. The two men returned to Cache Lake. With that issue resolved, August resumed his boarding school career. While I accompanied Antoine and Jeremy on a few forays, I spent much of the time between January and May traveling and working with other hunting teams. Exposure to middle-aged and older men, and to other parts of the territory, I hoped, would deepen my understanding of the larger community of hunters.

Prolonged daylight and warmer temperatures in April heralded a period of intensive muskrat trapping. It was a perilous time for traveling, however, owing to rapidly deteriorating ice conditions. The complete break-up of ice on the Churchill and its major tributaries in early May ushered in another period of intensive hunting, this time for beaver.

By the end of May the annual fur hunt was over. The largest lakes were finally breaking free of ice. Yet, there was little time for rest or reflection. The most favorable time for commercial fishing was quickly approaching. Men who had spent the winter hunting together now sought out new partners. Fishing teams would spend several weeks furiously netting pickerel, whitefish, lake trout, and jackfish. Raven Lake, a major expansion of the Churchill River near Dipper Lake, was a particularly favored destination. Its deep waters, abundant fish populations, and large harvest quotas insured substantial food supplies and cash returns for many fishermen and their families.

When Antoine's older brother, Norbert Ptarmigan, asked me to team-up with him at Raven lake I jumped at the opportunity. Apparently, his usual partner wanted to fish elsewhere. I had spent some time on Norbert's trapline and was eager to learn more from this soft-spoken man who seemed wise beyond his 32 years.

We made our base camp at Joe and Mary Ptarmigan's old cabin in the small seasonal village at Dipper Lake. About 35 other men, organized into 14 teams, were operating in the same vicinity. From our base camp Norbert and I made daily forays by skiff to Raven lake, setting out a series of 100-yard gill nets at strategic locales. These we inspected two or three times per day. After removing and cleaning the fish, and packing them into 100-pound wooden boxes covered with chipped ice, we would relocate some of the nets and begin the process anew. It was not uncommon for fishing teams to log 18-hour days.

"Dastloze, you paid the lake, eh?" Norbert inquired suspiciously one morning.

"Sure I paid." The Chipewyan viewed large lakes and rivers as potentially lethal forces which required "payments" or offerings of tobacco, coins, matches and other objects. This ritual insurance protected the fisherman or traveler from storms and other hazards. It was a particularly compelling gesture for first-time travelers in new country. Antoine had shown me how to pay Cache Lake. I had done the same at Dipper and Raven. "Remember that pipe tobacco I threw in?"

"Yah, okay then." Norbert sounded unconvinced.

"Well, I can pay again."

"Maybe. Something bad is coming, I think." Norbert puttered around with our breakfast fire, but he was sullen and preoccupied.

Something bad is coming. Where had I heard that line before? Wasn't it a favorite quip of Labidsas, the renowned Chipewyan magician? He always knew when his enemies were sending bad medicine his way. It was 4:00 A.M., and the sun was already breaking the eastern horizon. A few fishing teams were shoving off in their skiffs, the men heavily bedecked in rubberized pants and knee boots.

But half an hour later the early risers were back in the village. They were walking about in an anxious manner. Loud agitated voices could be heard. Something was amiss. Norbert went over to investigate while I hauled supplies to our skiff.

Norbert joined me a few moments later cursing a blue streak, "Damut'a fuckin' ta'gai!"

"Is something wrong?"

"Damn DNR is here!" Norbert shook his head in disgust. "Every year they try to stop us. Bad for fishing now."

As frustrated fishermen gathered in Dipper Lake village, news of an impending showdown emerged. The head of the Department of Natural Resources for the district, Ted Merck, had suddenly appeared for an unannounced inspection tour. Suspecting equipment violations and other transgressions, Merck and an RCMP officer had been covertly deposited by bush plane at a remote northern corner of Raven Lake. There they transferred to a motorized canoe and began pulling up illegal nets by means of a weighted dragline. Anyone caught using nets with a mesh size smaller than five inches faced certain conviction and penalties.

It was a touchy and volatile situation. Many fishermen had at least some older nets with three-inch mesh. Since part of the catch was intended for home consumption, the Chipewyan viewed the old nets as a valid means of fishing for food. But the DNR saw Raven Lake essentially as a commercial fishery where strict legal equipment requirements applied. With Merck prowling about, fishermen feared inspecting their nets. Yet, not checking them risked spoilage of the fish and loss of food and income. The anger of the fishermen increased throughout the day as the futility of their situation became apparent.

Frustrated by inactivity, fishermen assembled on a small island in Raven lake where an ice storage shed and fish weighing scale served as the transfer point for freighting out loads of fish by chartered bush plane. Ordinarily Billy Yarmchuk and other pilots would haul out several plane loads per day to fish dealers in Ile-a-la-Crosse. But the skies were empty on this day. The men milled around the ice shed feeding off each others' state of excitement and indignation. "DNR no good!" and "Damn DNR, we should shoot him!" quickly became favored invectives.

It was soon discovered that four men, who had gone to check their nets before sunrise, were probably unaware of the DNR's presence and in a vulnerable position. While vague plans were made to send a warning to the fishing team, a group of men climbed a high rock dome capped by a tall jack pine near the center of the island. A young man with binoculars scaled the tree and scanned the distant perimeter of the lake in all directions. When the DNR canoe was spotted several miles to the north, the island crowd became greatly excited. The fishermen hurled insults and obscenities from afar, becoming euphoric with laughter.

"DNR, sneaky guys, eh! Sneaky guys!" Norbert shouted from a perch near the top of the tree. "Well, let's see how sneaky we can get. Hey, Joachim, let me have your rifle. I think I can shoot them from here."

Joachim Deneyou passed his .308 rifle to Norbert who drew a sharp bead on the offending visitors. He paused to adjust for the distant trajectory. I winced as he squeezed off an imaginary round. "DNR no good!" Norbert yelled. The point was made, and the crowd howled with laughter. But their giddiness was matched by nervous anticipation of the confrontation which would surely follow.

Shortly before noon the DNR canoe appeared on the western horizon, heading full speed for the island. Piled high with confiscated gill nets, glistening fish still intact, Merck's canoe rode dangerously low in the water and nearly capsized in the choppy waves along the shore. The fishermen sat silently a few yards away, hunkered around several fires laden with roasting whitefish and simmering tea pails. Their eyes focused intently on the two officers walking slowly up the embankment.

Merck wore a perpetual smirk, strained and ingenuous. The young RCMP officer trailing a few feet behind maintained an expressionless demeanor. The pair stopped and stared accusingly at the assembled crowd, but no words were exchanged. Merck shot a peevish look in my direction and quickly turned away. I imagined him thinking: "Research, my ass! Goddamn American up here running with these outlaw Chips."

It was an awkward moment. The last time I had seen Merck was nine months earlier at the trapper's meeting when his assistant had tried to scuttle my plans. But I had no quarrel with Merck. He had a thankless job to perform, and the cards were stacked against him. The problem was that the Chipewyan detested him. Indeed, they despised all hard-nosed DNR officers. Merck was like Scrooge coming to take food from children's mouths and hard-earned cash from people's pockets. Nonetheless, getting hauled in on an illegal fishing charge would do my project no good. As far as I knew Norbert's outfit was clean, but what about the other teams?

The awkward impasse was broken by George Muskrat, a young talkative band councilor who strode boldly out of the ice shed and greeted the visitors jovially:

"Hi, Mr. Merck! How's your trip? Didn't think you'd get here so soon!"

Merck was irritated by these insincere pleasantries, and he moved closer to the assembled fishermen. He sat on his haunches facing the crowd a few feet away. The RCMP officer remained nearby, but he turned his back to the crowd and stared grimly at the lake. Another uncomfortable silence ensued.

"Catch a lot of fish?" Muskrat asked with deadpan sarcasm. He pursed his lips in the direction of the visitors' canoe.

"Yup!" Merck exploded in anger. "There's a helluva lot of small mesh nets in this lake!" His face turned several shades of red as he glared at the fishermen. A silent face-off continued for another moment.

Norbert then disarmed Merck with an unexpected query: "When are you going to pay us for that portage job?" It was a reference to trail maintenance work around rapids on the Churchill River. The work was directed by the DNR and carried out by local Chipewyan.

Merck was compelled to explain delays in the distribution of paychecks. During this distraction August McLeod, one of the oldest fishermen at Raven lake, beached his skiff nearby. Several of his nets had been confiscated during the DNR's morning patrol. He was profoundly angered by this loss. The old man ran with alarming speed up the embankment.

"Why is RCMP here?" McLeod bellowed at Merck. "Is there trouble here? Somebody call for RCMP?"

"No, no! No trouble," Merck backpedaled with forced calmness. "He's my friend, and he's never seen the country up here . . ."

"You're afraid of the people here!" McLeod interrupted. His booming voice echoed off the granite dome behind us. "That's why you bring RCMP. You're afraid!"

"No. He just wanted to see the country, and I brought him along," Merck repeated wearily.

Incensed by this explanation, McLeod had the final word before storming off to his skiff: "You're just afraid of the people here, that's all!"

In the wake of McLeod's angry display, indignant murmurs spread through the crowd. Norbert became less circumspect. He bluntly questioned Merck: "What time are you going to leave?"

"As soon as a plane comes in," Merck muttered. "I guess that'll be after you guys have checked your nets."

Sensing the futility of further interrogation, Merck retreated from the crowd and sat in silence with the RCMP officer. This was a welcome sign for the fishermen who sensed that the confrontation was nearing an end. They talked with renewed enthusiasm about their fishing plans. George Muskrat entertained the men with a comic tale of a former close call with DNR officers in the bush. While the narration was in Chipewyan, Merck and the RCMP officer had little trouble interpreting Muskrat's animated style or the howls of laughter from the crowd.

Hours passed before a small bush plane arrived. After loading on their cargo of confiscated nets and fish, however, Merck and the officer returned to their canoe and headed toward the south end of Raven Lake. The bush pilot followed the wake of the canoe, making long taxis punctuated by brief low altitude flights. The fishermen were mystified by this development. Uncertain of the officers' intentions or whereabouts, they were reluctant to resume fishing.

"Bad day, Dastloze," Norbert shook his head. "C'mon, now we go hunting for DNR."

Norbert and I, and several other teams, rode skiffs into a maze of islands near the lake's south end. From a distant vantage point, we spotted the officers caching their canoe on a rocky island before boarding the plane. But the overloaded Cessna had difficulty taxing. After several futile attempts to lift off, the plane returned to the small island where hundreds of pounds of fish and nets were jettisoned on the shore. The fishermen watched with growing fascination, and then horror, as Merck and his partner soaked the heap with gasoline and set it ablaze. Moments later the plane ascended through rising plumes of black smoke and disappeared over the horizon.

The aftermath of the fish burning was marked by a rapid exodus from Raven Lake. "Everybody's scared of the DNR now," George Muskrat observed. Within a day most teams had collected their remaining nets and supplies and returned to Patuanak.

A few fishermen were reluctant to leave without harvesting some of the 25,000 pounds of fish remaining on the legal commercial quota for the lake. They alone, however, could not catch enough fish per day to finance the necessary bush plane transport. These men, too, quickly departed. It was a bitter pill to swallow. In effect, the DNR had shut

Fishing partners John Day (left) and Louis Janvier (right) spread gill nets to dry at La Ronge village.

down the Chipewyan's highly productive fishing operations on Raven Lake for two consecutive summers. This was no trifling matter, since half the annual income for most families derived from commercial fishing.

Most of the fishing teams traveled back to Patuanak together caravan-style. Norbert and I were among them. We helped one another portage around Dipper Rapids, a treacherous set of falls that had destroyed many skiffs and claimed a few lives over the years. It was said that Patuanak's old missionary priest, Father Moraud, once took a canoe-load of lumber through this maelstrom. The canoe and lumber were destroyed. Moraud emerged unscathed, a fact which enhanced his reputation among the Chipewyan.

At the head of the portage, a large fire was built. Tea pails were produced for a final collective meal before reaching the village. Despite the somber mood, men took pleasure in walking around the fire, retrieving pieces of dried moose meat and other morsels from each other's open grub boxes. This simple expression of reciprocity and solidarity, and the leisurely meal which followed, brought immense satisfaction.

After the men had repacked their skiffs for the final leg of the journey, George Muskrat remained alone near the fire. He seemed lost in thought as he chewed on the raw air bladder of a jackfish, considered a delicacy by some people. Addressing no one in particular he asked: "So how are we going to put food on the table for our families now? Our families have to eat."

Word of the Raven Lake confrontation quickly spread, raising the ire of the Patuanak community. People had little time to speculate on the long-range implications of their battle with the DNR, however. Within a day of the fishermen's return, a monstrous forest fire broke out on the east side of Shagwenaw Lake, a mere four miles from the village. Hellish sounds from fire-fueled winds and exploding timbers carried ominously across the water. Day turned to night as the sun disappeared behind billowing pillars of smoke.

Rumors ran rampant. Some DNR officials believed the fire was a retaliatory act, that Chipewyan intentionally torched the bush to compensate for loss of income at Raven Lake. Others maintained that it was a lightning-induced fire. At that very moment there were 31 forest fires burning simultaneously across northern Saskatchewan, including a large conflagration in the rugged Buffalo Hills near Dillon. Despite the heavy snows of early winter, the spring had been rainless. Forests were tinder dry. Whatever the truth of the matter, the DNR was now compelled to hire local crews of fire fighters to combat a blaze that could burn for weeks.

Village life was thrown into turmoil as able-bodied men of all ages were literally grabbed on the spot. Recruits were permitted only enough time to pack a bedroll before departing. Within hours 35 men were sent to the fire. By the end of the day at least another 20 would be needed. All of this was happening on Treaty Day, the annual ceremonial occasion when the federal government acknowledged the registered status of English River Band members with an annuity payment of five dollars per person. On this day, however, the proceedings were cut short. Even the attending RCMP officer arrived in a drab work uniform rather than his ceremonial reds.

The chaotic scene in Patuanak mirrored my own conflicting emotions. My year of fieldwork was rapidly coming to an end. Only a few weeks remained to wrap up dozens of loose ends, including map work, family histories, and subsistence ecology questionnaires with key informants. Did I want to spend that time battling flames and smoke? I felt it would be selfish not to volunteer. Moreover, if the fire grew out of control, the DNR had the authority to conscript every last soul. At that very moment locally designated fire foremen were scouring the village to fill out their crews. Some men who claimed to get "sick on smoke," or otherwise detested fire fighting work, hid out in caches and storehouses.

"Dastloze, you're still here?" A strange man in ragged, grimy clothing stood in the doorway of my cabin. He was out of breath and perspiring heavily. Bloodshot eyes burned like coals in his soot-blackened face. But his knowing smile was the giveaway.

"Holy shit! Norbert, is that you!"

"Yup!" Norbert Ptarmigan flashed a grin. "I need one more man for my crew."

"I was afraid of that. Don't you want experienced people on the fire?"

"*Ta'gai!*" Norbert cursed and shot me a dirty look. "Remember, we're sits'eni now."

"Okay, okay. Count me in. When do we leave?"

"We go now! My skiff's here. Don't worry. If fire burns down, maybe you can quit after a week."

And if the fire becomes a raging inferno, what then? Maybe I'd be pinned down in fire camps for the rest of the summer. As we drifted across the lake I brooded about my future. We traveled with Charlie Charles, another of Norbert's last-minute recruits. Charlie was a lummox of a man, a strapping 6-foot 6-incher with broad shoulders and ham-sized hands. He had done time in the slammer in Prince Albert, apparently on larceny charges. Yet, he was remarkably good-humored and reserved even by Chipewyan standards. Charlie seemed like the proverbial gentle giant.

The eastern half of Shagwenaw Lake was shrouded in thick smoke pouring off the fire. Norbert slowed the skiff to a crawl and navigated by sheer instinct. An eerie background din of fire-fueled updrafts and groaning, snapping timbers grew louder as we approached land. Occasionally, flaring pillars of fire shot up hundreds of feet above the trees. A childhood memory of an old engraving flashed through my mind. It was a medieval artist's depiction of hell.

A cluster of tents emerged in the swirling smoke ahead. It was the temporary fire camp nestled at the head of a small inlet near an old dogsled trail. Suddenly the skiff began rocking violently. Charlie was on his feet. His huge frame lurched from side to side as he did a frantic 360° scan of the murky surroundings. He talked in agitated tones with Norbert whose gaze was now riveted on something faintly visible across the inlet to the northwest. Charlie's behavior was unsettling. Did he know something about this fire that could save our hides?

"Charlie, what's wrong?" I asked as our skiff drifted to shore.

"I don't know how to say it in English," Charlie winced as he held a wet bandanna over his nose and mouth. "Something bad."

"You don't mean the fire?" I expected to see a monstrous wall of flame engulf the camp at any moment.

"No, not fire. It's over there on that *hochela* [peninsula]." Charlie gestured with his head across the inlet to a small point of land. "No good. Screaming place."

The screaming place. Months had passed since anyone had mentioned it in my presence. I had not forgotten Jimmy Stonypoint's alarming stories about the dreadful cries that emanated from this part of the lake. Whether a bushman, a bushman's ghost, or some other unspeakable thing lurked here, the Chipewyan ordinarily avoided the area like the plague. It was a cruel twist of fate that they were now forced to fight a forest fire in this extraordinarily bad place.

For several days any concerns about the screaming place took a back seat to more urgent demands. Warm daytime temperatures and high winds fanned the fire into a roaring conflagration. It quickly advanced southward, jumping the old dog sled trail, and burned for several miles before coming to a momentary halt at a small river. Fortunately, the fire was contained to the west by Shagwenaw Lake and to the east by *Tabiketwe* or "fish net lake." The country to the north was a major problem, however. It stretched unobstructed for eight miles or more to the Churchill River. That land was filled with mature stands of white spruce, a promising source of timber if the community ever became involved in commercial logging in future years.

Preventing the blaze from advancing northward became the top priority. A several-mile fire line was built, primarily with shovels, pickaxes and portable water bags. Eventually, a couple gas-powered pumps were hauled in to draw water out of streams and ponds and keep the line dampened. Eight crews of six to eight men each maintained the line for 12-hour shifts. Four crews worked during the day while the other four tackled night duty. As a member of Norbert's crew, I pulled the day shift. But that distinction soon became meaningless. One quickly lost track of shifts and days. The long daylight hours of approaching summer solstice, combined with oppressive heat and smoke, seemed to suspend time. People staggered around the bush looking like dazed coal miners and smelling like Smithfield hams.

Our camp soon split into two units to better patrol the east and west ends of the fire line. In addition to the line crews, there were cooking crews, usually older men who kept large pots of coffee and kettles of boiled beef tongues and other fare at the ready. Joachim Deneyou, one of the cooks, also had the unenviable task of rousting sleeping men out of their tents to begin their shifts. It seemed fitting that Joachim, the official village child chaser, was herding adults as well. Another man was in charge of the supply tent. It held the food provisions and the ledger where crew signed on for duty. It was also a small canteen where men could make minor purchases against their paychecks. Ironically, cigarettes were the commodity of choice.

Overseeing the entire operation was the fire boss, Nap Malboeuf, a middle-aged Métis Cree man from Ile-a-la-Crosse. Of excitable temperament, Malboeuf spoke little English. Rather, he communicated in Cree with the older Chipewyan men who were also fluent in that language. Malboeuf worried incessantly about cooping. Exhausted fire crews sometimes were known to wander away from the line and sleep. It was a dangerous practice which could imperil an entire operation. Norbert, at least, kept a tight reign on his crew.

By the fifth day it appeared that the northern line was holding. There was hope that the fire would burn itself out in the center. To be certain, however, Malboeuf radiophoned DNR headquarters for a "waterbomber." The lumbering amphibious aircraft could suck up thousands of pounds of water from the lake and dump them on flaring "hot spots" at the core of the fire.

On the evening of the fifth day the retiring day crews were in an exuberant mood. Someone produced a deck of cards, and in mere minutes the supply tent was emptied of cigarettes. The latter became valued currency in spirited sessions of "lowball" poker. A circle of men knelt around a canvas tarp, in the same way that elderly folks knelt on the floors of tents and houses in the village. No one ever gambled sitting at a table. After each hand was dealt, the victor tucked the winnings emphatically between his knees with the forceful sweep of one arm. In less than an hour, 70-year-old Isaac Saizi, widely regarded as a fearless lowball player, picked all his competitors clean. After tossing a few packs to the losing players, he strolled back to his tent with a flour sack bulging with cigarettes.

Charlie Charles, also a card player of some repute, was not to be outdone, however. He stood in the center of the camp and bellowed loudly: *"Bal'ai, bal'ai, bal'ai!"*

Several men who had been sleeping peacefully near the supply tent suddenly scrambled to their feet and ran into the bush. Others moved furtively toward the edge of the camp. Yet others, wearing sheepish grins and shaking their heads in a resigned manner, congregated around Charlie. A couple of men attempted to extricate Isaac from his tent with little success. The air was suddenly tense with anticipation. Charlie beckoned me with head signals to join the crowd.

"Norbert, what the hell is going on?" I asked.

"I don't like this bal'ai," Norbert Ptarmigan snorted contemptuously as he slinked away toward the bush.

"But what is it?"

"Go ask Charlie. You'll see."

On impulse, I joined a dozen men assembled near Charlie. A couple dozen others observed from a safe distance, giving the distinct impression that something unpleasant was in the offing. With mock solemnity, Charlie ordered: "Okay, give me your shirts!"

We obediently removed our shirts, an odd assortment of soiled and torn garments, and threw them in a pile at Charlie's feet. The latter did a quick about-face to avoid seeing the owners of the clothes. Then he marched off officiously toward the cook tent while scribbling the names of the participants on a piece of paper. Tension mounted as Charlie selected Joachim Deneyou as his henchman. Joachim approached the pile of shirts with the seriousness of a brain surgeon. He frowned and studied the pile cautiously. Then he thrust his hands in and removed the first shirt, holding it aloft for all to see.

From his hiding place behind the cook tent, Charlie announced the first name on his list: "Emilien Whitefish!"

A hefty older man stepped forward and received his gift from Joachim. It was a tight-fitting knit pullover which barely reached the top of his ample belly. As Emilien struggled with the shirt, the onlookers howled hysterically. And so it was with each succeeding selection. Moreover, the new shirts could not be given back. Bal'ai was for keeps. Smaller men invariably received over-sized garments that made them look ludicrous. A number of recipients were infuriated with the wretched condition of their new shirts and huffily threw them into the cooking fire. This too drew volleys of hysterical laughter. By the end of the session, participants and onlookers alike were rolling on the ground.

"Dastloze!" Charlie announced. I was one of the last on his list. He handed me what was once a fancy white cowboy shirt. It now resembled an oily gas station rag. Surely a few more days of fire fighting could do it no harm. As soon as I put it on, however, I began to itch. Nearly a week would pass before I discovered the lice.

While there were dissenters, most of the camp seemed genuinely appreciative of bal'ai. Was it the sheer spectacle, the opportunity to laugh at one's fellows, or indeed the act of exchange which made it compelling? Gambling with cards and other means of scrambling or redistributing wealth and property were also great passions among the Chipewyan. As I mused on this problem, Charlie added a new twist: "Okay, now give me your pants. Then I want your boots."

I was preparing to hide out in the bush with Norbert when our ceremony was interrupted. Something or somebody was moving through the smoke haze east of the camp. A moose outrunning the fire, perhaps? In the next instant, three men staggered into our circle. They belonged to a crew working out of the other camp on the west end of the fire line. Several miles out of their normal range, the men looked haggard and not at all amused by our antics.

Nap Malboeuf was the first to greet them: "Hey, we can't cover the line if you boys bunch up at our end. What's going on?"

"We're staying here," one of the visitors announced sullenly as he dropped his bedroll. His eyes had a vacant look that betrayed sleepless nights. "That thing, that screaming thing is back."

I could not place the man. His hair was disheveled, his face smeared with ash and grime. Yet his voice had a familiar raspy timbre. I glanced at Norbert who nodded and whispered: "Yup, that's John Lynx. I guess he's back too."

Since my strange dreams at Cache Lake, I had pushed John Lynx out of my mind. He had done his prison time months before but seemed to be steering clear of Patuanak. Now, out of the blue, he was at the forest fire. And awful screaming sounds were stirring the air. Surely this was coincidence?

According to Lynx and his companions the west-end camp was in turmoil. Sporadic, frightful cries and wails, "like somebody dying," or "something dying," had kept people on edge for more than a day. The noises unmistakably were emanating from the nearby peninsula. Men on the west-end crews were talking about a wholesale move to our camp or, barring that, an early return to the village. As Lynx's story unfolded, looks of excitement, consternation and alarm spread across the faces of his audience.

"Well, maybe we should go and look for that thing, eh?" Frank Whitefish interrupted with a display of bravado. "We should find out what it is."

"It's no use," Lynx replied shaking his head wearily. "Some guys already went over there. You can't find nothing." He described the trek of three daring souls who had probed the thick bush of the peninsula on the previous day. Each time they advanced toward the source of the dreadful wailing, the sound mysteriously shifted location. That was unnerving enough. When one of the searchers felt something grasping his shoulders from behind, he nearly lost consciousness. The badly shaken trio fled the scene. News of their strange encounter had only heightened fears and tensions at the west-end camp.

"Holy smokin' anyways," Joachim Deneyou muttered anxiously. "Fire's almost out now. I think we should go back to Patuanak."

"Nobody's going fuckin' nowhere!" Nap Malboeuf shouted as he stormed angrily out of the supply tent. He was outraged that people might be shirking work to chase phantom voices. Moreover, he had a potential mutiny on his hands. "Tag'ai! This fire's still hot. We need another week to kill it, eh. Now, I'm going over and check the other camp. Norbert, I'm making you the boss here, so keep these potlickers in line until I get back." Malboeuf grabbed a pick axe and waterbag and tramped off into the bush. Norbert Ptarmigan appeared a bit ill at ease with the sudden elevation of his status.

"Boss, eh?" Frank Whitefish snorted with mock derision. Although a few years younger than his cousin, he enjoyed a spirited joking relationship with Norbert, Antoine and the other older Ptarmigan brothers. Frank nodded knowingly to a few companions standing nearby. In an instant, the men pounced on Norbert. The latter struggled valiantly to slip away, but soon the men were carrying Norbert like a thrashing steer toward a nearby pond.

"Gotta be baptized to be a boss, Norbert!" Frank giggled as the men held their captive aloft over the edge of the water.

The camp crowd was amused by the diversion which, at least for a moment, took minds off the screaming thing. The baptizing crew hesitated for a mere second. Norbert seized the opportunity. Like a squirming anaconda, he wriggled and rotated furiously until his captors dropped him. Without uttering a word, Norbert strolled nonchalantly back to the cook fire and sat down for a cup of tea. His composure was hardly ruffled. In a sense, Norbert was playing out a scripted role. His strength was legendary in the community. Occasionally it had to be tested. After all, he was one of the few who could break a cooked beaver femur in his bare hands, a certain sign of power and hunting prowess. Indeed, Norbert had once broken a raw femur, an almost unheard of feat.

I looked around for John Lynx. Thankfully, he had not partaken in the dunking party. His competitiveness with the Ptarmigan brothers was far from benign. Nothing good could come from a confrontation between him and Norbert. But the man's absence made me nervous. What was he up to? Lynx was prone to dramatic appearances under unsettling circumstances. And if he had a stash of alcohol somewhere, the forest fire might become the least of our worries.

Later I discovered Lynx sitting with Charlie Charles in a secluded corner of the camp. They had an affinity borne of common prison experience. Both men sported an assortment of jailhouse tattoos. The normally quiet Charlie was now quite voluble. Together the pair exuded a jaded cynicism and knowledge of the outside world that few locals questioned. They boasted at length of sexual conquests in farflung communities, each man claiming women that the other had not "tried."

"Well, I know one thing," Lynx said wistfully. "Those guys hiding out in Patuanak have all the women now."

"Yah, those little potlickers should be fighting fire," Charlie replied shaking his head. "You know, Isaac Saizi was just talking about old times when we all used to travel around together. It was much easier for us men to control our women in those days, eh. But now? The women are in the village, and the men are always in the bush. It's no good."

A Chipewyan man breaks a cooked beaver femur, a ritual path for obtaining power and hunting prowess.

"No, it's not right. But I think we've got some girls right here."
Lynx's voice became menacing as he gestured toward a young man with
delicate facial features and shoulder length hair standing near the supply tent.

"Who? Isaac's kid?" Charlie laughed in disbelief. "Sure, he's pretty.
Maybe he'd better watch out with you around. He's a friend of Gilbert's,
you know."

"So what. Gilbert's kinda pretty himself."

"Yah, but he's in for two months down in P.A. [Prince Albert]."

"Tag'ai! Nobody told me." Lynx's hard edge dissolved. "What's he in
for?"

"Went haywire on bootleg wine, just before you got back. Pulled a
knife on some guy in Buffalo," Charlie confided. "But I don't think it was
Gilbert's fault. Must be some way to get our friend out of there."

An invisible curtain had lifted. The presence of others in the camp
became a painful reality for John Lynx. He hung his head dejectedly.
When he looked up a few moments later his jaw was trembling and his
eyes glared venomously. With alarming fury, he began beating the
ground with his fist. Then, addressing no one in particular, he bellowed
out his rage: "These people around here don't care. All they know is a
little deuces wild and a few prayers. Shit, they don't know bugger-all!
Nobody helped me. They were all glad to see me go. Four fucking months
for breaking a few 50-cent windows!"

The camp grew uncomfortably quiet. Men scattered to their tents.
For a few seconds Lynx's voice punctuated the silence in a frenzied wail.
It approached the tortured cry that had alarmed the entire village on
that terrifying night nearly a year before. It was a sound that still
haunted my dreams. I retired to Norbert's tent, but nagging questions
kept me awake. What dreadful thing was really out there on that peninsula? What could create such havoc? Was it more desperate or
frightening than what faced us in our own camp?

When the day crews were rousted the next morning, Malboeuf had
not returned. More disturbing, perhaps, was the fact that John Lynx
was gone. No one knew where he was or when he had departed. In my
morning fog, I began to wonder whether his presence the previous
evening had been some kind of collective dream or hysteria.

Not one for idle speculation, Norbert soon had the crews out
patrolling the line. But the men's hearts were not in the work. They
wandered about in a desultory fashion picking at the occasional smol-
dering tree root. It was a windless day, and the remnant smoke hung
over the landscape like a heavy shroud.

Late in the day our people encountered a crew working out of the
west-end camp. Aside from Lynx and his companions, it was the first

time we had seen any west enders since the screaming started. While none of these men had been members of the exploring trio on the peninsula, they all had endured several sleepless nights listening to unearthly cries echo across the inlet. They seemed eager to share their burden with us.

"It's bad, for sure, slini [evil]. It's like somebody dying out there," one man said with a shudder.

"You mean like what the old Rats heard?" Charlie Charles asked. This was a reference to an elderly couple, Prosper and Cecile Rat, who had been among the first to hear the disturbing sounds nearly a decade earlier. They had camped on the peninsula for fall hunting and were greeted by blood-curdling cries. After the third night they had fled to the village never to return to the east side of Shagwenaw Lake.

"The Rats, yah. Must be. It sounds like no animal, you know. It's hotet'slini [bushman], for sure."

"Could be a bushman," another man added tentatively. "It's like somebody crying, somebody hurt real bad. But sometimes it sounds a little bit like a dog or a wolf too."

"A dog or a wolf?" I inquired. I felt reluctant breaking into the conversation, but suddenly Eredk'ali, the wolf-turned-man, was on my mind. "Would a bushman sound like that?"

"Could be. I don't know. I heard something like it before, long time ago. When I was a boy my family lived up on Cree Lake. It was mostly us Kesyehot'ine, us Chips up there. But there was one family of Crees staying up there on the west side of the lake. Their people were from Waterhen Reserve, you know. And they were up hunting for the winter. That was in 1945. The old man in the family was a pretty strong magician, a medicine man. But he died in the springtime. Well, his family buried him on a little island there on the west side of the lake. Later when our people traveled by that island you could hear a voice crying. It was a man crying, but then it changed to a wolf, and then a loon, a raven, and a coyote, and then back to a man crying again."

"I remember that!" Isaac Saizi replied excitedly "My family was up at Cree Lake too. We heard that old *manitukasiu* [Cree for magician or medicine man] crying after he died."

"But this thing here on Shagwenaw is different," one of the visitors insisted. "It sounds more like a human, not like different animals."

"Well, maybe it's not a medicine man, eh." Isaac replied. "But could be it's *nedi*, old Indian medicine. Sometimes that little orange plant we collect can make a noise. That's what the old people say."

Old people? At 70 years, Isaac was our camp elder. My head ached as I attempted to digest the rapid-fire conversation. It was conducted in a mix of Chipewyan and English, and new theories about the screaming were emerging by the minute. The suspense was horrendous. Some deep cultural truth, a hidden layer of meaning, was about to be revealed, or so it seemed. And I would I miss it because I was exhausted and out in the bush fighting a forest fire without a decent notebook. I could not shake the feeling that something momentous was about to happen now that I had to end my fieldwork.

"I don't think this is medicine, Isaac," one of the west enders said shaking his head gravely "It sounds real bad. Remember, it's the place where that bushman died back in the '30s. Died from poison my Grandpa said."

"Yah, it must be hotet'slini. Or ghost of hotet'slini," Norbert concluded. He rose from the circle of seated men and scanned the charred landscape. "Wind's coming up! Better get back to work. Hurry, hurry, before fire boss comes!"

Reluctantly, the crews fanned out over the line. Hours later, toward the end of our shift, I overhead snatches of conversation between Isaac and Charlie. They were eager to return to Patuanak, and they noticed my interest.

"Dastloze, we think the screams could be something else," Charlie muttered in a low voice.

"You don't think it's a bushman?" I asked.

"Maybe" Isaac inserted. "But maybe it's really *wiligo*."

"Wiligo?" My heart raced. The term sounded like a variant of *witigo* or *Windigo*. Many of the Algonquian-speaking peoples, including the Cree, believed in a cannibalistic monster, the Windigo, that prowled the forest depths and devoured people. It was not common in the beliefs and mythology of the Athapaskans. Yet, the Patuanak Chipewyan lived on the edge of Cree country. Over the years they had intermarried with some of the Crees, and they had both great respect for and fear of Cree magico-medicinal power. "What is wiligo?"

"It's some kind of beast," Charlie whispered nervously.

"Yah, it's a beast. But it's very greedy," Isaac added.

"How do you mean greedy?" I inquired.

"You can tell if it's wiligo because it eats a lot. It even eats its own lips away. That's how greedy it is, eh." Isaac pulled his own lips back in a ghoulish grimace and circled his teeth with a forefinger.

"Yah, wiligo eats itself, and it eats other people too," Charlie observed with revulsion. "That's what the Cree people say."

Magicians, medicinal plants, bushmen, Windigos. What next? As we trudged back to camp my mind sifted the possibilities. I feared there would be no resolution to the dilemma, even though the prevailing view seemed to hold a bushman or bushman's ghost accountable. The Chipewyan themselves were struggling to make cultural sense of the experience. And at that very moment the awful thing continued screaming as the forest burned.

When we reached our camp, I had a premonition that we were not alone. There was a shadow near Norbert's tent. Someone was hovering over it. The image gave me a start as it replicated a chilling scene near my own tent in the village months before.

"John, is that you?" I called. "People have been looking for you."

"Tag'ai," a voice cursed. Then John Lynx stepped out of the shadows. "I've been looking for the fire boss. Where the hell is that guy? I gotta get back to Patuanak today."

"He's at the other camp, I think. What's going on in Patuanak?"

"I don't know. There's bugger-all to do here. I should be out hunting, eh. I'd like to get a nice moose for my family. There's a good *enagure* [wallow] up the Studer River where I can hunt. After I get that moose, I'll have a good meal. Boy, my mouth will just be covered with fat!" John drew his lips back in a grinning grimace and circled his teeth with a forefinger.

A couple weeks after the fire had burned out, I sat on the HBC dock with my year's worth of supplies and field notes waiting for a bush plane to take me away. Rose Deneyou was busy scraping a moosehide nearby. Her husband, Armand, sat in the shade of a storehouse with Isaac Saizi swapping stories and puffing on Black Cats. Young children shrieked with glee as they leaped off the dock into the chilly water. A team of fishermen offloaded boxes of whitefish and pickerel from their skiff.

The scene was a haunting replay of my arrival day. In a year's time I was back where I had started. Yet, I had learned a great deal from my Chipewyan hosts. Not the least of this was a new awareness of my own frailties and capabilities. It was an untouted reward of fieldwork. My apprenticeship, I finally realized, was just beginning. As the bush plane buzzed over the village, I had a sudden desire to flee back to my cabin. What if I simply stayed? Some of my friends had suggested that I could settle in Patuanak and make a life here. Now, the very idea of it filled me with an unexpected and painful longing.

Antoine Ptarmigan strolled down to the dock. I had said my good-byes to almost everyone I knew, but Antoine had been away fishing.

"So Dastloze, when are you coming back?" he asked.

"I wish I knew. Could be a couple years, maybe more."

"There's a lot of fur up on Ass Wiped Lake. If you stay, we'll be sits'eni."

"I'd like nothing better, Decak'ai."

"You know, next time you come here, this place could be different."

Indeed, monumental and ominous changes already were afoot in northern Saskatchewan. Uranium deposits had been discovered at remote places like Cluff Lake far to the north. A couple of Antoine's cousins had just departed to help clear the bush from one of the mine sites. A network of new roads was proposed to lessen the isolation of some of the smaller communities. By the end of the 1970s, Patuanak could have its own gravel spur road to the outside.

"I've heard the talk," I replied. "What do you think about this road business?"

"I'll be a hunter and fisherman 'til I die. But if that goes haywire, we're gonna need work. The road could bring jobs. That's the good part."

"And the bad part?"

"A road will bring more kontue [liquor], more stealing, accidents, outsiders, fighting, murders, and . . ." Antoine paused as he gazed across Shagwenaw Lake toward an expanse of blackened forest, " . . . even worse, the road will bring more bushmen."

Aftershock

After departing Chipewyan country in 1972, returning to my previous life proved more difficult than I had imagined. I felt perpetually distracted by thoughts of Patuanak, Cache Lake and the bush beyond. Ravens, wolves and forest fires haunted my dreams. I sorely missed my partners and friends. I even missed Dastloze, an alter ego that had no relevance in Minneapolis.

At the same time, however, I suffered a strong reluctance to intellectualize about my experiences. Living with the Chipewyan had seemed too personal and emotionally freighted to become grist for some academic mill. Yet, without analysis and interpretation of the field data, I could hardly expect to write a dissertation, let alone pursue a career as an anthropologist. As time dragged on I feared I had made a big mistake in rejecting Antoine's parting offer: "If you stay, we'll be sits'eni again."

H. Russell Bernard (1994:158–64) perceptively identifies typical stages of participant observation. These are a sequence of situations and responses which ethnographic fieldworkers commonly experience:

1. Initial contact.
2. Shock.
3. Discovering the obvious.
4. The break.
5. Focusing.
6. Exhaustion, the second break, and frantic activity.
7. Leaving the field.

With some modification, Bernard's stages reflect the progress of my own fieldwork. For better or worse, I had no prolonged "break" period to achieve distance and perspective and to provide my hosts with some distance from me. In effect, my real break was the year between the Han and the Chipewyan work.

Nonetheless, the Han prepared me in unforeseen ways for the Chipewyan. "Culture shock," that state of anxiety produced by unfamiliar surroundings and unpredictable behavior, typically is experienced early in one's fieldwork. The shock I felt in adjusting to Chipewyan society was probably lessened by having worked in a related Athapaskan community a short time previously.

What might be added to Bernard's model is the reverse culture shock or "aftershock" many researchers experience after leaving the field. Once-familiar behaviors at home now seem strange, inappropriate and irritating. Distance and separation from one's newfound field friends and newfound community create a profound sense of loss. The enormous task of facing a pile of field notes and translating them into persuasive, intelligible anthropology stir feelings of ambivalence, dread and incompetence. Depending on the circumstances, aftershock can last for months or years.

With the benefit of hindsight, I have come to view aftershock as a necessary, if not desirable, outcome of the research process. It is the humbling realization that the cultural assumptions underlying one's own life, as well as the lives of others, can never be taken for granted. The shock of confronting these assumptions firsthand, close-up in the field over a prolonged period eventually fosters an understanding of their salience. It is one of the great lessons of anthropology, too easily overlooked in an era when short-term projects and literary critical approaches threaten to remove anthropologists from fieldwork and distance scholars from people.

In retrospect, becoming an active apprentice hunter-fisherman and sits'eni among the Chipewyan offered both advantages and disadvantages in the conduct of my fieldwork.

On the positive side:

1. *Internalization of productive behavior.* The most obvious advantage of active participation is an understanding of the technical aspects of daily work routines, scheduling practices, interrelationships between environment and behavior, and the dynamics of labor allocation. By learning to work as a Chipewyan male, I internalized considerable knowledge about traveling across the landscape, hunting techniques, bush camp maintenance, and related matters.

2. *Access to the larger community.* As a working partner in several hunting and fishing teams, I was linked through prerogatives of friendship and reciprocity to my partners' families and kin. These ties quickly ramified, paving the way for relationships with a broad spectrum of individuals in Patuanak and other communities.

On the negative side:

1. *Time and energy commitments.* At times the apprentice role was taxing physically and psychologically. The daily demands of bush work, social interaction, and data gathering and processing could be overwhelming. The problem was compounded by the lack of privacy which accompanied active participation.

Since I frequently shared the same tent with the people I studied, it was difficult to move in and out of an observational mode. Relevant behavior was omnipresent.

2. *Observational constraints and bias.* The active participant is in a position to comment most pointedly on behaviors that are condensed in time and space: productive routines, technological procedures, economic tasks, and the like. Even if these areas are the focus of research, however, the fieldworker may be isolated from much useful information. While I became knowledgeable about the male bush economy, I had limited exposure to women's work and women's lives generally.

3. *Identity and detachment.* The close personal relationships developed through active participation can cloud the boundary between such roles as "researcher" and "friend" and, therefore, call into question the objectivity or neutrality of the anthropologist. While the intimacy of this style of fieldwork permits internalization of much knowledge, there is also the potential for internalizing attitudes and perspectives which are not widely held in the community or which poorly reflect economic and social realities. There is little question that I empathized most strongly with the hopes and fears of the Ptarmigans and their immediate network of kin. Hopefully, I did not project their views on other families, or worse, ignore the actions and attitudes of people they disliked.

Many years later in northern Finland I would confront the same challenges of apprenticeship again, this time as an ethnographer-farm laborer. However, the Chipewyan had prepared me well for this new experience. On balance, I would argue that the advantages of active participation outweigh the deleterious effects. The potential for internalizing meaningful skills and behaviors, combined with accessibility to important social categories and dynamics, readily offset the considerable time and energy expenditures and problems of bias and detachment.

Moreover, some useful insights about ecology and culture emerged from my first year's work with the Chipewyan. The community's "annual economic cycle" had an identifiable temporal and spatial structure defined, in part, by the movements and extractive activities of dozens of hunting, trapping and fishing teams. The cycle was a cultural means of distributing people across a vast territory at appropriate intervals to intercept needed resources which could be converted to food products and cash income. Moreover, the very rhythm of the cycle, the repetitive ebb and flow of teams in and out of the settlements, the exchange of fishing camp for trapping camp, was socially and psychologically reinforcing. And since seasonal population dispersions and concentrations had been part of Chipewyan life for generations, the cycle was compatible with the people's way of viewing the world.

My early analyses emphasized the locational or spatial organization of communities as a fundamental form of ecological adaptation for boreal forest hunter-gatherers. More than any other activity, trapping accounted for the most dramatic fluctuations in seasonal settlement patterns among the southern Chipewyan and was also responsible for the greatest spatial dispersion of people at any point during the annual cycle. Moreover, trapping productivity (as measured by numbers of animals harvested and cash income) varied positively with trapping area size and distance away from the central village. That is, the most productive hunters operated the largest traplines in the more remote sections of the territory. Even so, status and prestige were not linked directly to economic "success" in the Western sense. Chipewyan individuals and families alike could not maintain their integrity in the community without participating in a reciprocal flow of money, goods and services. By the same token, a Chipewyan trapper of average ability who could provide for his family and also share food and possessions with others was truly successful by community standards. He would have an esteemed reputation as a "good hunter" or "good trapper."

Since the early 1970s my career has developed in several new directions. In addition to the Finnish research, I conducted fieldwork on political ecology and agrarian change in Costa Rica. In the late 1980s I had an opportunity to return briefly to Han country. Sadly, most of my acquaintances there had long since passed away or moved elsewhere. I enjoyed a reunion with John Bacon who, at nearly 90 years of age, was still alert and gregarious.

The numbers of summer visitors in Dawson City had easily tripled since 1970, ushering in an expansive new era of tourism and a more active commoditization of Klondike gold rush history and sourdough imagery. As in former years, Indian history and culture remained marginal to this promotional image making. Nonetheless, the local native community was beginning to prosper economically. Han Fisheries was established by the Dawson Band to organize the salmon fishing business for its members. A new Chief Isaac Memorial Centre housed the Band's administrative offices and a number of businesses and services utilized by tourists. The Band was exploring possibilities for constructing a hotel and an RV campground. Their old village of Moosehide was declared "dry," making it a haven for nondrinkers, and there was talk about making it more accessible to visitors as well. For the first time in history the native community was significantly tapping the tourist economy.

The reoccupation of Moosehide was tied to a spiritual awakening and renewal of identity among local Indians. *Han* was becoming a more self-conscious form of identity and self-ascription for a large segment of the native community, overriding local band designations such as Troncik and Ezan. Moreover, these changes in economy and identity were emerging at a time in the late 1980s when the various Indian bands of the Yukon Territory, represented by the Council for Yukon Indians, were on the brink of negotiating and signing with federal authorities the Yukon Indian Land Claims Agreement.

Chipewyan country has continued to exert the strongest pull on me. I have returned to Patuanak and surrounding communities seven times as my interests shifted to technological and social change, Chipewyan-Cree relations, and Indian-European relations. Some of the earlier research comprised my doctoral dissertation, eventually revised and published as *The Trappers of Patuanak* (1980), while other material has appeared in numerous journal articles, books and book chapters. Occasionally, I have taken my students to the field, hoping to recycle some of the wisdom imparted to me by Dr. McClellan. I married Hetty Jo Brumbach, an archaeologist. Our joint investigations have probed fur trade ethnohistory, women's lives and gender relations, among other issues. Using ethnoarchaeological methods which incorporate local Chipewyan consultants as research team members, we mapped and inventoried a regional network of former encampments, settlements, and trading outpost communities. The past came vividly alive for us as our companions commented, often with great emotion, on remains of structures and artifacts that they or their ancestors had once constructed and used.

In 1977 the long-awaited spur road into Patuanak was completed, linking it forever to the outside. That very summer disturbing rumors of a threatening bushman spread through the community when a young girl wandered away from her berry picking party. In the space of a few years, pick-up trucks, telephones, televisions, and other consumer goods, never seen in the village before, became commonplace. A boom in new house construction changed the visual landscape of the settlement as the population swelled beyond 600 people. A number of young Chipewyan became "commuter laborers," traveling by bush plane to the new uranium mines at Cluff Lake and Key Lake. Families with pickups often drove to Beauval, Ile-a-la-Crosse, and Buffalo Narrows, and occasionally to distant destinations like Meadow Lake which offered more exotic opportunities for trade and amusement. The allure of the outside could be heard in the self-denigrating speech of some young people: "We should go to Meadow Lake, eh. There's bugger-all to do around here."

At the same time, other people were journeying toward Patuanak as it blossomed into an annual religious pilgrimage site of some renown.

Local Chipewyan had begun observing the anniversary of missionary Louis Moraud's death, but what had once been a simple commemoration quickly evolved, by the mid- and late-1970s, into a rather complex ceremonial occasion known colloquially as the "feast for Father Moraud" or the "Patuanak pilgrimage." Hundreds of pilgrims from Chipewyan, Cree and Métis communities throughout northern Saskatchewan were arriving every July to pay homage to their old priest, and also to obtain his spiritual power, to seek out native magico-medicinal healers, and to renew kinship ties with farflung, seldom-seen relatives. For the Patuanak Chipewyan, and the Kesyehot'ine generally, the pilgrimage was becoming an important symbolic means of defining their identity.

As a bustling summer tent community, the pilgrimage site physically and kinetically resurrects sights and sounds associated with three familiar sociosettlement forms from the nineteenth and early twentieth centuries: (1) regional band aggregations of Chipewyan and Cree at summer fishing stations; (2) annual trade gatherings of native families at HBC headquarters in Ile-a-la-Crosse; and (3) summer religious instructional encampments of Chipewyan, Cree and Métis at the Roman Catholic mission in Ile-a-la-Crosse. A massive new summer tent gathering in Patuanak has become in modern times a primordial characteristic of Chipewyan and Upper Churchill pan-Indian identity. Recreating the summer gathering fundamentally distinguishes the "Chipewyan" or the "Indian" from all others and is, thereby, a uniquely *cultural interpretation* of identity.

I was at home in upstate New York one day in 1982 when the first news of the tragedy reached me. Something had gone horribly wrong in Patuanak. A brief letter in an urgent hand-written scrawl arrived from a Chipewyan friend. It was sketchy on details, but there was no mistaking one fact: a young woman and two young men from the village had been shot to death in the primes of their lives. A rifle-wielding assailant had sent them to the great beyond in the early morning hours of New Year's Day. I knew two of the victims and their families well. Their parents and other relatives would be devastated. As my own grief took hold, I could scarcely finish reading the letter.

As was customary, there had been a lot of celebrating in the village between Christmas and New Year. The bootleggers had been working overtime. But a triple homicide in Patuanak? An awful feeling welled in the pit of my stomach as a nagging thought kept surfacing: old John Lynx finally had gone off the deep end.

But the final shock came at the end of the letter. There was no mention of Lynx. The authorities had arrested someone else. It was a man I knew quite well, well enough to address as sits'eni. I had worked with him in the bush and had spent time on his trapline. We had developed a special friendship that had grown over the years. Now, he was charged with taking the lives of three fellow villagers, one of them a first cousin. The ties of blood and marriage ran thick and deep between all the families involved, compounding the horror of the situation. The crime would rip the community apart, creating emotional and social wounds that might never heal. Yes, this was a man I had known quite well. Now I wondered.

Many years later I made a trip to another part of Canada. The only sign of human life in the bleak stretch of short-grass prairie was a massive stone building looming fortress-like from the top of a commanding hill. It was surrounded by miles of chain-link fence and concertina wire. After signing a register and emptying out my pockets, I passed through a series of electronically operated steel doors and into a sparsely furnished visiting room. Several inmates huddled quietly in the corners with wives and girlfriends.

At first I paid little attention to the man seated alone. When his eyes followed me around the room, however, I felt a twinge of recognition.

"Dastloze?" the man whispered hoarsely.

"Hey, I'm sorry. I should've known . . ."

"It's okay. I haven't been eating right. Hard to get whitefish and bannock in this place, eh."

The man's altered appearance startled me. He had lost considerable weight. His face had an older, wiser, more determined countenance. But there was no mistake. This man was truly my old friend and partner. We easily fell into conversation about our past experiences together on the Churchill River, about our families and recent lives, and yet, by some unstated code, avoided the most delicate and painful subjects. Several hours passed.

"Dastloze, I have to ask you something." My friend's voice was suddenly urgent as a guard came by to end the visit.

"Sure, anything."

"You've been to Patuanak so many times. Maybe you know better than me what it's like now. Why do you keep going back there?"

"Why?" I felt anything I could say on the subject would sound trite and inadequate and wondered what my friend really wanted to hear. "We Beschokdene [Americans] are a pretty rootless bunch, you know. Patuanak's like a second home to me. I have good friends there. I guess going back is like going home."

"Really?" My friend stood up and scanned the distant treeless horizon from a grimy wire-mesh window.

"Yah, that's how I feel."

"Dastloze, if I ever get out of this place, do you think . . ."

An uncomfortable silence ensued as my friend ran out of words. But it didn't matter. I knew what he was thinking. Could he return to Chipewyan country? Could he ever go home?

Bibliography

Adeny, Edwin Tappan. 1900. *The Klondike Stampede of 1897–98.* New York: Harper and Brothers Publishers.

Archer, F. A. 1929. *A Heroine of the North: Memoirs of Charlotte Selina Bompas (1830-1917) Wife of the First Bishop of Selkirk (Yukon) with Extracts of Her Journals and Letters.* London.

Bernard, H. Russell. 1994. *Research Methods in Anthropology: Qualitative and Quantitative Approaches.* Thousand Oaks, CA: Sage Publications.

Berton, Laura Beatrice. 1954. *I Married the Klondike.* Boston: Little, Brown and Company.

Berton, Pierre. 1958. *Klondike: The Life and Death of the Last Great Gold Rush.* Toronto: McClelland & Stewart.

Brumbach, Hetty Jo, and Robert Jarvenpa. 1989. *Ethnoarchaeological and Cultural Frontiers: Athapaskan, Algonquian and European Adaptations in the Central Subarctic.* New York: Peter Lang.

Calder, Ritchie. 1957. *Men Against the Frozen North.* London: George Allen and Unwin Ltd.

Clark, Donald W. 1991. *Western Subarctic Prehistory.* Hull, Quebec: Canadian Museum of Civilization.

Coates, Kenneth. 1985. *Canada's Colonies: A History of the Yukon and Northwest Territories.* Toronto: James Lorimer & Company.

Coates, Kenneth. 1988. Best Left as Indians: The Federal Government and the Indians of the Yukon, 1894–1950. In Robin Fisher and Kenneth Coates, eds. *Out of the Background: Readings on Canadian Native History.* Toronto: Copp Clark Pittman.

Cohen, Erik. 1988. Authenticity and Commoditization in Tourism. *Annals of Tourism Research* 15:371–86.

Department of Natural Resources. 1950. *The Fur Act* (1953 Amended Version). Regina, Saskatchewan.

Dominion Bureau of Statistics. 1957. *Canadian Mineral Statistics 1886–1956.* Ottawa: Queen's Printer.

Epstein, A. L., ed. 1967. *The Craft of Social Anthropology.* London: Tavistock Publications.

Findlay, D. C. 1969. *The Mineral Industry of Yukon Territory and Southwestern District of MacKenzie 1967.* Ottawa: Geological Survey of Canada, Paper 68.

Formazov, A. N. 1970. Ecology of the Major Species of Subarctic Fauna. In *Ecology of Subarctic Regions: Proceedings of the Helsinki Symposium.* Paris: UNESCO.

Foster, George M. 1955. Peasant Society and the Image of the Limited Good. *American Anthropologist* 67:293–315.

Fowler, William R., Jr. 1977. Linguistic Evidence for Athapaskan Prehistory. In J. W. Helmer, S. Van Dyke and F. J. Kense, eds. *Prehistory of the North American Subarctic: The Athapaskan Question*. Calgary: The Archaeological Association of the University of Calgary.

Gillespie, Beryl C. 1975. Territorial Expansion of the Chipewyan in the 18th Century. In A.M. Clark, ed. *Proceedings: Northern Athapaskan Conference 1971*. Ottawa: National Museum of Man Mercury Series, Canadian Ethnology Service Paper No. 27.

Greenberg, Joseph H., Christy G. Turner II, and Stephen L. Zegura. 1986. The Settlement of the Americas: A Comparison of the Linguistic, Dental and Genetic Evidence. *Current Anthropology* 27:477–97.

Guedon, Marie-Francoise. 1974. *People of Tetlin: Why Are You Singing?* Ottawa: National Museum of Man Mercury Series, Canadian Ethnology Service Paper No. 9.

Harris, A. C. 1897. *Alaska and the Klondike Gold Fields*. Chicago: Monroe Book Co.

Hearne, Samuel. 1795. *A Journey from Prince of Wales Fort in Hudson's Bay to the Northern Ocean in the Years 1769, 1770, 1771 and 1772*. London: A. Strachan and T. Cadell.

Helm, June. 1965. Bilaterality in the Socio-territorial Organization of the Arctic Drainage Dene. *Ethnology* 4:361–85.

Helm. June. 1969a. Remarks on the Methodology of Band Composition Analysis. In David Damas, ed. *Contributions to Anthropology: Band Societies*. Ottawa: Anthropological Series 84, National Museums of Canada Bulletin 228.

Helm, June. 1969b. A Method of Statistical Analysis of Primary Relative Bonds in Community Composition. In David Damas, ed. *Contributions to Anthropology: Band Societies*. Ottawa: Anthropological Series 84, National Museums of Canada Bulletin 228.

Helm, June, and David Damas. 1963. The Contact-Traditional All-Native Community of the Canadian North. *Anthropologica* 5:9–21.

Holy, Ladislav. 1984. Theory, Methodology and the Research Process. In R. F. Ellen, ed. *Ethnographic Research: A Guide to General Conduct*. London: Academic Press.

Hosley, Edward H. 1977. A Reexamination of the Salmon Dependence of the Pacific Drainage Culture Athapaskans. In J. W. Helmer, S. Van Dyke, and F. J. Kense, eds. *Prehistory of the North American Subarctic: The Athapaskan Question*. Calgary: The Archaeological Association of the University of Calgary.

Jarvenpa, Robert. 1976. Spatial and Ecological Factors in the Annual Economic Cycle of the English River Band of Chipewyan. *Arctic Anthropology* 13:43–69.

Jarvenpa, Robert. 1977. The Ubiquitous Bushman: Chipewyan-White Trapper Relations of the 1930s. In J. W. Helmer, S. Van Dyke, and F. J. Kense, eds. *Prehistory of the North American Subarctic: The Athapaskan Question*. Calgary: The Archaeological Association of the University of Calgary.

Jarvenpa, Robert. 1980. *The Trappers of Patuanak; Toward a Spatial Ecology of Modern Hunters*. Ottawa: National Museum of Man Mercury Series. Canadian Ethnology Service Paper No. 67.

Jarvenpa, Robert. 1982. Intergroup Behavior and Imagery: The Case of Chipewyan and Cree. *Ethnology* 21:283–99.

Jarvenpa, Robert. 1987. The Hudson's Bay Company, the Roman Catholic Church, and the Chipewyan in the Late Fur Trade Period. In Bruce Trigger, Toby Morantz, and Louise Dechene, eds. *Le castor Fait Tout: Selected Papers of the Fifth North American Fur Trade Conference*. Montreal: Lake St. Louis Historical Society.

Jarvenpa, Robert. 1990. The Development of Pilgrimage in an Inter-Cultural Frontier. In Robert H. Winthrop, ed. *Culture and the Anthropological Tradition: Essays in Honor of Robert F. Spencer*. Lanham, MD: University Press of America.

Jarvenpa, Robert. 1994. Commoditization Versus Cultural Integration: Tourism and Image Building in the Klondike. *Arctic Anthropology* 31:26–46.

Jarvenpa, Robert, and Hetty Jo Brumbach. 1988. Socio-Spatial Organization and Decision-Making Processes: Observations from the Chipewyan. *American Anthropologist* 90:598–618.

Jarvenpa, Robert, and Hetty Jo Brumbach. 1995. Ethnoarchaeology and Gender: Chipewyan Women as Hunters. *Research in Economic Anthropology* 16:39–82.

Kari, James, and James Fall. 1988. *Shem Pete's Alaska: The Territory of the Upper Cook Inlet Dena'ina*. Fairbanks: Alaska Native Language Center.

Kelsall, John P. 1968. *The Migratory Barren-Ground Caribou of Canada*. Ottawa: Department of Indian Affairs and Northern Development.

Koolage, William W., Jr. 1975. Conceptual Negativism in Chipewyan Ethnology. *Anthropologica* 17:45–60.

Krech, Shepard III, ed. 1984. *The Subarctic Fur Trade: Native Social and Economic Adaptations*. Vancouver: University of British Columbia Press.

Kroeber, Alfred L. 1939. *Cultural and Natural Areas of Native North America*. Berkeley: University of California Publications in American Archaeology and Ethnology, Volume 38.

Krauss, Michael E. 1973. Na-Dene. *Current Trends in Linguistics* 10:903–78.

Krauss, Michael E. 1988. Many Tongues-Ancient Tales. In William W. Fitzhugh and Aron Crowell, eds. *Crossroads of Continents: Cultures of Siberia and Alaska*. Washington, DC: Smithsonian Institution Press.

Li, Fang-Kuei. 1946. Chipewyan. In Harry Hoijer et al. *Linguistic Structures of Native America*. New York: Viking Fund Publications in Anthropology 6.

London, Jack. 1903. *The Call of the Wild*. New York: Grosset & Dunlap.

Lotz, J. R. 1964. *The Dawson Area: A Regional Monograph*. Ottawa: Department of Northern Affairs and National Resources, Yukon Research Project Series No. 2.

Lotz, Jim. 1970. *Northern Realities: The Future of Northern Development in Canada*. Toronto: New Press.

Malinowski, Bronislaw. 1922. *Argonauts of the Western Pacific: An Account of Native Enterprise and Adventure in the Archipelagoes of Melanesian New Guinea*. London: Routledge and Kegan Paul. Reprint, Prospect Heights, IL: Waveland Press, 1984.

McClellan, Catharine. 1964. Culture Contacts in the Early Historic Period in Northwestern North America. *Arctic Anthropology* 2:3–20.

McClellan, Catharine. 1970. Introduction: Athabascan Studies. *Western Canadian Journal of Anthropology* 2:vi–xix.

McClellan, Catharine, and Glenda Denniston. 1981. Environment and Culture in the Cordillera. In June Helm, ed. *Handbook of North American Indians*. Volume 6: Subarctic. Washington, DC: Smithsonian Institution Press.

McConnell, R. G. 1891. *Report on an Exploration in the Yukon and Mackenzie Basins, N.W.T.* Geology and Natural History Survey of Canada, Vol. IV, 1888–1889.

McKennan, Robert A. 1959. *The Upper Tanana Indians*. New Haven: Yale University Publications in Anthropology No. 55.

McKennan, Robert A. 1969. Athapaskan Groupings and Social Organization in Central Alaska. In David Damas, ed. *Contributions to Anthropology: Band Societies*. Ottawa: Anthropological Series 84, National Museums of Canada Bulletin 228.

McQuesten, Leroy N. 1952. *Recollections of Leroy N. McQuesten: Life in the Yukon, 1871–1885*. Dawson City, Yukon Territory: Copy of original ms. in possession of Yukon Order of Pioneers.

Mercier, Francois Xavier. 1986. *Recollections of the Yukon: Memoires from the Years 1868–1885*, translated, edited and annotated by Linda Finn Yarborough. Anchorage: Alaska Historical Commission Studies in History No. 188, the Alaska Historical Society.

Middleton, John. 1970. Entree into the Field: Africa. In Raoul Naroll and Ronald Cohen, eds. *A Handbook of Method in Cultural Anthropology*. Garden City, NY: Natural History Press.

Mooney, James. 1928. *The Aboriginal Population of America North of Mexico*. Washington, DC: Smithsonian Miscellaneous Collections 80 (7).

Morrison, W. R. 1985. *Showing the Flag: The Mounted Police and Canadian Sovereignty in the North, 1895–1925*. Vancouver.

Murray, Alexander Hunter. 1910. *Journal of the Yukon 1847–48*. Ottawa: Publications of the Canadian Archives No. 4.

Nelson, Richard K. 1973. *Hunters of the Northern Forest: Designs for Survival Among the Alaska Kutchin*. Chicago: University of Chicago Press.

North, Dick. 1972. *The Mad Trapper of Rat River*. Toronto: Macmillan.

Osgood, Cornelius. 1936. *Distribution of the Northern Athapaskan Indians*. New Haven: Yale University Publications in Anthropology No. 7.

Osgood, Cornelius. 1953. *Winter*. New York: W. W. Norton & Company, Inc.

Osgood, Cornelius. 1971. *The Han Indians: A Compilation of Ethnographic and Historical Data on the Alaska-Yukon Boundary*. New Haven: Yale University Publications in Anthropology No. 74.

Osgood, Cornelius. 1975. An Ethnographical Map of Great Bear Lake. In A. M. Clark, ed. *Proceedings: Northern Athapaskan Conference 1971*. Ottawa: National Museum of Man Mercury Series, Canadian Ethnology Service Paper No. 27.

Pelto, Pertti J. 1973. *The Snowmobile Revolution: Technology and Social Change in the Arctic*. Menlo Park, CA: Cummings. Reprint, Prospect Heights, IL: Waveland Press, 1987.

Pelto, Pertti J., and Gretel H. Pelto. 1978. *Anthropological Research: The Structure of Inquiry*. Cambridge: Cambridge University Press.

Priutt, W. O. 1978. *Boreal Ecology*. London: Edward Arnold Limited.

Ridington, Robin. 1987. From Hunt Chief to Prophet: Beaver Indians and Christianity. *Arctic Anthropology* 24:8–18.

Ridington, Robin. 1988. Knowledge, Power, and the Individual in Subarctic Hunting Societies. *American Anthropologist* 90:98–110.

Savishinsky, Joel S. 1994. *The Trail of the Hare: Environment and Stress in a Subarctic Community.* New York: Gordon and Breach.

Schwatka, Frederick. 1892. *A Summer in Alaska.* St. Louis: J. W. Henry.

Service, Elman R. 1962. *Primitive Social Organization: An Evolutionary Perspective.* New York: Random House.

Service, Robert. 1907. *The Spell of the Yukon and Other Verses.* New York: Barse and Hopkins.

Service, Robert. 1909. *Ballads of a Cheechako.* New York: Barse and Hopkins.

Sharp, Henry S. 1988. *The Transformation of Bigfoot: Maleness, Power and Belief Among the Chipewyan.* Washington, DC: Smithsonian Institution Press.

Slobodin, Richard. 1963. "The Dawson Boys"—Peel River Indians and the Klondike Gold Rush. *Polar Notes* 5:24–36.

Smith, David M. 1973. *Inkonze: Magico-Religious Beliefs of Contact-Traditional Chipewyan Trading at Fort Resolution, NWT, Canada.* Ottawa: National Museum of Man Mercury Series, Ethnology Division Paper No. 6.

Smith, David M. 1982. *Moose-Deer Island House People: A History of the Native People of Fort Resolution.* Ottawa: National Museum of Man Mercury Series, Canadian Ethnology Service Paper No. 81.

Smith, James G. E. 1975. The Ecological Basis of Chipewyan Socio-territorial Organization. In A. M. Clark, ed. *Proceedings: Northern Athapaskan Conference 1971.* Ottawa: National Museum of Man Mercury Series, Canadian Ethnology Service Paper No. 27.

Spradley, James P. 1980. *Participant Observation.* New York: Holt, Rinehart and Winston.

Spurr, Josiah E. 1900. *Through the Yukon Gold Diggings.* Boston: Eastern Publishing Company.

Stone, T. 1979. The Mounties as Vigilantes: Reflections on Community and the Transformation of the Law in the Yukon, 1885–1897. *Law and Society Review* 14:83–114.

Turner, Christy G. II. 1988. Ancient Peoples of the North Pacific Rim. In William W. Fitzhugh and Aron Crowell, eds. *Crossroads of Continents: Cultures of Siberia and Alaska.* Washington, DC: Smithsonian Institution Press.

Valentine, V. F. 1954. Some Problems of the Metis of Northern Saskatchewan. *The Canadian Journal of Economics and Political Science* 20:89–95.

VanStone, James W. 1965. *The Changing Culture of the Snowdrift Chipewyan.* Ottawa: National Museums of Canada Bulletin 209.

VanStone, James W. 1974. *Athapaskan Adaptations: Hunters and Fishermen of the Subarctic Forests.* Chicago: Aldine Publishing Company.

Yukon Indian Agency. 1969. *Dawson Band.* January 1969 Roster. Dawson City, Yukon Territory.

Study Guide

prepared by Karla Poewe
University of Calgary

This story about a young man who starts his fieldwork career among some Han and Chipewyan people in Alaska, the Yukon Territory, and northern Saskatchewan is not only a good read, it is also a powerful experience. The author captures the sights and sounds, the moods and feelings of landscape and people. The book is also an experience because it is structured and worded in such a way as to invite (a) shifts in the reader's perception and (b) engagement of the reader with specific individuals, situations, things, and nature.

In this time of questions about the nature of ethnographic writing, we read this book not only for the events and reality it portrays, but also for how it is written. Ask yourself the following questions: (1) On what material is the book based? (2) When did the experiences described in this book actually occur? (3) How does the structure, style, and rhetoric of the book make it effective? (4) How do the author's words guide your eyes, ears, thoughts, and feelings? Finally, (5) what about the book makes you aware that some things are left out?

Accounts of fieldwork make explicit what is left implicit in descriptive ethnographies, namely, the effects of active participation on both the researcher and his or her project. What is notable about this account of fieldwork, however, is that Jarvenpa's active participation in one set of events, trapping, makes the reader curious about other sets of events. As we learn to understand the issues on which Jarvenpa's attention is focused, we become concerned and curious about peripheral research problems: native spirituality, the undercurrent of violence, the role of Christianity and gender.

Two other things teased my mind as I read this book. They are Jarvenpa's use of "shifting perception" and "helping locals." The structure of the book reminds me of John Bunyan's *Pilgrim's Progress,* and shifting perception and helping locals have something to do with it. Shifting perception is used to construct a text that is as exotic as it is mysterious. Helping locals is used to structure the research design that is as intuitive as it is rational.

Jarvenpa, although he does not deal explicitly with Native spirituality and Christianity, nevertheless directs the reader's attention to periodic shifts of perception. Thus we find that he and his trapping part-

201

ners read certain, seemingly fortuitous, events or dreams as signs or premonitions inviting decision, action, avoidance, or caution. Where, how, and why does Jarvenpa do this? Find the pages on which perceptive changes are depicted or hinted at. Second, while Jarvenpa concentrates his research and active participation on certain groups of Dene, it is specific local whites and Indians who, in diverse situations and ways, give him concrete help. Who are they? In what situations does Jarvenpa encounter them? And how do they help him?

Other things may have teased your mind. What are they? Can you anticipate areas of research, barely mentioned in this book, that the author himself researched later?

Pages 2–3

According to Jarvenpa, in what two senses is the book a "journey"? What motivates him and, for that matter, other anthropologists to write a narrative account of fieldwork experiences? What does Jarvenpa mean by "burden of memory" and how is it related to genre choice?

Page 4

In what environment did Jarvenpa conduct his two stints of fieldwork? What people are of central concern in this book, what languages do they speak, and how are they socially organized?

Pages 6–7

How does Jarvenpa define environment? What is meant by *matrilineal* social structure and *bilateral kinship* and how are these forms of organization related to differential environmental accommodations? What is the relationship between space, mobility, and kinship?

Pages 8–9

How is the topographical landscape connected to peoples' history and lore? What do dreams and "supernatural" knowledge and power have to do with adaptation and environmental constraints?

Page 13

Jarvenpa and a fellow student had a relatively unique introduction to fieldwork. What was it? More importantly, Jarvenpa gives a succinct definition of *ethnographic fieldwork*. What is it?

Pages 14–15

Jarvenpa gives a concise definition of participant observation and relates it to empathy, interviews, being a neophyte, and note taking. What is his definition?

Pages 17–18

In Athapaskan country, the author, his mentor, and a fellow student spent two weeks on the road to familiarize themselves with land and people. They discovered, for example, that many Pacific-drainage Athapaskan peoples had a moiety system. What are moieties? With which moieties do Jarvenpa and Susanne become affiliated? As you read on, observe how the author uses his affiliation to interpret, and act upon, dreams and coincidences, in short, to bring about a shift in perception from the natural to the supernatural.

Page 20

The author creates a sense of mystery by identifying an anthropological puzzle. What is the ethnographic riddle, and which anthropologists expressed opposing viewpoints?

Pages 21–22

What role does history play in Jarvenpa's ethnographic research?

Page 23

As happens to many anthropologists in the field, Jarvenpa's research interests changed. What became his new focus?

Pages 24–29

What have alcohol, segregation, and radical shifts in the local economy to do with the Klondike rush?

Page 30

Dr. McClellan's advice to Bob and Susanne was: "Don't drink with your informants." The advice of white locals was rather different; it revealed their prejudice, cynicism, but also accurate knowledge and observation. What was their advice, was it valuable, and did Bob and Susanne follow it?

Pages 31–35

Karl Swenson was one of those local whites whose help in Jarvenpa's research was unorthodox and unexpected. Of what did it consist and what was learned?

Page 38

The famous anthropologist Max Gluckman once said that anthropology is like detective work. Jarvenpa indirectly reminds us of this aspect of research when he reflects about Dick North's "hunt." What quality inherent in North's activities does Jarvenpa think anthropologists need? How does this quality set the tone for the whole book?

Pages 38–45

Why does Jarvenpa jokingly call his experiences in the Westminster "baptism"? How did it further his research?

Pages 45–51

The author begins to "feel like an anthropologist" after working with Simon Isaac. Why? What did Simon's narrative reveal about Han society and history?

Pages 53–55

The significance of calling chapter 2 "Subarctic Skid Row" emerges fully in feelings of disgust, depression, and yearning. How did these emotions, indeed reflections, affect Jarvenpa's research?

Pages 59–62

If the "Westminster" brought home the extensive kin ties among local Indians, "Discovery Day" highlighted Indian-white relations. What were these like?

Page 62

What fortuitous event and chance meeting, the latter through the help of a local white, took Jarvenpa out of Dawson City?

Pages 62–63

Leaving Dawson City not only gave Jarvenpa a sense of release, it was also the occasion of considerable reflectiveness. About what aspects of research did he worry?

Page 64

Indian-white relationships could be summarized as a mythology of blame. It came up earlier in this book. How does it surface here?

Pages 64–66

What is the spellbinding vision Jarvenpa comes upon? To what extent is it real? To what extent is it illusion?

Pages 67–71

Jarvenpa learned several things in Dawson City that now come in handy. What were they and how do they help him gain rapport and converse?

Page 75

Jarvenpa uses the raven to signal something. Why and of what is the raven a good omen? On this page too Jarvenpa uses the image of baptism again. Into what had he been baptized?

Pages 80–81

After a break at his university, Jarvenpa started research for his Ph.D. On what issues would this research be centered? What method did Robert Spencer, his Ph.D. advisor, suggest Jarvenpa use to find a researchable community? How else did Jarvenpa prepare himself for his next field trip? Where was it and among which people would he work?

Pages 82–84

Jarvenpa links his choice of destination to ominous coincidences. What were they?

Pages 85–86

Which local white helps Jarvenpa find the native settlement for his fieldwork and what is the settlement's name?

Page 87

On what ethical consideration is responsible ethnographic research based?

Pages 88–90

Acceptance or rejection of the anthropologist by the community depends upon the nature of his or her entrance. How does Jarvenpa gain admittance?

Pages 90–91

Many researchers have commented on their vivid dreams in the field. Do you see any link between Jarvenpa's dream content and his relationship with the Chipewyan?

Pages 93–95

How is the relationship between Marcel Flatstone and the author prefigured in the latter's dream?

Pages 95–97

Casual conversations are a source of data. What does Jarvenpa learn from the banter of his young Chipewyan friends?

Pages 97–99

Some pages earlier we learned that alcohol plays a sinister, if subdued, role in Patuanak. What other undercurrent threatens the peace of this community?

Page 100

What is ethnoecology? Besides listening to banter, what else does Jarvenpa do and how is this activity related to ethnoecology?

Pages 100–103

Certain knowledge and experiences are crystalized into powerful images conveyed by specific Chipewyan words. How are these words and the lore behind them connected to Chipewyan ecology?

Page 103

Jarvenpa describes the various aspects of participant observation in some detail. What kind of participation does he want to practice and how does it make him an apprentice?

Pages 104–5

How does Jarvenpa find a trapping partner? As well, now that Jarvenpa is relatively settled in the community, different local Chipewyan help him progress in his research. What does Jarvenpa do in the book to bring out the wonderfully unique and ever so human qualities of each Chipewyan who is significant to his work? He starts with Joachim Deneyou. Who is next?

Page 105

What theme is mentioned but not pursued? Jarvenpa seems to do this deliberately to show something about the nature of active participation and focused research.

Pages 107–9

Jarvenpa mentions that in earlier times the Chipewyan were sandwiched between two types of whites. Who were they?

Page 110

Which other whites, belonging to which specific institutions, are part of the local environment and form links to the larger world?

Pages 110–12

Which meeting depicts the uneasy relationship between Chipewyan and the Canadian government?

Pages 113–16, 119

It is important that anthropologists let all local authorities know that they are in the area in order to do research. How does the revelation that Jarvenpa made his research plans known to the DNR backfire?

Page 120

What theme does Jarvenpa discuss briefly but not pursue at this point because of his specific research approach?

Pages 120–21

What is the legal difference between being a Treaty and a non-Treaty man? What is the difference for a woman?

Pages 121–22

Various kinship arrangements are discussed. What are they and what role do they play in Chipewyan ecology?

Pages 123–25

Jarvenpa uses a common motif as a premonitory device to warn him, as much as the reader, of a problem while giving him, as well as the reader, hope for a solution. What is it?

Pages 127–28

A bush pilot flies Jarvenpa and his trapping partner to the latter's hunting territory. Even from the plane Jarvenpa learns more ethnoecology. How is this brought out?

Page 130

Of what did the temporary encampment consist?

Page 132

What did Jarvenpa find disconcerting about the partners on the trapline?

Pages 133–34, 150

What is meant by a trapline? What technology and skills are involved in setting it up?

Page 134–35

Partner or *sits'eni* was a social fiction. What was the prevailing social structure among Chipewyan trappers, and what were its multiple functions?

Pages 137–39

When Antoine Ptarmigan explains beaver sociology he summarizes a knowledge based on keen observation. But then comes a shift in perception, and the subject-object distance between Antoine and the beaver is erased. How does this happen? How does the world of magic, immanence, power, and dreams merge with that of observation and objectivity?

Page 140

What two problems worried the Ptarmigan brothers?

Pages 141–44

What is the significance of place names? Do they only tell something about the environment? How does Jarvenpa's "amusing" mishap play into this?

Page 145

How was the problem of writing up field notes solved?

Pages 146–47

Inkonzedene was mentioned earlier. Now the term is linked to a story that reveals something of Chipewyan beliefs and justice. What are the main elements in the story and what does it say about Chipewyan-Cree relationships?

Page 148

The outside world breaks into the mystery of environment and magic. How?

Pages 149–50

How does Jarvenpa highlight the disparity between explanatory theory and human experience?

Page 151

What did fire making test?

Page 152

What marks a shift in perception on this page?

Pages 153–54

What new technology has eased travel between base camps in northern Saskatchewan?

Pages 155–56

In the bush, the concept of power is mentioned frequently. According to Chipewyan beliefs, what is its source?

Page 157

What was particularly abhorrent in the environment?

Pages 157–59

Bush life is not without its tensions. What are some of the mishaps that make tempers flare up?

Page 160

Here is another shift of perception. It is associated with danger. Which fortuitous event is interpreted as a sign that leads Jarvenpa to safety?

Pages 160–62

The author shifts continuously between "supernatural" and "natural," or specific and general, explanations of human and animal life in the bush. Can you give some examples?

Pages 163–64

Why is Jarvenpa anxious upon his return to Patuanak?

Page 166

Did the experience in the bush result in total acceptance of the researcher?

Page 167

What did Jarvenpa do to get a greater overview of trapping life and other seasonal economic activities?

Pages 168–70

Doubts about the execution of appropriate rituals served as premonition of something bad to come. What caused the new flare up of anger?

Pages 171–73

Jarvenpa uses different kinds of fires to contrast different sets of relationships. Can you describe these?

Pages 174–83

Did the fire-fighting spectacle reveal a deep cultural truth?

Pages 178–83

In addition to the forest fire, what other problem confronts the fire-fighting crews? How do the men interpret their situation?

Pages 184–85

On leaving his field site, Jarvenpa and his trapping partner Antoine anticipate change. Is the change anticipated with equanimity?

Page 187

Upon his return home, Jarvenpa expresses a classic conflict about fieldwork. What is it? Do Bernard's stages of participant observation reflect the progress of Jarvenpa's fieldwork?

Page 188

What is meant by "reverse culture shock"?

Pages 188–89

Jarvenpa carefully analyzes the advantages and disadvantages of active participation in fieldwork. What are they?

Pages 189–90

What insights about culture and ecology did Jarvenpa gain from his intensive fieldwork? Did these insights and experiences benefit his later research career?

Page 191

Did Jarvenpa return to Han and Chipewyan country? Did he research some of the tantalizing issues mentioned in this book on his return trips?

Pages 191–92

What radical changes occurred in Patuanak? Why is it appropriate that Patuanak became a religious pilgrimage site? How is the pilgrimage an apt new symbol for pan-Indian identity?

Pages 192–94

Jarvenpa ended chapter 6 with Antoine's anticipation of bad things to come. Does the tragedy with which the book ends prove Antoine right?